"MEMORABLY DELICIOUS."
—*House & Garden*

Former food and restaurant critic for *The New York Times,* Mimi Sheraton grew up in a home where every meal was a small, important ritual for her family. Snowy mornings started with a special hot cereal: "to many, I know, the very mention of hot cereal summons up memories of being loved and cared for." Friday evenings brought "tantalizing aromas of the day's cooking. Roast meat, hints of garlic and onion, the almost sunny, airy scent of chicken soup, the pungency of sweet and sour cabbage, the sugary smell of a pie or coffee cake that might be baking." Each season every event from a funeral to the "Joys of Being Sick in had a special food that enhanced the occasion. So om Mimi Sheraton's mother's kitchen to yours, is one be avorite after another. . . .

"A real treasury of Jewish ot-so-Jewish cuisine."
—*Publishers Weekly*

"...embrace it with unreserv sure."—*Kirkus Reviews*

FROM MY MOTHER'S KITCHEN

MIMI SHERATON is the former food and restaurant critic for *The New York Times,* food editor for *Seventeen Magazine* and a contributor to *Good Housekeeping* and *House Beautiful.* She is author of *The German Cookbook, The New York Times Guide to New York Restaurants, Visions of Sugarplums,* and (with Alan King) *Is Salami and Eggs Better Than Sex? Memoirs of a Happy Eater.*

FROM MY MOTHER'S KITCHEN

Recipes and Reminiscences

Mimi Sheraton

Illustrative drawings by Marisabina Russo
Decorative drawings by Nancy Stahl

A PLUME BOOK

NEW AMERICAN LIBRARY

NEW YORK AND SCARBOROUGH, ONTARIO

NAL BOOKS ARE AVAILABLE AT QUANTITY DISCOUNTS
WHEN USED TO PROMOTE PRODUCTS OR SERVICES.
FOR INFORMATION PLEASE WRITE TO PREMIUM MARKETING DIVISION,
NEW AMERICAN LIBRARY, 1633 BROADWAY, NEW YORK, NEW YORK 10019.

This is an authorized reprint of a hardcover edition published by Harper & Row,
Publishers, Inc. Published simultaneously in Canada by Fitzhenry & Whiteside
Limited, Toronto.

Illustrative drawings © 1979 by Marisabina Russo

Decorative drawings © 1979 by Nancy Stahl

Grateful acknowledgment is made for permission to reprint:
Excerpts from "The Joys of Being Sick in Bed." First appeared in the January 12,
    1977, issue of *The New York Times.* © 1977 by The New York Times
    Company. Reprinted by permission.
Excerpts from "Sour Pickles." First appeared in the August 3, 1977, issue of
    The New York Times. © 1977 by The New York Times Company. Reprinted by
    permission.
Excerpts from "Breakfasts." First appeared in the March 8, 1978, issue of
    The New York Times. © 1978 by The New York Times Company. Reprinted
    by permission.
"Passover" first appeared in somewhat different form in the April 4, 1979, issue
    of *The New York Times.* © 1979 by The New York Times Company. Reprinted
    by permission.
Portions of this work first appeared in *Quest/78.*

Library of Congress Cataloging in Publication Data
Sheraton, Mimi.

From my mother's kitchen.

Reprint. Originally published: New York : Harper
& Row, c1979.

1. Cookery, International.   I. Title.
TX725.A1S443   1985   641.5   84-25416
ISBN 0-452-25667-4

PLUME TRADEMARK REG. U.S. PAT. OFF. AND FOREIGN COUNTRIES
REG. TRADEMARK—MARCA REGISTRADA
HECHO EN WESTFORD, MASS., U.S.A.

SIGNET, SIGNET CLASSIC, MENTOR, PLUME, MERIDIAN and NAL BOOKS are
published *in the United States* by New American Library, 1633 Broadway,
New York, New York 10019, *in Canada* by The American Library of Canada
Limited, 81 Mack Avenue, Scarborough, Ontario M1L 1M8

First Plume Printing, March, 1985

1 2 3 4 5 6 7 8 9

PRINTED IN THE UNITED STATES OF AMERICA

TO MY DEAR BROTHER, ARTHUR SOLOMON

and

To the memory of

MY DEAR AND DEVOTED MOTHER, BEATRICE SOLOMON

whose untiring efforts and talents in the kitchen
taught me what good food was all about and

MY WONDERFUL FATHER, JOSEPH SOLOMON

who was her most appreciative audience

Contents

Acknowledgments

In addition to my mother and numerous relatives who helped me to recall and recreate the family recipes gathered in this book, there are a number of others to whom I must express thanks. Among them are Rhena E. Vaughns, for her careful typing and checking; Rena and Gary Coyle, for their help in testing and advising on so many of the cakes, breads, and cookies; and to John Clancy, the professional chef, master baker, and teacher who also advised on the baking recipes and did much to perfect the long-lost recipe for challah, as my grandmother made it.

I would also like to thank Ann Harris, my editor, for her four years of patience and persistence, and Margery Tippie for her painstaking and corrective copyediting.

FROM MY MOTHER'S KITCHEN

Introduction

"Are we going to measure or are we going to cook?" my mother asked in exasperation as we began the first of the many joint sessions it took to prepare this book.

Like so many old-fashioned, great, natural cooks, my mother rarely measured or used recipes, and did so only when trying a completely new dish. If I asked her how much water to add to the gefüllte fish mixture, her answer was, "Until it looks right." And when I asked her how long it would take to bake her cinnamon coffee cake, she said, "The longer the better." In fact, my measuring so unnerved her that she ruined several dishes before she got used to my slipping around with measuring cups and spoons.

Once she did, she begged me to drop the project entirely, knowing it was going to become detailed and bothersome. "I'll pay you not to do the book," she said.

"How much?" I asked, certain I would be the first writer to be subsidized for not producing.

"Fifty dollars," she answered, obviously her estimation of my worth on the open market.

In actual fact, this book was begun twenty-eight years ago, after I had been living away from home for five years and had begun to miss some of the more intricate dishes my mother cooked. I started a notebook titled "Mother's Recipes," and as a table of contents I included some forty favorites I wanted to be able to reproduce. Twenty-five years later—three years ago—only eight recipes had been set down.

Knowing how many of my grandmother's wonderful recipes had been lost because they were never recorded, and realizing my mother was aging, I began the project in earnest and quickly discovered I was on my way to a full-fledged cookbook.

But as I worked, it became obvious that recipes alone would have left the book incomplete. So many of the dishes were more than what they were, evoking as they did vignette memories of family life. And so what began as a cookbook expanded into at least the partial autobiography of a family. This is not really surprising, considering how much of our life cen-

1

tered around food, how important it was at ordinary as well as special occasions, how much time my mother spent in its planning and preparation,
and how incessantly we talked about food, not only while eating it, but between meals as well. At every dinner we gave a critique, briefly or at length,
of the dishes being served, and as we ate one meal we discussed and
planned the next one.

The immediate family behind all this eating was small, consisting of my
parents, my younger brother, and myself, and in most ways it was typical of
families in that middle-class, primarily Jewish, Midwood section of Flatbush
in Brooklyn. Although this was not the older Flatbush with its neoclassic
mansions and lavish Victorian-inspired houses, it was an attractive if undis-
tinguished neighborhood that, miraculously, looks today much as it did when
I was growing up. Streets were lined with builder's houses, usually duplicated
three or four in a row. None were noteworthy architecturally—if, in fact, the
word "architecture" can even be used in connection with those simple, two-
story brick-and-stucco affairs. But they were brightened by small neat
patches of front lawns rimmed by clipped hedges, and by window boxes
overflowing with ivy, gray-green ice plants, geraniums, and petunias.

Pocket-sized back yards were filled with flowering springtime bushes of
lilacs, pink and red rambler roses in June, azaleas, yellow forsythia (Brooklyn's official flower), rhododendron, and a white flowering bush called
"bridal wreath," which I especially loved for its languid fragility. Big, sprawling
maple trees cast dappled light on the sidewalks and in spring dropped their
winged seedlings, which we used to open and paste onto the bridges of our
noses, calling them "polly-noses" because of their resemblance to parrots'
beaks.

I remember this neighborhood most fondly as it was in summer, when
the tinkling bells of the slow-moving, gleaming white Good Humor and
Bungalow Bar trucks lured us out for evening Popsicles, and when we were
allowed to put on bathing suits and run under lawn sprinklers or take turns
spraying one another with garden hoses. On the hottest nights, when the air
was close and still, my father rounded us up—usually with a friend or a
cousin or two—and in his high, black 1928 Buick took us to Coney Island,
where we walked the boardwalk that stretched over the beach, rode the roller coasters, and had hot dogs at Nathan's, then steaming corn with butter,
then frozen custard, then cotton candy, then more but tamer rides on
merry-go-rounds or Ferris wheels. At other times, we drove to Sheepshead
Bay and ate clams at Lundy's outdoor clam bar and walked onto the piers
and watched the sightseeing launches come and go.

When it was too hot to do anything but sit on deck chairs or the glider in the back yard, my father would take a big glass pitcher to Gold's, the local bar, and have it filled with golden, foam-capped draught beer, all for twenty-five cents with pretzels added free.

I felt as though we were a very ordinary family in almost every way. "Almost," because of a few circumstances that I felt set us a bit apart; and in a child's world even the smallest distinctions take on mammoth proportions. For one thing, my father had what was considered an unusual occupation. He was a commission merchant in the wholesale fruit and produce business in Washington Market, whereas the fathers of my friends were in what *I* considered ordinary professions—manufacturers of coats, suits, or dresses, furriers, lawyers or accountants, doctors or dentists—jobs that did not need explanations when you were asked aloud in class what your father "did."

Our family was also prominent locally in a minor way because my father's father was a well-known, highly respected rabbi, and his brother, my uncle, was one of the leading physicians in Brooklyn and also had a national reputation. For those reasons, I was perhaps unduly proud of my last name, Solomon. I suppose I really believed my grandfather when he told me we were direct descendants of *the* Solomon, and it was with some reluctance that I exchanged it for Sheraton when I married; I have often regretted not resuming it when I was subsequently divorced.

My paternal grandfather, Kalman Solomon, was a feisty, cantankerous, but dignified, loving, and gentle man, with silky, snowy white hair and a neatly trimmed short beard. He looked his most dignified when he was dressed for outdoors in winter, wearing his black homburg, a black silk scarf, and a black, velvet-collared Chesterfield coat, and carrying a walnut-burl walking stick with a gleaming gold ring just below the curved handle. He married three times, outliving his first two wives. Born in Poland, he had worked his way to America in stages, as did so many Jews of that time, and with his young German wife made his first stop London, where he spent five years.

During that time he officiated at a synagogue on Old Castle Street in Whitechapel. It was there that my father was born, along with a sister and a brother. When my grandfather moved his young family to this country, he settled in the Williamsburg section of Brooklyn. There my grandma, Miriam, for whom I was named, died. My grandfather remarried, had four more children, and prospered. Later he moved to the Prospect Park area, where he was the rabbi of two congregations and the official mohel at the Brooklyn Jewish Hospital, where he performed the ritual circumcisions on newborn Jewish boys.

As I began to bring boys home to meet my parents, the first and certainly the most embarrassing question my mother invariably asked was, "Have you any idea who circumcised you?" No amount of tears, pleas, or threats of suicide could fend off that query. Almost as astonishing as this most peculiar of social icebreakers was the fact that each boy actually went home and asked his parents. Indeed, most did turn out to be products of my grandfather's handicraft, endearing the boys to my parents and, oddly enough, me to theirs.

As proud as I was of the Solomon side of my family, and as much as I adored my grandfather, our visits to them were infrequent, relegated for the most part to holidays and special occasions.

We were much closer to and more informally familiar with my mother's family, the Breits. My grandparents, four aunts, and one uncle lived nearby, and three other uncles who were scattered around the country came back for frequent visits, which were great treats and the occasion for party-sized meals. My mother's parents had come from Galicia, the area that was southern Poland bordering on Rumania, and which in those days was part of the Hapsburg Empire. For that reason, my mother always insisted her family was Austrian, *not* Polish.

My Breit grandparents, Morris and Greta, also emigrated to America in stages, stopping for a few years in Bremen, Germany, and finally landing in Williamsburg, where my grandfather did "fine tailoring for ladies" and made a comfortable living, and where my grandmother spent her days having babies, cleaning, and cooking.

And how she cooked! She was by far the best home cook and baker I have ever known, and it was her repertory of Polish-Rumanian-Austrian-German-Hungarian specialties that formed the basis of my mother's cooking as well as of my aunts', all of whom cooked identically. Each had a specialty or two, but it was otherwise impossible to tell whether it was Aunt Estelle, Aunt June, Aunt Sadie, Aunt Pauline, or my mother, Beatrice, who had made the gefüllte fish, the chopped liver, the cold beet borscht or the Passover nut sponge cake. All shared utter contempt for the cooking of Russian Jews, who, they said, "put sugar in everything."

Ours was in every way a cooking house. Whenever we wanted to find my mother, we first looked in the kitchen. Sometimes I did my homework on the big kitchen table, and as I worked and we talked, I absorbed the basics of cooking simply by observing, however subliminally, the general goings-on. As a result, I cannot remember a time when I did not know how to cook.

My mother's collection of specialties was interesting and varied, for in spite of the fact that both sets of grandparents were Orthodox and kosher, my mother did not keep a kosher house. We ate not only the Jewish-European dishes she learned from her mother, but a great many American specialties, including shellfish such as boiled or broiled lobsters, clam chowder, steamed clams, deviled crabmeat, shrimp Creole or Newburg, and fried oysters. Dairy and meat were combined in creamy chicken à la king and chicken pie. Ham and bacon were served often, as were legs of lamb, sirloin steaks, and other nonkosher cuts of meat. Although my mother had only one cookbook (and that a baking book premium offered by the Royal Baking Powder Company), and usually cooked by rote or from memory, she did clip recipes from magazines and food packages, and scribbled down others from friends on countless scraps of paper, most of which she handed to me at the start of this project. With their brown, frayed, and ragged edges and their always incomplete recipes (usually a list of ingredients followed by the instructions "Combine as usual . . ."), they were more frustrating then helpful. She always liked to try new things—a cheesecake tasted at a friend's party, a seafood dish eaten at a restaurant, cookies served at a resort hotel.

All this cooking was done with the worst sorts of utensils. Except for a few ancient, lethally sharp carbon-steel knives, my mother's kitchenware made a mockery of all recipes calling for well-insulated heavy pots and enameled interiors. Her pots were of the thinnest aluminum, except for the one or two that were thin enameled steel and for her cast-iron skillet. As they grew older, the aluminum pots became so dented on the bottom that they could not stand upright when empty. None of this seemed to affect the excellence of her soups and stews, her cakes and pies. Nor did her distinct proclivity for setting fire to the kitchen. This she generally accomplished by carelessly putting down a burning cigarette or a taper used to light the broiler on a pile of newspapers just in front of the window, where the curtains caught the flame. Several times I arrived home from school to find fire engines outside our house. I remember rushing in to see if the canary had been safely removed from the kitchen. I knew my mother was all right. She was at the door as I approached, laughing and telling me it was all a big joke and that everything was fine, a view my father did not share in spite of his notorious sense of humor.

My mother was small and round, with beautiful jade-green eyes, a regally elongated nose, a firm mouth and chin. She was funny when she meant to be and often when she didn't. Popular and sociable, she loved to entertain. Apart from family occasions, she gave fund-raising card-party luncheons, dinner parties, and late-night suppers, and I loved the preparation that included not only the special and elegant foods, but the setting out of table appointments as well.

I gladly helped polish the heavy silver bowls and baskets, and after the party would put away the "good" silver flatware in the dark red flannel rolls in which it was kept. All silver was stored in a wine-velvet-lined cabinet that matched the heavily carved fumed-oak dining room furniture, and it was in that same cabinet that my mother "hid" candy in a futile attempt to conceal what we all knew was there. The fact that the key had been turned in the lock (though not removed), was no deterrent, of course, least of all to my father, who alone could, and often did, consume a three-pound box of chocolate bonbons in a single sitting. "What will I do if someone drops in and I want to put out a dish of candy?" my mother would ask when she discovered her reserves had been devoured. "Anyone who drops in here should bring candy," my father would answer.

In addition to the planned company meals, there were impromptu family visits, usually preceded by a phone call on a Sunday afternoon. "We're in the neighborhood and thought we'd drop in for a few minutes," was the standard message. My mother's equally standard reply was, "My God! I don't have a thing in the house to eat . . ."

"Don't worry," an aunt or uncle would answer ritualistically. "We don't want a thing . . . just fix a little something for the kids."

And a little something for the kids would turn out to be a groaning board of festive proportions based on the "nothing" in my mother's refrigerator and pantry.

My mother's mothering extended beyond the bounds of family. She died as this book was going to press, and I received a condolence note from Sheila Hochman, a young woman whose mother-in-law, Marjorie Hochman, was my mother's loyal, helpful, and loving neighbor. Much of that note seemed particularly appropriate for this book, and I quote with Sheila Hochman's kind permission.

". . . I have such fond memories of your mother. When I was a newly married woman, living across the street, your mother helped me cook my first seder meal. I'll never forget her beating fourteen eggs and 'yelling' at me to chop the charoses finer. Her sponge cake was wonderful.

"I talk about food because food is supposed to nourish us. Your mother nourished me and my son and my husband with her care, her sense of humor and her wonderful 'kvetching.' "

1

Sauces and Some Basic Preparations

Schmaltz (Rendered Chicken Fat) with Griebenes (Cracklings)

This was an ingredient we were rarely without, and each week a fresh batch would be prepared with the trimmings of the Friday soup chicken. While a fowl provides the most fat for rendering, trimmings from any chicken can be used. Ducks and geese provide even more savory fat and cracklings. It is possible to save bits of fat and skin until you have a cupful and then render it all together. Store scraps in the freezer, well wrapped in foil, but do not keep more than a month, as fat never freezes completely. This homemade schmaltz is far superior to any I have ever purchased. When I have none, I prefer substituting butter. Those who are kosher will prefer margarine or that traditional substitute, Nyafat. My mother never kept a batch of chicken fat more than two weeks, and always under refrigeration.

In addition to the uses of schmaltz in cooking, when very fresh it was considered a treat spread on rye bread, challah, or matzoh and sprinkled with coarse salt. The cracklings (griebenes) also went into certain dishes, unless my father saw them first, in which case they disappeared in a single swallow. Sometimes my mother would save them for him and serve them lightly salted as an appetizer. Duck and goose cracklings are especially good in omelets or scrambled eggs (page 95).

2 cups cut-up skin and diced fat   ¾ cup cold water
    trimmed from any chicken (but
    preferably a fowl) or a duck or
    goose

In trimming the fat and skin from the poultry, try not to include bits of meat. Place the cut-up skin and diced fat in a heavy-bottomed saucepan, add the water, and simmer very, very slowly over low heat. When all the water has evaporated and pure yellow fat begins to collect, pour it off and reserve. The fat is completely rendered when the skin forms crisp, brown cracklings. Drain the cracklings on paper towels and use in recipes where called for or sprinkle with salt and eat before someone else does.

Although it is not strictly necessary to pour off the fat as it accumulates, it is safer to do so; it will not then become brown by the time the cracklings are finished. The fat should be a bright butter yellow without any tint of brown in it. Store the fat tightly covered in the refrigerator. It will last about one week. Cracklings should be used as soon as possible after they are made, or they will become soggy.

Einbrenne

[Roux]

An einbrenne is a combination of sautéed flour and fat and is the basic thickening for many soups and sauces. It is, of course, a roux by its German name. The flour may be sautéed in the fat to any color from pale blond, as for cream sauces or white soups, to its darkest tone—the color of dark brown sugar—for dark sauces. The fat might be butter, chicken fat, or margarine, although butter was the most frequently used at our house, even for meat-based soups.

In many dishes, finely minced onion or garlic was browned in the fat before the flour was added. In that case it would be known as an "onion (or garlic) einbrenne."

Great care must be taken in browning the flour, especially if you want it dark. For a long while it will seem that the flour is barely turning color. But suddenly it will darken rapidly and burn. Although you may want it dark brown, there should never be the faintest hint of blackness to it. Since the browning must be done in a heavy pan that holds heat, it is a good idea to remove the pan from the heat before the einbrenne is quite as dark as you want it to be because it will keep darkening in the pan. If any blackness shows, you will have to throw away what you have and start over, as that blackness, indicating burning, will result in a bitter, acrid flavor that will ruin the completed dish.

As with a cream sauce, 2 tablespoons of fat and 2 tablespoons of flour will thicken 1 cup of liquid to a sauce. In thickening soups, 1 tablespoon of fat and 1 tablespoon of flour should be used per cup of soup, if it is a clear soup. Less einbrenne may be called for in recipes in which the liquid is already otherwise thickened (as in pea soup and potato soup), but which need a slight additional binding and a touch of flavor.

To make an einbrenne, melt the fat in a small, heavy saucepan or skillet. When hot, stir in the flour all at once; consistency should be smooth and like a very thick liquid. If dry and lumpy, add a little more fat. If too thin and watery, add a little more flour. Cook over low heat, stirring almost constantly, until you reach the desired color. It will take 7 or 8 minutes to reach the darkest, brown-sugar color.

Some of the liquid to be thickened can be poured into the einbrenne and beaten smooth, as when making cream sauce, but I have always followed my mother's practice of simply turning the einbrenne into the potful of simmering liquid and stirring until it has dissolved into the soup or sauce. It is important that it be turned into simmering or even gently boiling liquid so the roux will dissolve. If the liquid is cold or even tepid, the flour-and-fat combination will form lumps.

If you are adding minced onion or garlic, add to the hot fat and sauté until light golden brown. Then stir in the flour and proceed as above.

Basic Cream Sauce

2 tablespoons sweet butter
2 tablespoons flour
1 cup hot, scalded milk or half-and-
   half milk and cream (see note 1
   below

Salt and white pepper to taste
Nutmeg or other seasoning called
   for in individual recipes

Melt the butter in a small, heavy-bottomed saucepan. When hot and bubbling, stir in the flour, all at once. Cook, stirring frequently, over low heat for
3 or 4 minutes, or until the mixture is bright yellow. Pour in, all at once, the
hot, scalded milk, and using a wire whisk, beat and simmer over low heat
until the sauce is thick and smooth—about 5 minutes. Season to taste and
simmer a minute or two longer.

If the sauce is simply to be poured over a finished dish, simmer an additional 15 minutes over low heat, half covered and stirring frequently. If it
becomes too thick, thin with a little hot milk. If the sauce is to be added to a
food in which it will be cooked again (as when making creamed spinach or a
cream soup), you may add it to the other food after the first 5 minutes of
cooking time.

Yield: 1 cup

Notes: 1. Today's milk is less rich in cream, and half-and-half seems closer
to what it used to be, so use that if you prefer the added richness.

2. Cream thickenings for soups are included with the recipes for those
soups.

Cheese Sauce

Add 2 tablespoons grated Cheddar, Gruyère, or Parmesan to the basic
cream sauce (see above) along with the scalded milk. (Cayenne pepper was
always added instead of white pepper in a cheese sauce.)

Tomato Sauce

Although this sauce tastes best made with fresh tomatoes, it will be rich and
full-flavored only if the tomatoes are darkly red and completely ripe. Late

summer is the best time to get such tomatoes. And if they are not available, good canned tomatoes are preferable.

2 pounds fresh tomatoes, any size or variety as long as they are ripe, or 2 cans (1 pound each) tomatoes
4 tablespoons sweet butter or margarine, or corn oil
2 tablespoons finely minced carrots
3 tablespoons finely minced onion
2 tablespoons finely minced celery

1½ tablespoons flour
1 cup water, if fresh tomatoes are used
½ teaspoon salt
1 to 3 teaspoons sugar
1 teaspoon thyme
1 small bay leaf
1 clove garlic, peeled
3 sprigs parsley
1 sprig celery leaves

Cut the tomatoes up coarsely. It is not necessary to peel or seed them, as the sauce will be strained. If using canned tomatoes, drain well, reserving the liquid, and chop.

Heat the butter or margarine in a heavy-bottomed saucepan and sauté the minced vegetables slowly, stirring frequently, until very soft but not brown. Stir in the flour and cook slowly for about 5 minutes, or until it turns a bright yellow. Add the tomatoes, water or 1 cup canning liquid, and all the remaining ingredients. Cover and simmer slowly for 1 hour. Add more water (or liquid from canned tomatoes) if the mixture becomes dry. Uncover and simmer for 30 minutes longer, until the sauce becomes quite thick. Strain and press the vegetables through a sieve with a wooden spoon. Simmer for 5 minutes and check the seasonings.

If the sauce seems a little pale or thin, a tablespoonful of canned tomato paste can be added and simmered with it. However, the natural color should be a bright, rich orange red, and it seems too bad to spoil the delicate flavor in order to achieve a more customary color. Freeze, can, or store in the refrigerator.

Yield: About 2½ cups

Variations: 1. Although this sauce tastes best prepared with herbs, it is more flexible if cooked without them. In that case, herbs can be added when the sauce is reheated and will be better suited to the food it will be served with.

2. To give the sauce a Creole flavor, add 3 tablespoons diced sautéed green pepper and reheat together.

Mayonnaise

As a rule my mother used Hellmann's (Best Foods) mayonnaise for most occasions. She liked to thin it with a little fresh lemon juice and add a dab of prepared mustard when making salads, although she used it plain and thick for spreading on sandwiches.

But for special occasions, such as her almost endless luncheons and card parties, she made her own.

2 egg yolks, at room
      temperature
½ teaspoon salt
   Pinch of white pepper
½ teaspoon dry mustard
2 teaspoons lemon juice, more
      as needed

1 to 1¼ cups light vegetable oil, at
            room temperature (see
            note below)
1 to 2 tablespoons hot water
            (optional)

Use a mixing bowl made of porcelain, glass, or stainless steel. Rinse the bowl in hot water to warm it, then dry thoroughly.

Drop the egg yolks into the bowl; add the salt, pepper, mustard, and 2 teaspoons lemon juice; beat well.

Using a bottle or a small pitcher, trickle oil very, very slowly into the egg mixture, beating with a wire whisk between each addition. Do not add more oil before the previous amount has been absorbed.

Add a little lemon juice from time to time to keep the mixture workable. When the mayonnaise has reached the consistency of thin sour cream, add the remaining oil in a thin stream, beating constantly as you do so, until the desired thickness is reached. Check the seasonings and adjust to taste. If the mayonnaise is to be stored, beat in the hot water. Store in the refrigerator for no more than one week. If it curdles, reconstitute by dropping 1 room-temperature egg yolk into a mixing bowl and very slowly beating in the curdled mayonnaise.

Yield: About 1½ cups

Note: For most tastes, olive oil will be too overpowering for mayonnaise, but it can be used in half-and-half combination with vegetable oil; I prefer corn or peanut oil.

Russian Dressing

Russian dressing was a great favorite of ours. To make it my mother followed the simplest method of mixing ketchup or chili sauce with mayonnaise. Although I loved that as a child, I now find it a little sweet, possibly because those two tomato products are sweeter than they used to be, or because my palate has changed. A little fresh lemon juice will help unless the mayonnaise is good and lemony. I now prefer tomato puree blended into homemade mayonnaise; some fresh herbs are also desirable.

Russian dressing was served on seafood salads and on the wedges of iceberg lettuce I hated and never ate, and on sliced turkey and cole slaw sandwiches on rye bread, a combination I loved to have at the old Tip Toe Inn on upper Broadway, and which my mother approximated at home.

Tartar Sauce

We were never fond of sweet pickles in tartar sauce, so my mother devised the following version. The touch of curry powder was added now and then, and was especially good on cold fried fish.

¾ cup mayonnaise
1 tablespoon lemon juice
½ teaspoon grated lemon rind
1 tablespoon finely minced parsley
2 teaspoons finely minced green and
  white portions of scallion

2 teaspoons minced green olives
1 teaspoon drained, minced capers
1 small hard-cooked egg, peeled and
  finely chopped
Salt and white pepper to taste
Tiny pinch of curry powder
  (optional)

Beat the mayonnaise with the lemon juice and rind. Fold in the remaining ingredients, seasoning to taste. Chill several hours before serving.

Yield: About 1 cup

Sour Cream and . . .

This thick and piquant stand-by was used as a ready-made sauce for many dishes.

In addition it was the basis of several light main courses that we ate for summer lunches or dinner, especially if the other meal of the day had been a heavy one. Some of the following may be mentioned elsewhere, but a summation seems in order here. When using sour cream as a sauce or garnish, beat it with a fork, in a bowl, so it will become smooth and thin. Yogurt can be substituted in every case below for the diet-conscious, but the effect is not quite the same.

Sour Cream with Boiled Potatoes

Old potatoes were generally used, but new potatoes could be used also. Potatoes when done were returned to the dry, hot pot in which they had been cooked and were shaken over low heat until dry and floury. The hot potatoes were placed in deep individual fruit or cereal bowls, and the sour cream spooned over them. They were seasoned with salt and pepper, and sometimes with minced chives or chopped scallions. The contrast of hot potato with cold sour cream is one of my great taste memories. One medium or 3 small new potatoes covered with cream makes a portion.

Sour Cream with Vegetables and/or Pot Cheese

The Greek salad combination of cucumbers, scallions, radishes, and green peppers (see page 201) would be spooned into a deep fruit or cereal bowl and the cream poured over it. We would also pour sour cream over pot cheese—not cottage cheese, which is already creamed. Pot cheese and vegetables might be combined at one time. Be sure you do not make Greek salad with tomatoes if you intend to serve it with sour cream; in this instance the flavors will not mix and the liquid in the tomatoes will break down the cream.

Sour Cream with Rye Bread or Pumpernickel

As strange as it may sound, my mother sometimes served sour cream with chunks of either of these breads mixed into it. The rye bread was especially good because it had caraway seeds. This dish may have been a peculiar family taste, so I cannot guarantee that anyone else will like it. I liked some of the rye bread (in chunks with crusts) mixed in with the vegetables described above, which is somewhat like the Tuscan bread and vegetable salad.

Horseradish

Freshly grated horseradish root, when available, is preferable to the bottled variety. The fresh root is generally available in Jewish neighborhoods around Passover, but it may also be found at other times of the year.

The bottled variety is packed in vinegar, as it must be to prevent blackening. Freshly grated horseradish without vinegar is quite different and more interesting. To prepare it, peel a piece of horseradish root and grate on the fine side of a grater, or better yet in a blender or food processor. Grate only as much as you need for a meal. If you want to grate a lot in advance, then add a dash of salt, place in a narrow jar, and cover with white vinegar.

Yield: A horseradish root weighs about ¾ pound and will make about 1 cup when grated.

Beet Horseradish

Beets, or beet juice, color and sweeten horseradish. Beet horseradish can be bought bottled. To make your own, add about 2 teaspoons finely grated cooked beets to 1 cup of grated horseradish. For a milder color and sweetening, simply cover freshly grated horseradish with the juice of canned beets, or russell (page 60), and add a little vinegar and salt.

Vanilla Sugar

This sweetly fragrant confectioners' sugar makes a delightful topping for waffles, French toast, and cakes, or over any dessert for which confectioners' sugar is the final garnish. My grandmother kept hers in a sugar shaker which she covered with waxed paper so the scent of the vanilla bean did not evaporate. Plastic wrap or foil will do this more easily, or, if you prefer, keep it in a tightly closed jar and shake into a caster before using.

All you need for this is confectioners' sugar and a vanilla bean. A bean about 6 inches long will flavor 4 cups of confectioners' sugar if left in it for 2 weeks, but you can keep replacing the sugar for months before needing a new bean. For smaller amounts, such as a cup of sugar, use 2 to 3 inches of bean.

Cinnamon Sugar

This is a lovely sprinkling for French toast, blintzes, coffee cakes, and the like. Premixed cinnamon sugar purchased in stores is usually long on sugar, short on cinnamon. It is preferable to make your own, again in a shaker or a covered jar. The proportions I like are 2 tablespoons cinnamon to 1 cup granulated sugar. Combine in a jar, cover, and shake until well blended. You can also make cinnamon confectioners' sugar for a finer topping on cakes.

2

Washington Market

Whenever I drive downtown on West Street, along the Hudson River with its crumbling piers, and come to the area from Fulton Street to Canal Street, what I always see in my mind's eye is Washington Market, the old wholesale produce market that served New York and which has moved to the dismal concrete compound that is Hunt's Point. Except for a few of the restored market buildings that have been declared landmarks (many of the buildings used by the produce companies were originally homes built by the early Dutch settlers), no trace remains of the lively, colorful complex that once stood there. All is a wasteland cleared for construction or, in some parts, with apartment-house construction already underway.

But what I see in memory are long, narrow, dark streets lined with three-story buildings, all fronted with big black sheds that hung over the streets to protect them from snow, rain, and sun. For in this market the selling was done on "The Street," a composite name for all of the streets that crisscrossed the area.

The Street was my father's life. He was a commission merchant in Washington Market, contracting for crops from farmers in Florida, Georgia, the Carolinas, California, Texas, and just about everywhere else that crops were grown.

My father was something of an expert in this field and wrote two books—one on the distribution of fruits and vegetables, another advocating the use of railroads instead of trucks for transporting these perishables. And he was a frequent contributor to the trade paper, the *Produce News*. He was interviewed several times on a morning market program hosted by Mayor Fiorello La Guardia, and was the subject of stories in local papers. The tributes he was proudest of were two invitations from Henry A. Wallace, then Secretary of Agriculture, asking my father to go to Washington and discuss the views expressed in his books. Small wonder that Wallace was for years a hero in our household and, in a way, has remained one to me.

In those days the produce business was an exciting gamble, for, since commission merchants obviously worked on commission, they had to get the best possible price for the merchandise. My father left home in the dark hour between five and six in the morning, and though he was home by six in the evening, he remained on call all during the night as the trucks pulled in under the West Side Highway and unloaded their crates onto the streets. Toward three or four in the morning, buyers would go to market and the bargaining began. But in the middle of the night, when truckers were still hauling their produce from the farms, they would stop at checkpoints and call the New York produce merchants for whom they worked, so they could be given instructions as to which wholesale markets were getting the best prices. New York companies had agent firms in the markets of Baltimore, Washington, Philadelphia, and Boston, as well as in nearby markets in Newark and the Wallabout Market in Brooklyn.

If New York had a glut of string beans and prices were low, the truckload would be diverted to Baltimore or Philadelphia or wherever prices were holding up, or where the goods could be dumped at a low price before they spoiled and became a total loss.

Because of such imminent emergencies, and because only my father was empowered to make such decisions for the companies he worked for, he had to be reachable all through the night. If my parents went visiting, telephone numbers were left behind, and I can remember having him paged at local movie houses when urgent calls came from The Street.

Aside from the workings of the market itself, which made up much of my father's dinner table talk, there was conversation about the fruits and vegetables as well. I learned early that not all varieties of apples are equal in flavor and quality, that thick asparagus that fetch a premium price may not be as tender or flavorful as the thinner, less costly specimens, and that if anyone buys a head of cauliflower or cabbage without turning it over to look at the condition of the bottom of the core, he or she is a fool.

It meant too that we ate more unusual vegetables than most of the families around us. My father brought home eggplants and artichokes when they were rarely seen in the markets of Flatbush, as well as the season's first strawberries, asparagus, and corn, weeks before they were in middle-class, middle-price shops.

My mother was always pleased to see my father arrive with a crumpled brown bag filled with something special, and she would adjust her dinner menu to include the latest offering. Artichokes were quickly boiled and dressed with melted butter and lemon to be served as appetizers, eggplant slices were crisply fried as an extra vegetable, strawberries were given a brief washing and a bath of heavy sweet cream.

I loved going to Washington Market, as I often did with my father on Saturdays or Sundays when he had a few hours of work to clear up. Usually we would spend the morning there and then go to lunch and a movie up-town, but several times, during school vacations, I spent entire weekdays there. I can still remember the smell of the cool, damp streets, with their sweet, fresh orangewood crates, the pungent scent of crushed wet spinach or lettuce leaves, and the intermittent warm whiffs emanating from the sidings of dealers who handled onions and garlic.

The insides of those buildings were wobbly and, even then, tilted and askew. The narrow wood staircase we climbed to the second-floor offices was tipped away from its wall, and the office itself was a maze of various levels, leaning desks, hanging green-glass lampshades and heavy golden oak furniture that listed with the floor. I remember the bookkeeper wearing his green eyeshade sitting at a high oak counter desk, and the office manager, a tough, henna-haired woman who always wore black dresses, an old red sweater over her shoulders, high heels, and chunks of gold (fake or real I never knew) jewelry. My father said she had a big mouth, and her raucous voice bore evidence to his description, but I have a feeling she needed it in that time and place.

While my father worked, my favorite diversion was rolls of adding machine paper—oh, long and wondrous strips of blank paper waiting to be written on, not with some ordinary message but saved for an endless list.

For lunch on The Street we would go to a corner tavern restaurant, a place of tiled floors, star-etched mirrors, dark bentwood chairs, snowy tablecloths. Usually we sat at a big round table with friends of my father (most of the men who owned the businesses on The Street were Jews or Italians), and they began by downing shots of whiskey. The Italians all said "Lachaim," and the Jews all answered "Salud" in a show of camaraderie that was habitual but heartfelt.

I remember with joy and longing several dishes at that market restaurant. Among them were huge golden-brown Western omelets, flecked with green peppers, glassy onions, and dicings of pink ham, accompanied by crisp yet tender, oniony home fries. There was London broil in thick, bloody slices nestled under a beefy brown gravy full of fresh mushrooms and served with real mashed potatoes; or pink, gently saline corned beef and cabbage with dry, floury boiled potatoes; Yankee pot roast or sauerbraten with potato pancakes, applesauce, and a ruby mound of winy-red cabbage, one of the few vegetables I ever saw served in this restaurant in the heart of the vegetable market. Apple pie with cuts of Cheddar cheese was my father's dessert in winter; apple pie à la mode with vanilla ice cream was his daily dessert in summer.

A few times, when my parents took me to dinner and a theatre in New York to celebrate some special event and we were driving back to Brooklyn close to midnight, my father would stop on The Street for a minute to see if the unloading was underway or to warn his salesmen that a shipment of berries might be rotted because the farmlands had had an overabundance of rain. Late at night the black streets glowed with pools of light from electric bulbs strung under the sheds and from bonfires, burning in oil drums to warm the hands of market workers the night long.

His knowledge of fruits and vegetables made my father outspokenly intolerant of those who did not understand how to judge quality, whether they were professional buyers on The Street or housewives in our local stores. His pet peeve was the glowingly perfect, improbably huge hothouse fruit used in steamer baskets. He could go on for an hour at the dinner table about the high prices "the dopes" were paying for fruit that had no taste. When my mother would try to calm him and suggest gently that perhaps for the purpose of a special gift looks were important, my father would lose his temper and yell, "If it's looks they want, let them buy roses! Roses are to look at. Pears and apples are to eat!"

3

Appetizers, Snacks, and Sandwiches

"Nothing for vorspiese?" my father would ask with obvious disappointment in his voice if he thought my mother did not have an appetizer for dinner. *Vorspiese,* the German-Yiddish word for appetizer that means literally "before food," was a favorite course of his, second only to dessert. If my mother had nothing planned, she could always resort to a can of anchovies or sardines, which he loved on buttered toast, dressed only with a few drops of lemon juice. Although he was pleased with flat fillets of anchovies, he really preferred them rolled around capers, a variation I always thought looked like eyes. He also liked the cracklings or griebenes (left when the chicken fat was rendered), lightly salted all by themselves, and he was fond of starting with hot boiled artichokes accompanied by a pool of butter to which a few drops of lemon juice had been added.

My mother also made wonderful impromptu snacks and sandwiches, plain for our lunch boxes to school or beach, or fancy for one of her luncheons or late-night suppers.

Although I had no strong feelings about appetizers as a child, I now feel a meal is incomplete without one and would rather skip dessert if I had to choose.

In addition to the recipes in this chapter, appetizers were often merely smaller portions of main course dishes. See also the recipes for sweet and sour salmon (page 117), pickled jellied fish (page 113), fish in aspic (page 114), glazed sweet and sour stuffed cabbage (page 171), kofatellen (page 146), sweetbreads and mushrooms in patty shells (page 181).

For other salads used in sandwiches, see egg salad with green pepper (page 101), and the seafood salads on pages 119–20. See also the fried egg sandwich on page 94 and French-toasted cottage cheese sandwich on page 107.

Chopped Chicken Livers

I have had this favorite Friday night appetizer in other homes and in many restaurants, but I have never come across a version quite like my family's. It is much coarser, crumblier, and leaner than most, although my mother occasionally ground it very fine if she wanted to serve it as a spread, or if she wanted to mold it into a ring for a party. My grandmother used to broil the livers because it was the traditional way to kosher organ meats; my mother did so because she liked the flavor it imparted to the final result. Sometimes, however, she sautéed them, and both methods follow.

1 **pound chicken livers** (approximately 16 livers) Kosher (coarse) salt	3 to 4 **tablespoons schmaltz** (rendered chicken fat, page 7), or as needed
2 **extra-large eggs, hard cooked** and roughly cut up	2 **teaspoons salt, or to taste**
1 **medium onion, peeled and** coarsely chopped	¼ to ½ **teaspoon black pepper, or to** taste
⅓ to ½ **cup griebenes (cracklings,** page 7), optional but sensational	*Garnishes:* Sliced or grated black or white radishes or black radish and onion conserve (page 35)

Trim the chicken livers, removing any bits of fat adhering to them. It is not really necessary to remove the connective tissue. Dampen a large, clean sheet of brown wrapping paper by quickly passing both sides under cold running water. Place the wet paper on the broiler pan. Arrange the livers on the paper, leaving a little space between each. Sprinkle liberally with coarse salt. Broil for about 10 minutes, watching carefully to make sure the edges of the paper are wet enough to prevent them from burning. Moisten if necessary. You will not need to turn the livers over. They are done when the tops are brown but not black and the inside is firm but still faintly pink near the bottom.

Remove the livers from the paper, and brush off excess salt if any clings to them. The livers may be chopped on a board with a Fench chef's knife, or they can be chopped as my mother did them—in a big wooden bowl with a curved hand chopper, somewhat like a lunette. Cut up the livers coarsely and add the roughly cut-up eggs, coarsely chopped onion, and griebenes. Chop steadily until the mixture is well blended. The final texture should not be too fine, but rather like medium-fine chopped nuts. As you chop, add salt and pepper, tasting as you go along. The end result should be quite peppery and well salted.

Gently mix in only as much chicken fat as necessary to make the mixture hold together enough to be picked up on a fork. Since the mixture will be chilled, it will hold together more than when it was warm, so do not add too much fat. Pack into a crock or bowl, cover, and chill.

Chopped liver tastes better if it's allowed to chill for several hours before it is served, and I much prefer it after 24 hours. Remove from the refrigerator 15 minutes before serving.

Serve on lettuce, garnished with sliced or grated radishes or with the black radish and onion relish. Matzohs were considered essential to this dish, but crackers or toast can be substituted.

Yield: About 1 pound

Variations: 1. If you prefer, the livers can be sautéed instead of being broiled. To do this, place 3 or 4 tablespoons rendered chicken fat in a 10- to 12-inch skillet and slowly sauté the livers until they are firm and golden brown and just a tiny bit pink at the center. Place the livers and any of the sautéing fat that remains in the pan in the chopping bowl, and proceed with the recipe as above. In this case, it will probably not be necessary to add chicken fat at the end, but more salt will be needed.

2. To make a finer blend, to be served as a cocktail spread, put the livers, onions, eggs, and griebenes through the fine blade of a grinder twice, and add a little more fat. This method is best if you want to shape the liver in a mold. Grease an 8-inch ring mold lightly on the inside with mild-flavored vegetable oil. Then pack the liver mixture in firmly and chill for at least 5 hours, but preferably 24. Unmold onto a platter and garnish with radishes. A bouquet of curly, dark green chickory is a nice touch in the center of the ring.

Chopped Eggs and Onions

We always referred to this appetizer salad as chopped liver without the liver, for obvious reasons. Although it was often served with matzohs, we preferred it with very dark, moist Russian pumpernickel. It can also be used as a cocktail spread, if finely ground.

6 hard-cooked eggs, chopped
1 small onion, very finely minced
1 tablespoon crumbled griebenes
     (cracklings, page 7) (optional)
   Salt and white pepper to taste

2 tablespoons schmaltz (rendered
     chicken fat, page 7), or as
     needed
   Salty black olives, for garnish

Combine the eggs, onion, and griebenes and chop together until blended. Do not stir together or the eggs will become a paste. Season with salt and pepper and add just enough fat to bind the mixture. Serve with black olives.

Yield: About 1 cup

Chopped Mushrooms, Eggs, and Onions

This was much like a vegetarian chopped liver. As with chopped liver or eggs and onions, it can be served on a plate garnished with lettuce and black olives, or it can be spread on matzohs, pumpernickel, or toast. It also makes a delicious sandwich filling, especially suited to light whole-wheat bread.

2 tablespoons butter, margarine, or
     schmaltz (rendered chicken fat,
     page 7)
4 medium-sized mushrooms, cleaned
     and coarsely chopped

1 tablespoon minced onion
4 eggs, hard cooked and coarsely
     chopped
   Salt and white pepper to taste

Heat the fat in a small skillet, and when hot and bubbly add the onion. Sauté until it begins to wilt and add the mushrooms. Sauté a few minutes, stirring frequently, until the mushroom liquid evaporates and they begin to soften. Do not brown the mushrooms or onion.

Add the mushroom-onion mixture to the coarsely chopped eggs and continue to mix by chopping until evenly combined. Be sure to scrape in all fat and any liquid left from the sautéing. Season to taste. Chill several hours before serving.

Yield: About ¾ cup

Pickled Herring

A year-round favorite, this was a must for Yom Kippur, when a dairy dinner was served after the twenty-four-hour fast. It also appeared at post-funeral breakfasts, again featuring dairy dishes. I have never eaten store-bought pickled herring that even began to compare with this, and though it's a bit messy in the first stages of preparation, it is really simple and foolproof to produce.

My grandmother did not add sour cream until a few hours before the herring was to be served, for two reasons. For one thing, because she kept a kosher house, if there was no cream added the herring could be served as an appetizer before a meal that would include meat. It could also be kept longer if the cream was not in it to sour.

Many people prefer schmaltz herring to salt for pickling, but the fatter herring is really too soft and bland. Salt herring has a firmer texture and a more distinctive flavor.

Neither my mother or grandmother believed in skinning or filleting the herring before pickling. They thought there was a great loss of flavor and texture if that was done, and I agree with them. Nevertheless, if anyone prefers a more refined version, skin and fillet the herring—but only after it has been soaked. Otherwise it loses flavor. In addition, it is easy to pull the skin off the fish after it has soaked.

Do not use mixed pickling spices in making this recipe, as the combination contains sweetly aromatic spices such as cinnamon and cloves that are not correct for this dish.

The best herrings for pickling are those that have miltz, the milky sacs that are the spleen of the fish. Extra miltz can usually be purchased where raw herring is sold, and should be if the fish have none. If you buy roe herring, discard the roe.

(continued)

6 large salt herring, whole and
   unopened, preferably with miltz,
   plus extra miltz as needed to
   have 4 or 5 sacs
3 medium yellow onions (about 1
   pound)
3 cups distilled white vinegar
⅔ cup water
2 large bay leaves

10 to 12 white peppercorns
2 whole dried hot red chili
   peppers or ½ teaspoon
   crushed hot pepper flakes
15 to 18 whole coriander seeds
½ teaspoon mustard seeds
   Sour cream (optional)
   Boiled potatoes, for garnish

Salt herring needs a good deal of soaking before it can be pickled. Depending on saltiness and your preference, soaking time can take anywhere from 3 days to a week, plus at least 48 hours pickling time, so begin well in advance of the time you want to serve it. To see if the herring has soaked enough, taste it raw, or if that bothers you, sauté a small piece in some butter and taste it.

Place the whole unopened herrings and the extra miltz in a large deep glass or ceramic bowl and cover well with ice-cold water. Place in the refrigerator, loosely covered, and let soak as needed—probably between 3 and 5 days. Change the water twice a day, rinsing the herring under cold running water between water changes.

Have on hand a clean, wide-mouthed glass jar or ceramic crock of about 4-quart capacity. When ready for pickling, drain the water from the herrings. Place a thick sheaf of newspapers on the sink drainboard. Using scissors, trim off all fins and tail sections. Cut the herring open down their bellies and gently lift out the insides, discarding everything except the pinkish-white miltz sacs. Set those aside. If you want to skin the herring, make a small slit down the back and gently work off the skin, using your fingers and a sharp, pointed knife. Otherwise, just cut the cleaned herring, skin and all, into 1½- to 2-inch crosswise slices, cutting right through the bone.

Peel the onions and cut into very thin, round slices. Separate the slices into rings. Set aside.

Combine the vinegar, water, and all the spices in an enameled or stainless-steel saucepan and bring to a rolling boil for about 5 minutes. Add the onions and turn through the hot liquid. Set aside to cool. When cool, remove the onion rings from the liquid. Reserving the liquid, arrange herring pieces and the onion rings in alternate layers in the jar or crock.

Using a fork, mash all the miltz on a plate, pressing the insides out of the sacs, so you will be left with a smooth, thick, creamy substance and a membrane that can be discarded. Miltz can be creamed in a blender or food processor, but they then have to be strained to eliminate the membrane, so the mashing process seems simpler. Beat the pureed miltz into the cooled vinegar and spice liquid and pour over the herring and onions. Cover the jar or crock tightly and turn over so all air bubbles rise to the surface and the pickling liquid fills all corners of the jar.

If you are using a glass jar with a metal lid or a rubber gasket, place a double layer of waxed paper over the mouth of the jar before screwing on the cap. The metal will corrode when in contact with the pickling fluid, and the rubber gasket will take on a herring odor that cannot be removed.

Herring can be eaten after 24 hours, but a real pickled flavor begins to develop after 48 hours. I like it best after it has pickled for 5 days. I have never known herring to become too pickled or to spoil, mostly because I have never had any around for more than 10 days. If you do want to serve it after only 24 or 48 hours, boil the onion rings in the vinegar for about 10 minutes, or they will be rubbery. After 3 or 4 days, boiled or not, they become tender although firm, the ideal combination.

Herring can be served just with onions, without the addition of sour cream, but to prepare a sour cream sauce, beat 1 to 2 tablespoons pickling liquid into each ½ cup of sour cream you will need. Place the herring and onions to be served in a bowl and mix gently with the sour cream sauce. This can be served at once, but more flavor will develop after an hour or two in the refrigerator. Herring should be served cold, but not icily so.

Hot boiled potatoes are wonderful with this, as is black bread.

Yield: About 3 quarts of pickled herring or 16 pieces, from 4 to 16 servings.

Raw Herring with Onion Rings

Tender red maatjes herring is best for this, but schmaltz herring is also good.

4 maatjes or schmaltz herrings or 8 fillets	Boiled or baked potatoes, for garnish
Spanish, Bermuda, or red onions, peeled and sliced into thin rings	

If you buy maatjes fillets, they will probably have been soaked and are ready to serve. Whole raw herrings should be soaked as described for pickled herrings (page 25). Schmaltz herrings usually need no more than 2 days of soaking: their water should be changed twice daily.

(continued)

If using whole herrings, split, clean, and remove the skin after soaking, using a sharp, pointed knife and your fingers. Cut fillets off the bone. Arrange on a serving plate and top with onion rings.

Boiled potatoes, with or without sour cream, or buttered baked potatoes, are excellent foils for the saltiness of the fish.

Yield: 8 servings

Canned Salmon with Onions and Vinegar

A favorite appetizer for dairy dinners, this was usually based on red sockeye salmon or the Bumble Bee brand. Nothing else was considered acceptable.

1 can (7½ ounces) sockeye, blueback, or Chinook salmon	½ cup distilled white vinegar Black pepper (optional)
1 tablespoon finely minced Bermuda or Spanish onion	

Arrange the salmon in a serving dish, removing the center core bone and breaking the meat into fork-size pieces. Add the minced onion to the vinegar in a small bowl. Serve the salmon on individual plates and spoon onion and a little vinegar over each portion. Add pepper, if desired.

Yield: 2 servings

Gefüllte Fish

[Stuffed Fish]

Along with chicken soup and chopped liver, this dish completed the holy trinity of my mother's kitchen. Any woman who could not make proper gefüllte fish (by "proper" she meant fish that tasted exactly like hers) was barely worth socializing with. Hers was by all odds extraordinary, differing from most in that it was cooked in a broth loaded with onions and the fish itself was heavily peppered. There was not a trace of sweetness in it; only the tiniest pinch of sugar was added if the fish broth seemed acidic, and no carrots were grated into the mix, another practice that results in sweet fish.

Although it was ground finely enough to hold together smoothly, the fish was still coarse enough to have an interesting texture, not too solid or all of a piece. My grandmother chopped her fish in a big wooden bowl with a lunette, or half-moon hand chopper; my mother did hers in a grinder and then chopped as other ingredients were added. Blenders and processors produce too fine a mix for this. Anyone with patience should try the chopping method at least once, to see the fish at its most perfect. Sometimes my grandmother wrapped fish skins around the balls of fish before cooking so it really lived up to its name. My mother cooked the skins for flavor but did not wrap the skin around the fish balls because as kids we hated it. The fish was always placed in cold water; hot water tends to make it toughen and harden. Carp was added if my mother trusted the fish man and knew it would not taste of mud, as carp often does, thereby spoiling the taste of the entire batch. For that reason pike and whitefish were most often used, and carp eliminated.

It is possible to have the fish ground at the market, but my mother's belief that the mix will invariably include some scales has been transmitted to me, and though I have it filleted and trimmed at the market, I grind or chop it myself. Tiny balls can be made for cocktail use.

3 pounds pike (weight before cleaning, filleting), approximately	2 teaspoons salt
	½ to 1 teaspoon white pepper, depending on your tolerance
3 pounds whitefish (weight before cleaning, filleting), approximately	2 tablespoons matzoh meal
	5 very large or 7 medium onions, peeled
or	6 cups water, approximately
2 pounds each pike and whitefish and 1 pound carp, filleted	Small strip of knob celery, if available
Kosher (coarse) salt	3 large carrots, scraped and sliced into ½-inch rounds
All bones, heads, skin, and trimmings from above fish, with carp roe, if any	Pinch of sugar
	Red or white horseradish (page 15) and matzohs, as accompaniment
2 large onions, peeled	
2 extra-large eggs, lightly beaten	
½ cup ice water, approximately	

Rinse the fish fillets under cold running water, place in a bowl, sprinkle lightly with coarse salt, and store in the refrigerator for 4 or 5 hours or overnight, before beginning the preparation. Place all the trimmings in a separate bowl, salt, and store in the same way. Set the roe aside until ready to use.

(continued)

When you begin the preparation, rinse the fish and trimmings and drain well. Place all the trimmings in the bottom of a wide, 3- to 3½-quart Dutch oven-type pot. Set aside.

Chop all the fish together, either by hand, using a round wooden bowl and a half-moon chopper, or by putting it through the fine blade of a grinder. Grind or chop the two large onions along with it. Then grind all again, or keep chopping until smooth. Stir in the eggs, ice water, salt, pepper, and matzoh meal. Mix well. The consistency should be soft and thick, somewhat like thick, cooked oatmeal.

If you want to taste for seasoning, pinch off a small amount of fish, about the size of a hazelnut, and cook it in simmering salted water. Cool quickly in the freezer and taste. (Do not taste the fish raw, as it is freshwater fish and may be dangerous in an uncooked state.) Add salt or pepper to the raw mix as needed.

Slice the very large or medium onions in thin rounds and add to the pot with the fish trimmings. Pour in enough water to come very slightly above the onions; this should be between 4 and 6 cups. Shape the fish into slightly oval or round balls, each using about 2 tablespoons of fish. Shape with wet hands or with two wet tablespoons. Gently place the fish balls on top of the onion bed. Cover and bring to a boil, then lower the heat, and with cover slightly askew, simmer gently but steadily for 1 hour.

Add the knob celery, if you have it, along with the carrots and roe. Taste the broth and add a little salt and pepper if needed, and a tiny pinch of sugar if the broth is unpleasantly sharp. Cover and continue cooking at a steady simmer for another hour.

If the pieces of fish are touching and seem to stick together when first placed in the pot, don't worry. As they cook you will be able to separate them merely by shaking the pot gently several times during cooking.

Let the fish cool in the broth. When cool, gently lift the pieces out and place in a dish that is 2 or 3 inches deep and large enough to accommodate the fish in a single layer.

Strain the fish stock and reserve. Pick out a few of the onions and carrots and strew them over the fish and roe. Pour the strained stock over all and chill in the refrigerator. The fish tastes better if it stands overnight, although it can also be served freshly made and hot, something I detest.

The fish broth should jell. Serve, diced, with the fish and a piece of carrot, onion, and roe, and, of course, with horseradish, red or white. Matzohs are also a standard accompaniment. Stored in the refrigerator, the fish will keep for 3 to 5 days, and possibly even a week.

Yield: 10 to 12 pieces

Kalechla

[Mock Gefüllte Fish]

This is one more standard family dish that I have never come across elsewhere, although I have looked in dozens of Jewish cookbooks. We called it "fake gefüllte fish" because it was made with chicken and veal and was almost indistinguishable from the original. The only difference was an ever so slightly drier, meatier texture, noticeable only if one concentrated, and a total absence of a fish smell, although that smell is only faintly discernible in real gefüllte fish because of the mild fish used and the large quantity of onion.

1 pound lean, boneless shoulder of
   veal
2 pounds boned and skinned breast of
   chicken
4 large onions, peeled
2 teaspoons salt
1 teaspoon white pepper
2 extra-large eggs

2 to 3 tablespoons matzoh meal
1 large stalk celery with leaves
2 carrots, scraped and sliced into
   ½-inch rounds
4 cups water, approximately
   Pinch of salt
   Red or white horseradish
   (page 15)

Remove all membranes and cartilage from the veal and chicken so they will not jam in the grinder. As with gefüllte fish, you may chop by hand, but this is more difficult with meat, and it is best to grind both meats together through the fine blade of a food chopper. A food processor will make the mixture too fine. Grind 1 large onion in with the chicken and veal.

Add the salt, pepper, eggs, and enough matzoh meal to bind slightly. The mixture should be like thick, cooked oatmeal porridge.

Slice the remaining onions and place, along with the celery and carrots, in a 2½- to 3-quart enameled Dutch oven-type pot. Add just enough water to come to the level of the onions—about 4 cups. Add a pinch of salt to the water and bring to a boil.

Shape the kalechla as described for gefüllte fish (page 30), but use only about 1 heaping tablespoonful of the mix per portion. These should be a bit smaller than the fish pieces, or they will toughen from longer cooking. Gently place the shaped balls in the boiling water. Reduce to a simmer, half cover the pot, and simmer gently for 1 to 1½ hours, or until thoroughly cooked. Taste the broth during the cooking and add salt and pepper if needed.

Let the kalechla cool in the broth. When cool, remove to a deep dish. Pick out the carrot pieces and arrange around the kalechla.

Strain the cooking liquid into a bowl, rubbing through all of the cooked onion slices but discarding the celery. Pour this reduced, onion-thickened broth over the kalechla and let chill at least 12 hours before serving. This broth will not jell. Serve one or two kalechla as an appetizer with sauce, horseradish, and matzohs.

Yield: About 8 to 10 pieces

Calf's Brains Vinaigrette

1 **pound calf's brains**	4 to 5 **tablespoons mild vegetable oil**
1 **stalk celery with leaves**	**(see note below)**
Small piece of onion	**Salt and black pepper to taste**
4 or 5 **peppercorns**	1 **tablespoon capers**
1 **tablespoon fresh lemon juice**	**Minced parsley, for garnish**
1 **tablespoon white vinegar**	

Prepare the calf's brains by soaking and parboiling them with the celery, onion, and peppercorns as directed for sweetbreads on page 179. When the membrane and tubes have been trimmed away, slice the brains or cut in small sections. Combine the lemon juice, vinegar, and oil and beat or shake until blended. Pour over the warm brains, sprinkling with a little salt and pepper. Add the capers and toss gently. Chill for several hours, adjust the seasoning, and serve with minced parsley sprinkled on top.

Freshly made toast is excellent with this.

Yield: 4 appetizer servings

Note: I prefer a very mild olive oil for this dressing, but sunflower or corn oil can be substituted. If you like, a small clove of garlic, sliced, can be added to the dressing and removed just before serving.

Eggplant Caviar, Two Ways

My mother and grandmother prepared this two ways, the first as a puree bound with tomato that was kept for a day or two and was as rich as a conserve. The second is a fresher, lighter puree that should be served within two or three hours of the time it is made. In both, the smoky flavor of the broiled eggplant adds the distinctive and characteristic touch.

Eggplant Caviar I

1 medium-sized ripe eggplant
¼ cup vegetable oil, preferably olive, or as needed
1 small onion, peeled and finely minced
1 large clove garlic, minced
3 small canned tomatoes, drained and pureed, or 3 tablespoons tomato puree (not paste)

Salt, pepper, and lemon juice to taste

Garnishes: 1 tablespoon finely minced parsley, salty black olives, and (optional) chopped raw onion

There are two methods for broiling eggplant. The slightly better, if more tedious way, is to hold it over an open flame with a long-handled carving or barbecue fork, turning slowly until the outside skin is evenly charred and the inside is almost completely tender. This will take about 20 to 30 minutes.

The simpler method is broiling. Cut the whole, unpeeled eggplant in half vertically and remove only the leaves of the stem end. Place a piece of aluminum foil on the pan of your broiler. Brush the cut side of each eggplant half with oil, and place cut side down on the foil. Broil about 4 inches below the flame or coil until the skin is charred and the flesh is tender.

When the eggplant has been cooked by either method, peel, scrape out the seeds, and chop the flesh fine. Heat 2 tablespoons of the oil in a heavy-bottomed saucepan and in it slowly sauté the minced garlic and onion until soft but not brown. Stir in the eggplant and tomato puree and trickle in enough oil to enable the mixture to simmer.

Simmer over very low heat for about 30 minutes, adding trickles of oil as needed to prevent scorching, and stirring frequently and vigorously with a wooden spoon until the mixture is smooth and thick.

Add salt, pepper, and a few drops of lemon juice to taste. Chill at least several hours. Serve garnished with the minced parsley, salty black olives, and chopped raw onion, if you like.

Yield: About ¾ cup

Eggplant Caviar II

This is almost exactly like the Middle Eastern baba gannouj.

1 medium eggplant	1 to 2 tablespoons lemon juice
1 clove garlic, lightly crushed and peeled	Salt and white pepper to taste
Pinch of kosher (coarse) salt	*Garnishes:* 1 small onion, peeled and
About ¼ cup olive, sesame, or sunflower oil	finely chopped, and/or 1 small ripe tomato, cut in coarse chunks, and/or minced parsley

Cook the eggplant either over an open flame or under a flame, as described in the preceding recipe. Peel, remove the seeds, and chop. Rub a small mixing bowl with the crushed garlic clove and coarse salt. Leave the garlic in the bowl. Add the chopped eggplant and, with a wooden spoon, beat the eggplant as you slowly add trickles of oil, much as you would for mayonnaise. The final result should be thick and smoothly silky, but not liquidy. Stir in lemon juice, salt, and pepper to taste. Let stand from 1 to 3 hours in the refrigerator so the flavor will develop.

Serve with any or all of the garnishes sprinkled on top or stirred into the puree. This is especially good with dark bread or with Middle Eastern pita bread.

Yield: About ¾ cup

Radishes

Red, white, and black radishes were standard garnishes for appetizers at our house, most especially with chopped liver. For some reason, my mother in serving the red radishes would cut off all green leaves but leave the root.

White icicle radishes, whole if young and tender, sliced or grated if older and tougher, were also regulars.

But the ones we looked and longed for were the round, earthy black radishes of winter. These would be peeled, washed, then sliced into paper-thin rounds and crisped in ice water, or they might be grated in long, silky shreds with or without Spanish or Bermuda onions, or made into the conserve on page 35. Unlike the red and white radishes, the black were never served in salads or with sour cream. They ranged in flavor from mildly, pleasantly mustily earthy to bitingly strong and peppery.

In buying all radishes, be sure they are rock hard and not split, faded, or limp.

Black Radish and Onion Salad

This salad is a lighter, fresher variation on the conserve that my grandmother would prepare when a child or grandchild arrived at her house starving, a frequent occurrence. Pumpernickel seemed always to be on hand to go with it, but it is also very good on matzohs.

2 medium black radishes	Salt and black pepper, plenty
½ large Bermuda or Spanish	of both and to taste
onion	
1 to 2 tablespoons schmaltz	
(rendered chicken fat, page	
7), or to taste	

Wash and peel the radishes. Grate the radishes and onion on the coarsest side of a four-sided grater, to make long, slim slivers. Toss together gently with a fork, adding schmaltz, salt, and pepper.

Yield: 2 servings

Black Radish and Onion Conserve

A variation on the above, this radish and onion combination improves with age and is a rich, soft, and pungent accompaniment to chopped liver, or is equally good by itself spread on dark pumpernickel or matzohs.

(continued)

2 large black radishes	½ cup schmaltz (rendered chicken
3 tablespoons kosher (coarse) salt	fat, page 7), solidified
1 small onion	Black pepper to taste

Scrub and peel the radishes. Grate on the coarse side of a grater; you should have 4 cups. Toss with the coarse salt and place, loosely covered, in the refrigerator for 4 hours. Remove, place in a strainer, and rinse under very cold running water. Pick up handfuls of the radish and squeeze out as much water as possible. At that point you should have about 2 cups of compacted radish. Peel and grate the onion and toss with the radish, along with the chicken fat and pepper.

Pack into a clean jar, cover tightly, and place in the refrigerator for at least 4 days before eating. The relish will last for weeks, so double or triple this amount if you like the results.

Yield: About 2 cups

Creamed Mushrooms on Toast

Depending on her mood, my mother prepared these either with sweet or sour cream, with onions or without, and always as an appetizer. I find it is also a good accompaniment to breaded, fried veal cutlets, steak or roast beef, or as part of an all-vegetable main-course assortment.

1 pound firm white mushrooms	2 teaspoons flour
3 tablespoons sweet butter	⅔ to 1 cup sweet or sour cream
1 tablespoon finely minced onion	4 slices freshly made toast
(optional)	A few drops of water (optional)
Salt, white pepper, and nutmeg	

You may use small, medium, or large mushrooms. The small are best left whole, while the medium or large may be halved vertically or, if you prefer, sliced. If the mushrooms are sandy, wash quickly under cold running water and dry each individually. If they seem clean, just wipe with a damp towel. Trim off the bottom end of the stems and cut or slice as you prefer.

Heat the butter in a saucepan. If you want an onion flavor, sauté the minced onion until soft but not brown. Remove the onion and reserve. Sauté the mushrooms slowly until all liquid evaporates and the mushrooms begin to turn golden brown. Return the onion to the pan. Sprinkle with salt, pepper, nutmeg, and the flour. Stir until the flour is absorbed. Stir in the cream and mix until smoothly blended. Simmer gently for 2 or 3 minutes. If the mixture is too thick add more cream or, if you are using sour cream, a few drops of water. Serve at once, on the freshly made toast.

Yield: 4 servings

Mushrooms and Onions on Toast

1 **pound small or medium firm white mushrooms**	**Pinch of nutmeg (optional)**
1 **medium onion, peeled**	2 to 3 **teaspoons flour**
3 to 5 **tablespoons sweet butter, as needed**	3 to 4 **tablespoons water (see note below)**
Salt and black pepper	4 **slices freshly made toast**

If the mushrooms are sandy, wash quickly under cold running water and dry each thoroughly. If they are very white and clean, just wipe each with a damp towel. Slice off the bottom end of the stems. If the mushrooms are very small, leave them whole. If they are medium to large, cut in vertical quarters or halves, right through the stem.

Slice the onions and separate into rings.

Heat 3 tablespoons butter and add the onion rings. Sauté very slowly, and as they begin to soften, add the mushrooms and toss to coat with butter. Add more butter as needed. Sauté until the mushrooms begin to soften and their liquid evaporates—about 5 to 7 minutes. Sprinkle with salt, pepper, and nutmeg, if you are using it, and just enough flour to lightly bind the mixture. Stir in a little water, cover the pan, and simmer for 10 minutes, checking to see if more water is needed. Stir frequently with a wooden spatula. Adjust the seasoning and serve spooned on the toast slices.

Yield: 4 servings

Note: Although my mother always used water, I have sometimes used a light beef broth or a little dry white wine.

Sautéed Chicken Livers with Mushrooms and Onions

Prepare exactly as the above recipe, but begin by sautéing 1 pound of cleaned, well-trimmed chicken livers in the butter. Remove, set aside, then proceed with the cooking of the mushrooms and onions. Return the livers to the pan just before sprinkling on the flour and liquid and continue cooking as described. This will take a little more butter, flour, liquid, and seasoning, so adjust the amounts.

This can be served on toast or on a mound of steamed white rice, the latter being the way my mother served it as a light main course.

I have also used this as a brunch dish accompanied by scrambled eggs, toasted English muffins, and cottage cheese.

Yield: 6 servings

Meatball and Giblet Fricassee

This dish is prepared exactly like the chicken fricassee with meatballs on page 145 and was a standard appetizer on Friday night when the chicken giblets were on hand. It may be done with meatballs and giblets in combination or with either alone. The tiny meatballs prepared without giblets make good hot appetizers for cocktail parties, kept warm in a chafing dish. They are also delicious served on rice as a light main course. They may be flavored with either garlic or onion, something I vary with my mood. The garlic is preferable if the meatballs are to be served with cocktails. Proportion of giblets to meatballs is arbitrary.

1 pound chicken giblets, to include gizzard and heart (but not liver), neck, backbone, and, if you like, chicken wings

½ pound ground lean chuck

1 small egg

½ clove garlic, crushed in a press, or 2 teaspoons grated onion

Salt and black pepper

1 tablespoon fine, dry bread crumbs, as needed

2 tablespoons schmaltz (rendered chicken fat, page 7), margarine, or sweet butter

1 large onion, peeled and finely chopped

1½ tablespoons sweet paprika or 1 tablespoon sweet paprika plus 1½ teaspoons hot paprika

1 or 2 cloves garlic, peeled and cut in half vertically

1 cup water, or as needed

Clean the giblets, removing all skin and bits of fat. Gizzards should be scalded for 2 or 3 minutes in boiling water.

Mix the chopped beef with the egg, crushed garlic or grated onion, 1 teaspoon salt, and ¼ teaspoon black pepper (or adjust to taste); add just enough bread crumbs to make the mixture firm enough to mold into balls. Toss the ingredients lightly with a fork or the mixture will become too compacted and the meat balls will be hard. Shape into tiny meatballs, each about the size of a hazelnut.

Melt the fat in a 2-quart saucepan or casserole. Add the onion and sauté very slowly until it is completely soft and bright yellow; do not let the onion brown. Stir in the paprika and sauté for a minute or two, or until it loses its raw smell. Add the cut-up garlic and 1 cup water.

Place the giblets and meatballs in the pan and add more water as needed to come about halfway up the meats. Add a little salt and pepper, half cover, and simmer gently but steadily for about 30 minutes, or until the giblets are tender and the meatballs are well done. Check frequently to see if more water is needed. Serve plain or with steamed white rice.

Yield: 4 servings

Petcha or Feesel

[*Calf's Feet*]

The usual Yiddish name for jellied calf's feet is "petcha," a term I never heard at home where they were known as "feesel"—undoubtedly derived from the German *Fussen,* for "feet." Not only the name differed. Unlike the pale aspic that contains shreds of meat picked off the bone, my mother's calf's foot appetizer, reserved exclusively for Friday night, was really a braised dish of large chunks of feet, bone and all, flavored with paprika, onions, and plenty of garlic. It was served hot in soup bowls the first night, and I loathed not only the taste but the smell as well and so left the room during that course. A sign of its being really well cooked was if one's lips stuck together when compressed after eating this specialty. On Saturday, usually for lunch, my mother and father ate the remainder, now cold and set in the paprika-scented jell. I didn't mind being at that table then, but I never touched this until I was an adult. I can't say I like it entirely even now, not being fond of cartilagenous textures, but the sauce is wonderful and my husband happily consumes the whole thing, almost including the bones, which become very soft as they cook.

Many butchers keep scalded and cleaned calf's feet in their freezers. In other cases you will have to order them in advance and may have to clean them yourself. They should be plunged into boiling water and left there for about 10 minutes, then scraped clean of tough outer skin, hair, and whatever. (I have never seen toenails on calf's feet, for which I am thankful.) Even if they are not cleaned, you should have the butcher cut the feet with his electric saw—first split in half lengthwise, then cut across in 1- to 1½-inch chunks.

2 calf's feet, scalded, cleaned, split, and cut as described above

1 tablespoon schmaltz (rendered chicken fat, page 7) margarine, or sweet butter

1 medium carrot, scraped and coarsely chopped

1 large onion, peeled and coarsely chopped

1 generous tablespoon sweet paprika

2 teaspoons salt

1 teaspoon black pepper

2 tablespoons distilled white vinegar

4 cloves garlic, peeled, cut in half vertically, and sliced

Lemon juice or vinegar

Cleaned, scalded feet cut in pieces are ready for cooking if they have been scalded *after* they were cut, and are still warm. If they were purchased clean and cut, blanch in boiling water to cover for 10 minutes. Drain.

Melt the fat in a heavy 3-quart casserole and stir in the chopped carrot and onion. Sauté slowly, stirring frequently, until the vegetables are soft and just begin to take on color. Stir in the paprika, salt, and pepper and sauté for a minute or two. Stir in the calf's feet, sprinkle with the vinegar, and stir to coat with the paprika mixture. Add the garlic and enough water to barely cover the calves' feet.

Bring to a boil, reduce the heat, and simmer gently, loosely covered, for about 1½ hours, or until the meat is completely tender and coming away from the bones. During the cooking, add hot water as needed to keep the mixture from scorching. Stir several times with a wooden spatula. Let stand for an hour before serving so the grease can be skimmed off the top. Reheat and serve hot with lemon juice or vinegar to be sprinkled on individual portions at the table. My mother served this in warmed soup plates and everyone picked and nibbled at the bones, then used challah (page 247) to sop up the sauce.

Variation: To serve cold, place the pieces of feet in a deep baking dish or platter and pour the sauce and vegetables over. Serve chilled and set, also with lemon juice or vinegar and challah.

Yield: 4 servings

Roasted Peppers with Garlic

Although it is easier to roast several peppers all at once in the oven, the flavor is better if they are done over the flame or under the broiler, the latter being the trickiest to control.

6 large, firm, perfect green peppers
2 teaspoons salt
6 to 8 cloves garlic, lightly crushed
     and peeled

Olive or corn oil to cover, as
needed

Wash and dry the peppers. To roast over the flame, impale on a long-handled fork and turn slowly so the skin chars off. Or place on a piece of oiled aluminum foil in the broiler pan and broil about 4 inches from the flame, turning frequently. To roast, place the peppers upright in a roasting pan and set in a 400-degree oven for about 30 minutes, turning frequently so all sides blacken.

Whichever method you use, the peppers should be peeled, a simple matter if they were broiled over or under the flame. This can be trickier if they were roasted. In that case, place the peppers in a brown paper bag, close the bag, and let stand for about 10 minutes, after which the skin will be easy to pull off. It is important to understand, however, that for the true nature of these peppers to be realized, broiling is better; the roasted peppers become too soft. Those that are broiled are firmer.

Trim off the stem ends and discard the seeds. Place the peppers, in as large pieces as possible, in a tall, straight-sided jar. Add the salt and garlic and pour in enough oil to cover. Close the jar tightly and store in a cool place or the refrigerator for 5 days to a week. Before serving, let stand at room temperature for 20 to 30 minutes so the oil liquefies. Serve as an appetizer or as you would pickles, with a meat course.

Grilled Red Peppers

Ripe red sweet peppers, roasted over the flame or under the broiler, were something my grandmother also made, but without garlic. The rest of the recipe is exactly as above.

Deviled Eggs

My mother served these when she was stuck for an appetizer, but also at party luncheons and family picnics; and she often tucked a deviled egg, well wrapped in waxed paper, into a school lunch box.

4 extra-large eggs
   Salt
2 teaspoons mayonnaise, or as
   needed

½ teaspoon prepared mustard
   White pepper to taste

Garnishes: Capers, sweet paprika,
   minced parsley, or minced chives,
   or dill

Place the eggs in a saucepan with cold water to cover and a handful of salt, which, my mother said, prevented the egg white from running out of the shell should they crack. They are less likely to crack if begun in cold water. Bring to a boil, reduce the heat, and let bubble gently for 10 minutes. Do not boil rapidly or cover the pan.

Quickly drain off the hot water and let cold water run over the eggs for about 10 minutes to cool. Crack the egg shell lightly on all sides, then roll the egg gently between the palms of your hands so the shell cracks and loosens. To have attractive deviled eggs you will want eggs that have been peeled smoothly, and this makes the task easier. Remove the shell.

Cut each egg in half vertically and carefully remove the yolks. Place in a bowl and mash in the mayonnaise, mustard, and a pinch each of salt and white pepper to taste. Add enough mayonnaise to make a smooth, creamy mixture. The egg whites can be refilled with the yolks using a small teaspoon, or the yolk mixture can be pressed out of a fluted pastry tube for a fancier effect. Divide the egg yolk among the 8 halves of white and fill each.

Top with drained capers, or sweet paprika, or with minced parsley, chives or dill. Chill slightly before serving. If you are going to make these hours ahead of serving, place in the refrigerator ungarnished. Remove from the refrigerator 15 minutes before serving so they will not be too cold and then garnish.

Yield: 8 deviled egg halves; 4 servings

SANDWICHES

For as long as I can remember, I have been a sandwich lover, finding the instant satisfaction of sandwiches matched only by their adaptability to a wide variety of eating places—not only at table or desk, but on the sofa reading, in bed listening to the radio, at the beach and in school lunch boxes, or simply walking around the house doing other things.

We were rarely served sandwiches as meals at home; only on those days when we arrived home for lunch on school days, or late at night or on Sunday evening when we would have a sort of clean-up supper and there might be roast left from the midday meal.

In addition to such specialties as the chicken and tomato herring sandwiches described below, my mother relied on fillings such as egg salad, chicken salad, tuna fish or salmon salad, and halibut and shrimp salad (page 20), always on rolls or rye bread spread with mayonnaise and often with iceberg lettuce, for which I now substitute Boston or romaine.

Open grilled cheese with bacon and tomato sandwiches, cream cheese mashed and mixed with freshly shelled, chopped walnuts spread on raisin or date and nut bread (page 265), or cream cheese layered with stuffed green olives or mashed with pimento cheese or, on fancier occasions, red caviar, were all among our favorites. I hated peanut butter and jelly but did like peanut butter with bacon, and I also loathed jelly on cream cheese.

Chicken Sandwich

Generally these were in my lunch box on Saturdays in summer when I went to the beach, and were based on the soup chicken of the previous night. That means there was plenty of white meat on the large fowl and enough fat to keep it moist. The chicken meat, trimmed of all skin and bits of fat, was sliced. The sandwich bread might be sour rye with caraway seeds, challah (page 247), a big, crisp poppy seed kaiser roll, or, occasionally, a soft roll topped with poppy seeds and brown crisps of onion—in other words, an onion roll. Both top and bottom of the bread and roll were spread with rendered, solidified chicken fat. Then a leaf of lettuce was placed on the bottom. Next came a thick layering of chicken meat, sprinkled with salt and black pepper. The top of the sandwich was put on, and the whole thing was pressed down and wrapped and had several hours to ripen before eating, which, I think, greatly improved the flavor.

My mother generally added a few ripe Italian plum tomatoes to the lunch box to be eaten with this, and with them came a small paper packet of coarse salt. That, and iced tea from my thermos, made a perfect lunch . . . it still does. I sometimes vary the sandwich by using mayonnaise, but this must be kept in the refrigerator if it is not to be eaten at once. Butter is not bad either, but then I eliminate lettuce.

Tomato Herring and Onion Sandwich

For some reason, this is the only way I like canned herrings in tomato sauce, and it was a favorite Sunday night supper, served along with coffee and cinnamon coffee cake. I have often seen lettuce added to this sandwich, which I consider a mistake.

For each serving:

2 or 3 canned tomato herrings, with a little of their sauce
1 large, round, crusty but squashy kaiser roll, preferably with poppy seeds

Sweet butter, slightly softened
Lemon juice
1 large, thin slice of Bermuda or Spanish onion

Carefully split the herrings vertically and, with a fork, lift out the back vertebrae if still in the fish.

Cut the roll in half horizontally and spread the inside of both top and bottom halves with a fairly thick layer of softened sweet butter. Place the herrings on the bottom half to cover, and dribble on a little of their sauce and a few drops of lemon juice. With a fork, gently break up or semimash the herrings, right on the bottom half of the roll. Top with the onion slice and cover with the top of the roll.

Place the sandwich on a counter top and gently but firmly press the palm of your hand down on the sandwich to squash it together slightly. Cut in half so the sandwich will be easy to bite into.

Yield: 1 serving

Raw Chopped Beef on Rye Bread

This was a snack my mother would prepare if I arrived in the kitchen hungry while she was preparing hamburgers or meatballs, both made with the same seasonings as described for meatball and giblet fricassee (page 38).

She would simply take a slice or half slice of caraway sour rye bread and spread it with the raw beef, always saying as she did so that this was not really good for me to eat. It was, of course, steak tartar, much safer than that ground by the butcher. The raw egg and grated onion or crushed garlic gave it a wonderful flavor, and extra salt or pepper was sprinkled on top.

Vegetable Sandwich

Although the dark, round pumpernickel available now is a pallid version of what this hefty soured bread used to be, it still makes a delicious sandwich with this filling. This was something we loved when we came home from school starved (always) or for lunch on Saturday. I sometimes serve it as dinner on a hot summer night. It is a little more sophisticated made with butter, but I think the cream cheese variation is more luxurious.

For each sandwich:

2 large, oval slices of the darkest pumpernickel you can find
About 1 tablespoon sweet butter or about 2 tablespoons cream cheese
2 or 3 red radishes, washed and coarsely chopped

3 or 4 cucumber slices, peeled, seeded, and coarsely chopped
Green and white portions of 2 scallions, coarsely chopped
Salt and black pepper

Let the butter or cream cheese soften slightly at room temperature, then mash with a fork so it will spread easily without tearing the bread. Spread a thick layer of butter or cream cheese on one side of each slice of bread. Combine the chopped vegetables and pile on top of the butter or cream cheese on one slice of bread. Sprinkle with salt and pepper and top with the second slice, butter or cream-cheese side down. Hold firmly with one hand and use a saw-toothed bread knife to cut the sandwich carefully in half. If the slices are very large, cut each half again to form quarters. Delicious with a cup of fresh coffee or in summer with a glass of cold buttermilk.

Yield: 1 serving

Onion Sandwich

This was simply made with two slices of caraway sour rye bread, each spread with a thin layer of schmaltz (rendered chicken fat), between which was a layer of thinly sliced Bermuda or Spanish onion sprinkled with coarse salt and black pepper. Try it, but not if a visit to the dentist is in your near future.

Party Sandwiches

My mother also prepared a few fancy sandwiches for her luncheons or late-night suppers, and these are a few of her favorites.

Ribbon Loaf

The idea here is to have four layers of different-colored breads—usually a mix of white and whole-wheat slices—and three different-colored fillings. For large parties buy whole, unsliced loaves of whole-wheat and white, and, if you like, pumpernickel. Cut off the crusts and slice the breads in three or four layers horizontally. Spread the bottom three slices with a filling, then stack and cover with the top, unspread slice. Press down gently but firmly, wrap in a damp dishtowel, and chill for several hours. Cut downward into ½- to ¾-inch-thick slices to serve. The fillings used might be a layer of egg salad, one of cream cheese mixed with pimentoes or green olives or red caviar, and a layer of chopped black olives or tuna fish. Avoid sliced tomatoes, as they will make the loaf soggy. If the loaf is to be presented whole, whip cream cheese with a little sweet or sour cream and mashed pimento so it will resemble strawberry whipped cream and "frost" the loaf with it on tops and sides.

For small groups, use slices of these breads, laying them on top of each other with filling in between and then slicing downward.

Watercress Rolls

Spread a slice of thin-sliced white bread with softened butter, then trim off the crusts. Lay two washed and dried sprigs of watercress at one end of the slice, ends together at the middle and leaves extending over two sides of the bread slice. Roll cigarette fashion and secure with toothpicks. Wrap several rolls in a damp towel and chill for 2 hours. Unwrap and serve. The roll should stay closed after the toothpicks are removed.

Toasted Chicken Liver Pinwheels

Trim the crusts off a slice of thin-sliced white bread and spread one side with a thin layer of very finely chopped chicken livers. (Follow the recipe on page 22, but put the ingredients through the fine blade of a food chopper or use a food processor). Roll cigarette fashion, secure with toothpicks, and chill for several hours. Just before serving, cut each little roll into slices about 1 inch thick; you should get 3 or 4 pinwheels per slice, depending on the size of the bread. Place on a buttered cookie sheet, brush a little melted butter on each top side, and broil for about 5 minutes, or until toasted. Toast the second side lightly. Pass hot as an hors d'oeuvre.

4

Eating Out

The restaurant habit was one I developed early because my parents loved to "eat out" and often took me with them. Sometimes such occasions were planned long in advance, to celebrate a birthday, Mother's Day, or an anniversary; other times they were impromptu, as when, for example, my mother had had a busy day and did not feel like cooking or my father had a sudden longing for something at one of his favorite restaurants. Planned or impromptu, a visit to a restaurant was to me, perhaps prophetically, the most special of all events, no less momentous for being frequent. It meant (and still means) that one can decide where and what to eat at the very last moment, and so can order exactly what fits one's mood. Then, too, in a restaurant one is not bound by the choices of others. There is complete freedom, and options can be retained as long as possible, surely the most desirable of circumstances. There is also a wonderful feeling of expectancy. What had I really ordered? What would be on the plate? I often wonder, even now.

The restaurant that stands as a symbol of all restaurants is the one I first remember going to—F. W. I. L. Lundy Brothers in Brooklyn's Sheepshead Bay. My father and mother loved it, as did their friends, and we went often, especially in summer when seafood seemed particularly appropriate. In those days, some time before 1930, Lundy's was a small restaurant (it eventually became what was said to be the largest restaurant in the world, with three thousand seats) and was built on the bay side of Emmons Avenue across from its present location.

I remember a white wood house built on a pier over the water, and I can recall that when we walked to our table, my father clutched my hand tightly because the dining room listed slightly. In memory I see it all as a snow-white expanse of glossy, starchy linen—the sheen of the tablecloths, the huge rolled napkins, the white coats worn by the courtly, courteous black waiters whose approval I sought, so I watched my manners there far more than at home. Light reflections from the sunlit water outside bubbled onto the white ceilings, and the atmosphere was filled with the pulsating murmur of voices, the tinkle of ice, the clatter of silver, and laughter. My parents would nod to friends or stop to chat with them at the big wet and briny clam bar (one dozen cherrystones or littlenecks each was the warm-up while waiting for a table), and the whole adventure had about it the festive air of an ocean liner about to set sail.

I don't know just how old I was when I began going to Lundy's, but I know there were scenes about telephone books being piled onto chairs so I could reach the table, which means I was just a little too old for a highchair. I can still feel the topply sensation of being perched on three or four of those books as my mother tucked a napkin under my chin to protect what would probably have been my best dress of the moment.

It was a wise precaution, for the traditional New York shore dinners we ate at Lundy's were somewhat dripping affairs, what with steamers dunked in their own silvery, briny broth and then into hot melted butter, lobster meat that had to be picked from shells and also gilded with melted butter, on to corn on the cob, again with melting butter, the mouth-sized, fluffy white southern-style biscuits so hot they turned pats of butter into molten gold, and, finally, the lovely, runny huckleberry (not blueberry) pie, with its tiny, dark purple fresh-fruit filling that suggested liquid amethysts. After eating several mouthfuls, children showed purple-stained tongues to adults who would ask with feigned horror if their offspring had somehow, madly, swallowed indelible ink.

The shore dinner also meant shrimp cocktail, tomato-red Manhattan clam chowder with thick mincings of clams and the dry, Mediterranean scent of thyme. After the steamer clams and the lobster came half a broiled chicken, its inside sweet and glistening, its skin crackling with gold-brown blisters. There were bowlfuls of slim, crisp French fries, relish dishes of cole slaw, more biscuits, and again still *more* biscuits as the meal finally wound down with the pie (à la mode for most but not for me, since I did not and do not like the combination of cold ice cream with soothingly warm pie) and pitchers of iced tea.

The alternates on this standard Lundy menu were watermelon for dessert, and every once in a while one of my parents would decide to have "something different," which meant crab meat, lobster, or shrimp au gratin, blanketed under a bubbly golden-brown cheese and cream sauce, or covered with a gold-pink sherry, egg, and cream sauce Newburg.

In winter, when we went into New York to see a movie at one of the big houses, we might have a similar dinner at The Lobster, a now defunct seafood house that was near Times Square. Here my mother was inclined to order what seemed to me strange adult foods like gray sole, or broiled bluefish (of all things, I would think), or steamed codfish, or finnan haddie with an egg or cream sauce. I knew exactly who I was and ordered lobster, broiled or boiled, my only deviation being the method of cooking. As I remember it, and here memory could be clouded, the biggest differences between Lundy's and The Lobster were the settings and the oyster crackers—small, round, octagonal salted specimens in the Sheepshead Bay restaurant, but big, hard, dry-as-plaster, unsalted knobs in "the city."

Another restaurant my parents favored (expensive and therefore very special-occasion) was Fan & Bill's, now also gone from the New York scene. I recall its being a few steps below the street level, a big, low-ceilinged, noisy dining room where the main course we ordered still looms as devastatingly large in my memory as it appeared the first time I saw it. "Plank steak," my mother said to my father, who said the same to the waiter, and after we ate something like shrimp cocktail or oysters on the half shell, and my parents had lived it up with a Manhattan and my mother had said, as always, "It went straight to my legs," the waiter came up holding aloft a huge, thick cutting-board plank that looked like an entire table top to me.

If della Robbia had decided to forsake fruits as the subjects of his sculptures in favor of meat, potatoes, and vegetables, this brilliantly baroque* planked affair might have been one of his creations. In the center sat a high and mighty slab of seared Châteaubriand steak surrounded by concentric circles of red, green, orange, and white vegetables—beets and tomatoes, string beans, peas, broccoli, carrots, whole onions, grilled mushroom caps—

all wreathed by a ruffled border of mashed potatoes, gold crusted from a brief glazing under the broiler. All other memories of the meal, such as dessert, fade beside the image of that main-course blockbuster.

Several times a year, on Saturday afternoons, my father would take me to Radio City Music Hall or the late lamented Roxy, there to see a movie and a live stage-show extravaganza. We did that mostly during spring and summer, and I remember wearing the then-standard, still incomparably trim, navy blue spring coat with white collar and cuffs, a natural straw sailor hat with red streamers, black patent-leather pumps with pearl buttons, white anklets, or, in summer, an airy, balloon-skirted pastel cotton dress with polished white pumps. As we walked along Broadway to see Times Square, a sight I never tired of in those days, my father would stop and buy me a gardenia from one of the old ladies who sold them from huge baskets on street corners. This, of course, was the depression, and gardenia ladies alternated with apple Marys. Then we would go someplace to eat, and once I recall he took me to a large, formal French restaurant with a name that has faded with the years. I do remember that we went two or three steps down and through a doorway to a vestibule with a white tile floor, into which the restaurant name, "Maison de something," was set in darker tiles. I was so in awe of the large, carpeted, hushed room and the waiters whose speech I could hardly understand that the only dish I remember having is onion soup—not served gratinéed but just a wide, flat soup plate of golden broth with equally golden onion shreds into which the waiter sprinkled pale blond grated cheese. Onion soup is rarely served that way any more, at least not in this country, where the heavy layering of baked cheese seems to have more appeal. But that heavier coating, no matter how unctuously, sensually satisfying it may be, is much too filling on a first-course soup and is better served when it is to be the only thing eaten, as it was in late-night bistros.

We never went to Jewish restaurants because my mother said, rightly, that she cooked that food best, and aside from that one excursion to the French restaurant, the only other kind of "foreign" food I remember having was Chinese—the genre I think of as Brooklyn Jewish neighborhood Cantonese, and we ate it often. My mother and I would have it when we were shopping for clothes on a Saturday, or the whole family would go on Sunday, or I would go with friends before a movie. The restaurants were all done up in standard black, red, and gold lacquer with red-fringed pagoda motifs, like rickety souvenirs in Chinatown shops, and the prices were, in retrospect, unbelievable. A complete lunch for an adult was 40 cents and a child's meal was 25 cents. Both included egg drop soup or tomato juice, a choice of one of six or eight standard Cantonese dishes, crisp fried noodles, rice, tea, and ice cream, jello, or almond cakes, plus fortune cookies on the house. I still remember the mild, soothing taste of that food, primarily the flavors of celery, bean sprouts, and onions. It is far removed from the sophisticated (and truly better) Chinese food now fashionable, but there are moments when I would trade six of the best Szechuan meals in town for one plateful of that old chow mein (pronounced "sharmane") nostalgia.

In addition to neighborhood Chinese restaurants, my parents also went to Chinatown with friends, although not with me, for my father had succeeded in terrifying me about that part of the city, pointing out the pigtails still worn then under satin skullcaps by many Chinese workers as symbols of tong war gangs. But they always returned with reports of marvelous moo goo gai pan, and lobster in eggy Cantonese sauce, crisp spareribs, and fresh shrimp subgum. They brought me backscratchers and white porcelain soup spoons with which, my father said, one ate soup by filling the bowl of the spoon, then tipping the end of the handle toward your mouth and letting the soup run in. These instructions infuriated my mother because she knew I would try it, thereby ruining a freshly laundered dress.

Sometimes I was taken to a Horn & Hardart Automat, where, like most New York children of my time, I loved to drop coins in the slots of brass-trimmed glass compartments and withdraw the elements of a lunch—for me *always* fish cakes, cheese-baked macaroni and creamed spinach, and then pumpkin, blueberry, or apple pie.

I also loved to be taken to the dark old Schrafft's restaurants with their stern and precise schoolmarm waitresses, all of whom had lilting Irish brogues so fascinating I couldn't help staring into their mouths as they spoke, as if to see just where such extraordinary sounds could come from. My standard lunch there was an egg salad or cream cheese sandwich with the crusts cut off the bread (the height of elegance as far as I was concerned), and a whipped cream-frothed hot chocolate in winter, or a sunny peach ice-cream soda in summer.

Although it was hardly eating out in the formal sense, we often drove to Coney Island for hot dogs at Nathan's, where the salt-stung air, the smell of buttered popcorn, and the screams and crashing rattles emanating from the roller coasters were as much a seasoning for the sputtering frankfurters as the bright yellow mustard we spread on them. That, and sandwiches of corned beef or pastrami in kosher delicatessens that smelled mouthwateringly of the dilled pickles they kept in barrels, about made up our adventures in eating out. But they were more than enough to set me on an optimistic course of restaurant hopping that, at least so far, continues.

5

Soups

If I could remember the precise moment that I began to love soup, and especially soup that is volcanically hot, I think I could mark the turning point from childhood to adulthood.

There was no course with which I had less patience as a child than soup, partly because it seemed so boring and bothersome to splash my spoon around negotiating liquid and solids, but mostly because soup was served so steamily, endlessly hot. I can remember begging my mother to stop cooking the soup before it got so hot. Once in a while I would drop ice cubes into the soup and several times, in winter, I set a steaming bowl on a ledge in front of an open window. Such practices drove my mother crazy, as did my father's habit of liberally sprinkling soup with pepper and then having a coughing fit as he tried to eat it. "Who ever heard of pepper in soup?" she asked, year after year for almost half a century, as though each time it was a brand-new idea.

Soup is now not only my favorite course in a meal, it is beyond doubt what I most like to cook. How hot is hot enough is a personal question. My feeling is that one can always let it cool down, but there is obviously no way to get it hotter.

Only once have I been served soup that was too hot, and that was in the Troika, a small, dark, Russian restaurant in Helsinki, Finland, on a frozen white winter afternoon.

The soup was soldiers' shchi, made with sauerkraut, root vegetables, juicily fatty garlic sausages, and smoked pork. The already hot soup was ladled into small, individual terra-cotta bowls, then covered and baked. The result of hot bowl and lid, boiling soup and fat, was so unexpectedly incendiary that I swallowed a spoonful before I could stop, raising a blister on my upper lip and burning my tongue.

Chicken Soup

As might be expected in a Jewish family, this was the soup of soups, panacea for all ills whether physical or emotional and, to my mother at least, the measure of a cook's ability. "She can't even make a decent plate of soup," my mother would say of a woman she considered not only a bad cook, but a totally worthless individual in all other respects. It was always a "plate" of soup, and she was always self-congratulatory about her own. Each time she served it she announced to all assembled that this was the best she ever made. Never did I hear her say that last week's excelled this week's or that she was disappointed with the result. Only in recent years did she realize how difficult it is to make really good chicken soup with the chickens one has to work with today. For soup more than any other dish, the degree of flavor in a chicken is critical. Naturally fed chickens, which were allowed to scratch and which were then killed to order and bled to death—the kosher method of killing—did actually produce lighter, clearer, more golden soup of more delicate flavor. It is still possible to get chickens killed to order that way, even though the chickens are not nearly as good as their ancestors. Still, every little bit helps. Above all, do not expect to make good soup with frozen chicken, or any variety other than a fowl, which requires long, slow cooking and so imparts whatever flavor it has to the soup. If you do get a fresh-killed chicken, order it 48 hours before you intend to cook it, so it will be tender.

1 fowl (5 to 6 pounds), preferably freshly killed	1 small or ½ medium-sized parsnip
Salt	1 small petrouchka (root of
2½ to 3 quarts water	Italian parsley)

1 large or 2 small carrots
1 small or ½ large knob celery
1 medium onion
1 medium leek
2 stalks celery with leaves
3 or 4 sprigs parsley, preferably the
    Italian variety

White pepper, optional and
    to taste
Pinch of sugar, if needed

Garnishes: Parsley and/or dill;
    noodles, rice, eierstitch, matzoh
    balls, kreplach, or mandlen (pages
    78–83)

It is best to have the chicken quartered so it can be covered with as little water as possible. Singe the chicken to remove pin feathers, and trim off all excess fat from the neck opening and undersides of the quarters. Remove the skin from the chicken neck and wash the neck. Scrape the gizzard clean and rinse, along with the heart. Do not use the chicken liver in the soup.

Place the quartered chicken with giblets and 2 teaspoons of salt in a tall, straight-sided soup pot, preferably not of aluminum, and add just enough water barely to cover. Ideally, this will not be more than 2½ quarts. If much more is needed, your pot is too wide and the soup will lack strength. Bring the water to a boil, reduce the heat, and simmer uncovered, skimming scum off the surface as it rises. When the soup seems clear, cover and simmer slowly but steadily for about 45 minutes.

While the soup simmers, prepare the vegetables. Scrape the parsnip, petrouchka, and carrots; peel the knob of celery and onions, trim and wash the leek well to remove all sand. Add all of these, along with the washed celery stalks with leaves and parsley sprigs, to the soup pot, bring back to a simmer, and cook for 1½ hours longer, or until the meat begins to fall from the bone.

As the soup cooks, add a little bit of salt gradually, if needed. Do not add too much too early or the soup will become salty as it cooks down.

Remove the chicken and vegetables with a slotted spoon and set aside. Let the soup cool until it can be handled, then strain it through a very fine sieve. Rinse the original soup pot.

Season the soup with a tiny bit of white pepper if you like, and if the soup has an acidy edge, add the tiniest pinch of sugar. Actually, the root vegetables should have provided enough sweetening, but they vary as to sugar content, and sometimes the added sugar is necessary.

The soup should be served scalding hot. Never boil it in the reheating, or it will turn cloudy. At home it was always served in wide, flat bowls, ladled over noodles, rice, or other garnishes and liberally sprinkled with fresh parsley, dill, or both. My mother felt it was a mistake to cook the dill in the soup, as it had a souring effect, and having tried it once, I must report she was right.

Yield: About 2½ quarts soup

Variations: 1. A large, well-washed veal knuckle bone can be added to this soup to give it more flavor and body. Add the bone with the raw chicken. This makes a slightly heavier, fattier soup—a mistake, my mother felt, for someone who was ill.

2. Sometimes she put in a 2- to 3-pound piece of first-cut flanken along with the chicken and, in that case, added 2 or 3 cups more water. The meat should be served as boiled beef, with horseradish, as a second course. The beef alone can be cooked in the same way, using the vegetables indicated for the chicken soup.

Vegetable Split-Pea Soup

¾ cup yellow split peas (about ¼ pound) plus ¾ cup green split peas, or 1½ cups green split peas (about ½ pound)

Salt

1½ to 2 quarts water, approximately

1 large carrot, scraped and diced

1 large stalk celery with leaves, chopped

1 medium-sized onion, peeled and chopped

Leaves of 2 or 3 sprigs parsley, chopped

White pepper to taste

Minced fresh dill, for garnish (optional)

Wash and pick over the peas. Place in a 3-quart stainless-steel or enameled soup pot along with a pinch of salt and 1½ quarts water. Bring to a boil, cover, reduce the heat, and simmer for 1 hour. Add all the cut-up vegetables and cook for another 45 minutes to 1 hour, or until the peas are soft but not completely disintegrated. Add water during cooking if the mixture becomes too thick. Stir frequently to prevent scorching. Season to taste and serve garnished, if desired, with minced fresh dill.

Yield: About 2 quarts

Variation: For a slightly more elegant soup, puree the cooked peas with the vegetables when all are soft. Return to the pot, heat to the boiling point, and stir in ½ to ¾ cup heavy sweet cream. Reheat, add dill, and serve.

Split-Pea Soup with Meat

The meat used for this soup was always smoked, and might be the thick (schlung) end of the tongue or a leftover ham bone with some meat trimming from it. Smoked beef frankfurters were also used, with the other meats or alone. The wonderfully heady perfume of the sautéing garlic for the roux (einbrenne) usually told us in advance what the first course would be. This was considered a Sunday dinner soup, for reasons never explained and perhaps unexplainable.

Thick end of smoked tongue
or leftover ham bone with
any meat that is on it
1½ cups green split peas (about
½ pound), well washed and
picked over
1½ to 2 quarts water, approximately
Salt
1 carrot, scraped
1 large stalk celery with leaves
1 small onion, peeled

2 or 3 sprigs parsley
1 tablespoon sweet butter
1 clove garlic, finely minced
1½ teaspoons flour
2 tablespoons egg barley,
cooked in salted water
(optional)
Black pepper to taste
3 or 4 smoked beef frankfurters or
knackwursts, sliced
(optional)

Trim the fat from the tongue or ham. Place in a 4-quart soup pot. Add the washed split peas and about 1½ quarts water, which should amply cover the meat. Add a pinch of salt and bring to a boil. Reduce the heat, cover loosely, and simmer for 30 minutes.

Skim off any foam that has risen to the surface and add the vegetables and parsley. Cook for another 1½ hours, or until the peas are completely soft. Add water if the soup becomes too thick. Stir frequently to prevent scorching.

Remove the tongue or ham bone. Trim off all edible meat, cut into tiny pieces, and reserve. Discard the celery and onion; the carrot may be discarded or it can be sliced and served in the soup.

Strain and puree the remaining soup, either through a sieve or in a food processor. Rinse the soup pot and return the pureed soup to it, along with the cut-up meat. Bring to a simmer.

Melt the butter in a small saucepan. Add the garlic and slowly sauté until it is a medium golden brown; do not let it get dark brown or black. Sprinkle in the flour and continue sautéing until the garlic becomes a medium cocoa brown. Stir into the simmering soup until well blended. Add a little water if the soup is too thick. Add the cooked egg barley, salt and pepper to taste, and the sliced frankfurters, if using. Bring to a rapid boil, reduce the heat, and simmer for 10 to 15 minutes before serving.

This soup is much better if made a day in advance.

Yield: About 2 quarts

Note: A small piece of knob celery, parsnip or petrouchka (root of the Italian parsley), alone or in combination, can also be added when available. If no tongue or ham is available, half a small smoked ham butt can be used, but in that case blanch it for 20 minutes in boiling water. Discard the water, add the ham with the peas to fresh water, and proceed as above.

Lentil or Navy Bean Soup

My mother's lentil or navy bean soup was a variation on the basic recipe for split-pea soup with meat (see above). Lentil soup was made with smoked meat. Navy bean soup was often made with a cut of fresh beef such as flanken, chuck, neck bones, or brisket, or with smoked meat. Use 1 pound of beef for the quantities given above. Sliced frankfurters were always added to the lentil soup, as were a few drops of vinegar during the last half hour of cooking. Instead of browning garlic in the roux (einbrenne) for either of these soups, substitute 1 tablespoon minced onion.

Mushroom and Barley Soup

2 to 2½ pieces first-cut beef flanken
      1 small veal marrow bone (see note below)
         Salt
1½ to 2 quarts water, approximately
      1 carrot, scraped and cut in half vertically
      1 stalk celery with leaves
      1 small onion, peeled
         2-inch piece each of parsnip and/or petrouchka (root of Italian parsley), if available

      ½ small knob celery, if available
   2 or 3 sprigs parsley
   2 or 3 dried Polish mushroom caps, soaked 20 minutes in hot water
      2 tablespoons well-washed medium pearl barley
         White pepper to taste

Garnishes: 1 tablespoon minced fresh dill (optional) and 2 large or 4 small old potatoes, peeled, cut in half, if large, and boiled

Place the meat, bone, and a pinch of salt in a 3- to 4-quart soup pot. Add water to cover. Bring to a boil, skim the foam from the surface, cover, reduce the heat, and simmer gently for 1 hour.

Add the carrot, celery, onion, parsnip and/or parsley root, knob celery, and parsley sprigs. Remove the dried mushroom caps from their soaking liquid and chop coarsely. Add to the soup. If the soaking liquid is not sandy, add it to the soup. Simmer for 1 hour, then add the barley. Simmer for 30 minutes to 1 hour more, or until the meat is very tender. If the soup thickens too much, add a little boiling water as needed.

Remove the bone and discard. Remove the meat, trim off the fat, and cut in chunks or spoon-sized pieces. Return to the pot. Skim the fat from the surface of the soup. Season to taste and sprinkle in the dill, if desired. Serve each portion of soup and meat with half a large (or 1 small) boiled potato.

Yield: 1½ to 2 quarts

Note: Although the bone adds flavor, it also makes the soup greasy. This is no problem if you cook it a day or several hours in advance of serving so that the top layer of fat can be removed easily when coagulated. If the soup is to be served within an hour of the time it has finished cooking, eliminate the bone.

Hot Beef and Cabbage Borscht

3 pounds first-cut beef flanken
    or lean chuck or brisket, in
    that order of preference
1 veal marrow bone
2½ to 3 quarts water, or as needed
    Pinch of salt
2 large onions, peeled and
    coarsely chopped
2 cloves garlic, peeled and
    chopped

1 one-pound can whole
    tomatoes, with their liquid
1 head (2½ to 3 pounds) green
    cabbage, shredded
1½ tablespoons caraway seeds
3 tablespoons sweet butter
3 tablespoons flour
⅓ cup lemon juice, or to taste
2 to 3 tablespoons sugar, or to taste

Place the beef and bone in a 4- to 5-quart straight-sided soup pot, preferably of enameled cast iron. Add water to barely cover the meat. If you need more than 3 quarts, the pot is too wide. Bring to a boil, skim the foam from the surface, reduce the heat, cover, and simmer gently for 1 hour.

Add the onion and garlic. Crush or roughly chop the tomatoes and add to the soup pot, along with their liquid. Stir in the shredded cabbage and caraway seeds, then cover and simmer for 30 minutes. Remove the beef from the soup and trim off and discard the fat. Cut the meat into ½-inch cubes or spoon-sized pieces and return to the soup.

Heat the butter in a small saucepan or skillet, and when it is hot and bubbling, stir in the flour. Sauté slowly, stirring frequently, until the flour turns a medium cocoa-brown color. Turn into the simmering soup, beating or stirring for a few seconds until the roux (einbrenne) blends in.

Add the lemon juice and sugar, alternately and a little at a time, until a subtle sweet and sour balance is reached—a bit more sour than sweet. Simmer for another 30 minutes to 1 hour, or until the meat is meltingly tender. Discard the bone and skim the fat from the surface of the soup, a feat easier to perform after it is cold. Adjust the seasonings, reheat, and serve.

Yield: 3 to 4 quarts

Note: This is one of the many soups that improves as it ages. It is a good idea to make it a day or two in advance. Store it in the refrigerator and remove the layer of fat before reheating.

Russell

Although my mother never made this fermented beet juice, my grandmother always did for Passover when it became the basis of the most piquant, winy beet borschts of the year. It was used in place of the water or beet liquid called for in the recipes for clear beet borscht with beef and cold beet borscht that follow. It is so good that it seems a shame to relegate it to the short Passover week; I make it many times during the year because of the superior borscht it results in. Russell is a first cousin to Polish and Russian kvass, the fermented bread and fruit juice that is the basis for authentic borscht. In New York, russell can be purchased before Passover at Leibel Bistritzky's Kosher specialty store, 27½ Essex Street.

For this recipe you will need a 5- to 6-quart ceramic or stoneware pickling crock or bean pot.

About 10 pounds of beets, weighed   Water
after leaves and stems are removed

Scrub the beets and peel thinly. Cut into vertical quarters or eighths, depending on the size of the beets. The pieces should be about 1 to 1½ inches wide at the widest point.

Place in a thoroughly cleaned crock and pour in enough cold water to come within 2 inches of the top rim. Cover partially, setting the lid somewhat askew, then lay several layers of cheesecloth over the lid to keep dust out. Keep at room temperature for 1 week.

Skim off all scum on the surface. Stir well and skim again if more scum rises. By this time the liquid should begin to take on a faint pink color, and it will probably be cloudy.

Again, partially cover with a lid that in turn is covered with cheesecloth. Let stand in a cool but not cold corner for 2 to 3 weeks. The russell is done when it is a clear, deep ruby-red color. Refrigerate until ready to use. It will keep for several weeks.

Use for borscht as indicated, or as a coloring and flavoring for grated horseradish (page 15). The pickled russell beets can be substituted for those called for in the other recipes that follow, and if you run short, fresh beets can be cooked in the russell liquid.

Yield: 5 quarts of liquid, plus beets

Clear Beet Borscht with Beef

This extraordinary soup was more a specialty of my Aunt Pauline's than of my mother's, although we occasionally had it at home.

2 large onions, peeled and quartered or cut in half	½ small or ¼ large knob celery, peeled
5 medium to large or 8 or 9 small, fresh beets, or the equivalent in russell (page 60)	1 bay leaf
	Pinch of allspice
	½ teaspoon crushed caraway seeds
2 or 3 crystals sour salt	1 tablespoon long-grain converted rice (optional)
Cold water to cover	Sugar as needed
Salt	Juice of ½ lemon, or to taste
2½ to 3 pounds first-cut beef flanken	1 large or 2 small cloves garlic, peeled
1 marrow bone (½ to ¾ pound), washed	8 black peppercorns
1 carrot, scraped	

Preheat the oven to 400 degrees.

Place the peeled and cut-up onions in a baking pan or on a sheet of heavy-duty aluminum foil and bake in the preheated oven until they are golden brown—about 25 minutes. Remove and reserve.

Wash and peel the beets. Cut into very fine julienne strips or grate in coarse shreds. Place in a saucepan with the sour salt and water to cover (3 to 4 cups). Add a pinch of salt and cook, covered, for about 30 minutes, or until the beets are tender. Reserve.

Place the meat and the washed bone in a straight-sided stainless-steel or enameled soup pot and add cold water to cover—about 4 cups should do it. Bring to a boil, reduce to a simmer, and skim off the scum as it rises to the surface. When the soup is clear, add the browned onion pieces, the carrot, knob celery, bay leaf, allspice, and caraway seeds. Simmer, covered, slowly but steadily, for about 1 hour, or until the meat is almost completely tender. Remove the meat and vegetables from the soup with a slotted spoon. Discard the vegetables. Trim all fat from the meat and cut into spoon-sized chunks.

Return the meat to the stock and add the beets and their liquid. Add the rice, if using. The bone can be left in the soup. Cook for another 45 minutes, or until the meat is completely tender. Remove the bone.

Skim as much fat as possible from the soup. Taste the soup and adjust the seasoning with a pinch of sugar and several dashes of lemon juice. The final result should be a piquant and winy sweet-sour balance. Crush the garlic with a little salt and the peppercorns. Work to a fine paste, then stir into the soup. Bring to a boil and simmer gently for about 10 minutes, then serve the soup with the meat and grated beets.

Yield: About 2 quarts

Note: The rice will practically disappear, but it does serve to blend and mellow the flavors. Its addition was a bone of contention between my mother and my aunt: the former said always; the latter swore never. I alternate but have a slight preference for the clarity of the nonrice version.

Cold Beet Borscht

Beets for this refreshing cold soup were sometimes finely diced, other times coarsely grated. We liked best whichever we were being served, and I still alternate, indiscriminately.

3 large or 4 medium fresh beets, or the equivalent in russell (page 60)

Juice of 1½ lemons, approximately
Salt
Pinch of sour salt (optional)

5 cups water
2 extra-large whole eggs or 4 yolks
   Pinch of sugar, if needed
   White pepper to taste

Garnishes: Sour cream and (optional)
   boiled potatoes

Wash and peel the beets and cut into fine dice or grate on the coarse side of a grater. Place in a saucepan with the juice of ½ lemon, a pinch each of salt and sour salt, and the 5 cups water. Bring to a boil, reduce the heat, cover, and simmer until the beets are tender, about 40 minutes. Add the juice of another ½ lemon. Remove from the heat.

Using whole eggs results in a creamier, thicker borscht, but it is much trickier to add the hot beet soup to the whole eggs without having them co-agulate. If you feel inexperienced with this process, use just the yolks. In ei-ther case, beat the eggs with a fork until they are thin and watery. Slowly ladle some of the hot borscht into the eggs, beating constantly. When about half the soup had been added, pour the egg mixture back into the pot with the remaining soup; again pour slowly and beat constantly. When all the egg mixture is beaten into the soup, pour the soup back and forth between the pot and a bowl or pitcher about 10 or 15 times until the mixture is smooth, airy, and creamy. Halfway through, add more lemon juice to pro-duce a winy effect; add a tiny pinch of sugar, if necessary, and salt and white pepper as needed. Continue pouring to blend. Chill thoroughly.

It is best to add sour cream shortly before serving so that the borscht will keep longer. The sour cream can simply be served on the side, to be spooned in at the table. Or you can add sour cream (about 1 heaping table-spoonful per cupful of borscht) to the soup in a jar. Close tightly and shake vigorously to blend. Fluffy, dry, hot boiled potato is wonderful in the middle of this ice-cold soup.

Yield: 1 to 1½ quarts

Variation: Canned beets can also be used for this soup with excellent if slightly less flavorful results. Use whole beets even though you will dice or grate them, as they have more taste and better color. For the above recipe use a 1-pound can of whole beets. Dice or grate. Cook for 10 minutes in a combination of their own canning liquid plus 1½ cans of water, to make a total of 4 cups of liquid. Proceed with the recipe as described above.

Potato Soup

Although I tend to prefer whichever of my mother's soups I am eating at the moment, there is no doubt that this was a great family favorite, and we always welcomed its savory aroma of lightly browned onions, dill, and thyme as we came through the door. My mother also used it as the basis of one of her clam chowders.

3 or 4 large boiling potatoes (about 1¼ pounds), peeled	1 small carrot, scraped
	½ teaspoon salt
5 to 6 cups water	⅛ teaspoon white pepper, or to taste
3 stalks celery, diced	2½ tablespoons sweet butter
Celery leaves	2 tablespoons diced onion
3 sprigs parsley, preferably the Italian variety	2½ tablespoons flour
	¼ teaspoon thyme
3 sprigs dill	

Cut the peeled raw potatoes into approximately ½-inch cubes, making them a little smaller rather than larger, if you cannot be exact. Place them in a 3-quart stainless-steel or enameled soup pot or deep saucepan and add water, which should cover; do not add more than 6 cups. Add the celery. If you do not mind bits of leaves floating in the soup, do as my mother did and add them coarsely chopped. If you do not like them right in the soup, leave them on the stalks, so they can be picked out when the soup is done. Add the parsley, dill, carrot, salt, and pepper. Bring to a boil, skimming off scum as it rises to the surface, and when the soup is clear, cover and reduce to a slow but steady simmer. Cook until the potatoes are tender but not falling apart. Remove the parsley and dill. Keep the soup simmering gently.

In a small saucepan, heat the butter, and when it bubbles add the diced onion. Sauté slowly, stirring frequently, until the onion becomes golden brown. Do not let it get too dark, and if it blackens begin all over. Stir in the flour and sauté until it becomes cocoa brown. Stir in about ½ cup of soup liquid to this roux (einbrenne), then beat the mixture into the simmering soup. Add the thyme. Increase the heat to just below a boil and stir until the einbrenne is completely absorbed. Simmer for 10 to 15 minutes more. Check the seasoning and serve.

Yield: About 1½ quarts

Variations: My mother did not always include carrot. Sometimes she said it made the soup sweet, other times she said it made it look pretty. If she had a small slice of knob celery root around, she added that also. I like to add minced fresh dill to the soup along with the thyme after adding the einbrenne, instead of cooking the sprigs with it from the start. Minced fresh parsley is a pleasant garnish, as always.

Clam and Potato Chowder

Follow the above recipe exactly, but add 12 large chowder clams. Trim the hard parts from the soft parts, and add their liquor to the water with the raw potatoes. Add the soft sections of the clams after 20 minutes.

Manhattan Clam Chowder

About 1 quart large chowder clams, with their liquor (18 to 24 large quahogs, or 3 dozen medium chowder clams, or 4 dozen cherrystones)

2 medium carrots, scraped and diced

1 large onion, peeled and finely chopped

1 stalk celery without leaves, diced

2 to 3 tablespoons sweet butter

1 can (20 ounces) whole tomatoes, coarsely chopped, with the canning liquid

2 to 3 cups boiling water, as needed
Salt

1 medium old potato (about 3-to-a-pound size), diced

1 teaspoon thyme, or to taste
Black pepper to taste

Trim the hard portions of the clams from the soft. Reserve both, as well as their liquor. In a 2½-quart stainless-steel or enameled saucepan, sauté the carrots, onion, and celery in 2 or 3 tablespoons hot butter, as needed. Sauté for about 5 minutes, or until the vegetables just begin to soften and become bright; do not brown.

Add the tomatoes and their liquid. If there are 2 cups of tomato liquid, add only 2 cups boiling water; if there is less tomato liquid, add enough boiling water to measure 4 cups of liquid. Add the hard portion of the clams and a pinch of salt. Simmer gently for about 20 minutes.

Add the diced potato, the soft part of the clams, with their liquor, and the thyme; simmer for 30 minutes, or until all the ingredients are tender. Adjust the seasoning with salt and pinch of pepper.

Yield: About 1½ quarts

Note: This too is a soup that has more flavor if cooked the day before it is to be served.

Fish Soup with Noodles

This is another family favorite that I have never found in any other cookbook. The closest thing to it is the somewhat spicier Polish fish soup, *zupa z ryby,* which is finished with sweet or sour cream. This is one soup that was a complete meal, whether the fish was served in the soup or separately with boiled potatoes. Most often fish, soup, noodles, and potatoes were served to my father all at once. I hated the fish and survived on the soup and noodles, both of which I adored. This soup was always made with freshwater fish, and a combination of pike and white had the most flavor.

2 pounds each whole whitefish and pike, or 4 pounds of either
Kosher (coarse) salt
2 carrots, scraped and quartered vertically
2 stalks celery with leaves
1 medium onion, peeled and sliced
2 or 3 sprigs parsley
1-inch cube knob celery, approximately, if available

6 cups water
2 teaspoons salt
12 black peppercorns, approximately
1½ to 2 cups milk, as needed
2 tablespoons sweet butter
8 ounces ½-inch-wide egg noodles

Garnishes: Sweet paprika and (optional) boiled potatoes

To have enough flavor for this soup, the fish should be available whole, with head and skin. They should be scaled and eviscerated, then cut crosswise into pieces 2 inches wide. Rinse with cold water and sprinkle with coarse salt. Let stand in the refrigerator for 2 or 3 hours. Rinse.

Place the carrots, celery, onion, parsley, knob celery, and water in a 3-

to 4-quart stainless-steel or enameled soup pot. Add the salt and peppercorns. Let come to a boil, then reduce the heat and simmer gently for 10 minutes.

Add the pieces of fish, including the heads, and cook for 15 to 20 minutes, until the fish is done but not falling apart. Remove the fish and carrots carefully with a slotted spoon and keep warm. The heads may be served or not, depending on your preference. Strain the remaining soup and return to the washed soup pot.

Scald the milk, and while hot pour gradually into the fish broth, tasting as you go along so you add enough milk for a creamy look but not so much that you cancel out the flavor of the fish. Simmer for 10 minutes, then stir in the butter and adjust the seasoning. Use enough pepper for a lively taste.

Cook the egg noodles until tender in well-salted boiling water; drain thoroughly. Divide the noodles between 4 serving bowls, ladle in the soup, and sprinkle with paprika. Add a boiled potato and pieces of carrot to the soup, or serve those separately as a second course, along with the fish.

Yield: 4 generous servings

Oyster Stew

My father considered this one of the best of weekday dinners, and my mother loved to surprise him with it. She also served it as a late supper after a card-playing party. When it was made for the family she used a double boiler; a fancy silver chafing dish was used for guests.

12 freshly shucked oysters, with their liquor	3 tablespoons sweet butter
	Salt and white pepper to taste
2 cups half-and-half milk and cream	2 to 3 tablespoons sherry
1 stalk celery with leaves	Sweet paprika

Drain off and reserve the oyster liquor. Pick over the oysters carefully to remove any bits of shell.

In a small saucepan, scald the half-and-half with the celery stalk and leaves. Cover, remove from the heat, and let steep for about 5 minutes.

Heat 2 tablespoons butter and the oyster liquid in the top of a chafing dish or double boiler set over boiling water in the lower pot. Add the oysters and stir gently over low heat, only until the edges of the oysters begin to curl—about 4 minutes. Pour in the hot half-and-half, without the celery, and season with salt and pepper. Heat thoroughly but do not boil. Stir in the remaining tablespoon butter. Stir in the sherry and heat for 2 to 3 minutes. Ladle into two heated cream-soup bowls and sprinkle with paprika.

Yield: 2 servings

Variation: I like a dash of cayenne pepper or Tabasco sauce added with the sherry, a substitution my mother considered a sign of madness.

Beef Tea

This strong beef broth was a favorite treat when recuperating from illness, but it was also something my mother occasionally served when I came home from grade school for lunch. I was slightly partial to the broiled variety; the blander boiled version seemed better suited to being sick in bed. The broth was sometimes served in a cup, but more usually was poured over mashed potatoes.

Boiled Beef Tea

**½ pound lean, juicy cut of beef such   Pinch of salt
        as chuck fillet, round, rump, or
        sirloin trimmings**

This was always made in an old-fashioned, narrow-necked milk bottle, now virtually nonexistent. Instead use a glass jar that can be placed in boiling water; Pyrex or any jar that can be sterilized will do. Slice thin or, better yet, scrape the beef. Place in the jar with a tiny pinch of salt and cover the jar tightly with a cork, a lid, or several thickness of foil tied on. Set in a pot and pour in enough water to come halfway up the sides of the jar. Let the water boil about 1 hour, or until the meat is pale and all the juices are out of it. Serve very hot in a cup or pour over mashed potatoes.

Although my mother always used a bottle, it is possible to do this in a double boiler. Place the cut-up meat and salt in the top section and set over the lower pot, half filled with boiling water. Cover and steam about 1 hour.

Yield: 1 serving

Broiled Beef Tea

This produces a smaller amount of more intensely flavored juices.

1-pound slice rump, round, or   **Kosher (coarse) salt**
  shoulder steak, ½ to 1 inch thick

Trim off as much fat as possible from the meat. Sprinkle coarse salt on a heavy iron frying pan, and when the pan is hot place the steak in it. Sear rapidly and on both sides. The steak is ready when the juices begin to rise to the surface of the second side. This all should take no more than 7 or 8 minutes. Cut the meat into small strips or pieces, being careful to reserve the juices. To press all the juice out of the meat, the best device is an old-fashioned potato ricer (see the illustration below). Put in the meat, 1 or 2 spoonfuls at a time, then press down firmly, catching the juices in a bowl. Serve on mashed potatoes.

Yield: 1 serving

Note: The meat is not usable for any other purpose except pet food.

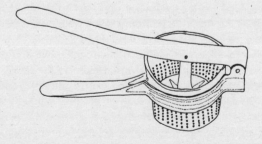

CREAM SOUPS

Although cooking at home was not kosher, cream soups were never made with meat stock, a combination that was foreign to my mother's palate. The results were very light soups flavored only by the vegetables in them. However, I often prepare the asparagus, spinach, mushroom, and celery soups with white stock made from chicken or veal. Simply substitute stocks for water as called for below.

Cream of Asparagus Soup

We had this only in spring when fresh asparagus were available. Neither canned nor frozen varieties are acceptable alternates.

1 pound fresh asparagus	2 cups hot, scalded milk
3 cups water, approximately	¼ cup heavy sweet cream
Salt	Salt, white pepper, and a pinch of
3 tablespoons sweet butter	sugar to taste
3 tablespoons flour	

Wash the asparagus thoroughly. Cut off the tough ends and discard. Trim off the tips and set aside. Cut the remaining asparagus into ½-inch pieces and cook in about 2 cups lightly salted water until very soft—about 10 minutes. Meanwhile, place the tips in ½ to ¾ cup salted water and simmer until firm but tender. Reserve both tips and cooking liquid.

When the asparagus pieces are soft, remove roughly half and puree in a blender or processor put through a food mill. Return to the soup.

Melt the butter, and when it is bubbling, stir in the flour and sauté slowly for 4 or 5 minutes, then pour in the hot, scalded milk and stir until smooth. Add to the asparagus stock with the reserved tips and their liquid and simmer for 10 minutes. Stir in the heavy cream, heat thoroughly, and season to taste with salt, pepper, and a pinch of sugar. Serve in heated cream-soup bowls.

Yield: 1 to 1½ quarts

Variation: If you prefer a thicker, more subtle soup, puree all the cooked asparagus pieces except the tips. Add them as indicated above.

Cream of Spinach Soup

This will not have enough flavor to be interesting if made with frozen spinach—only fresh will do.

1 pound fresh leaf spinach	2 tablespoons flour
1 tablespoon finely chopped	3½ cups milk
onion	½ cup heavy sweet cream
Salt	White pepper to taste
⅓ to ½ cup water	Croutons or hard-cooked egg
2 tablespoons sweet butter	slices, for garnish

Wash the spinach thoroughly. Discard stems. Combine the leaves with the onion, ½ teaspoon salt, and just enough water to cover the bottom of an 2-quart enameled cast-iron saucepan. Cover and steam the spinach and onion for 7 or 8 minutes, or until both are soft.

With a slotted spoon, remove the spinach from the cooking liquid and chop very coarsely, along with the onion. Empty the saucepan in which the spinach was cooked. Return the chopped spinach to it.

Melt the butter in a saucepan, and when it is bubbling, stir in the flour. Add the milk all at once and bring to a simmer, beating constantly with a wire whisk until well blended and smooth. Pour over the spinach and stir to blend. Simmer for 10 minutes. Pour in the sweet cream and adjust the seasoning with salt and pepper. Let stand, covered, for 15 to 20 minutes, then reheat and serve. Garnish with croutons or slices of hard-cooked eggs.

Yield: 1 quart

Cream of Mushroom Soup

1 pound mushrooms	2 tablespoons flour
6 tablespoons plus 2 teaspoons sweet	Salt, white pepper, and nutmeg to
butter	taste
1 quart milk	1 cup heavy sweet cream
1 medium onion, peeled and sliced	

Wash or wipe the mushrooms, as necessary. Cut off the bottom end of the stems. Coarsely chop the caps and stems together. Heat 3 tablespoons butter in a large skillet, and when the butter is hot and bubbling, stir in the

(continued)

mushrooms. Sauté and stir over moderate heat until the liquid evaporates. Add the onion slices to the milk in a saucepan, bring to a boil, and simmer for 10 minutes.

Add another 3 tablespoons butter to the mushrooms in the pan, and when hot, stir in the flour and sauté for 5 minutes, or until all is absorbed. Turn into a 2-quart saucepan.

Strain the hot milk into the mushroom mixture, discarding the onion. Bring the soup to a simmer and beat constantly until the mushroom mixture and milk have formed a smoother blend. Season. Simmer, partially covered, for 10 minutes.

Stir in the heavy cream and heat to just below the boiling point. Beat in 2 teaspoonfuls butter, a few pieces at a time.

Yield: 5 to 6 cups

Variation: I have found it a good idea to puree half of the cooked, unfloured mushrooms through a sieve, a food mill, a blender or a food processor, leaving the other half as is. Both the puree and chopped mushrooms can be added to the thickened, onion-flavored milk.

Cream of Corn Soup

1 can (12 ounces) dry-pack corn kernels	3 cups milk, or as needed
3 tablespoons sweet butter	1 teaspoon salt, or to taste
2 tablespoons finely minced onion	White pepper to taste
2 teaspoons flour	½ cup heavy sweet cream
	Pinch of sweet paprika

Measure out ¼ cup of corn and set aside. Put the remaining corn and any liquid in the can into a blender or food processor and puree.

Melt 2 tablespoons butter in a 1½- to 2-quart heavy-bottomed saucepan, and when it begins to foam, add the minced onion. Sauté slowly, stirring frequently, until the onion softens and turns bright yellow; do not let it brown. Sprinkle in the flour and sauté for about 5 minutes, but do not let color develop.

Pour in the milk, and with a whisk beat the flour and onion mixture into it. Stir in the pureed corn and reserved whole kernels; add salt and pepper. Simmer gently for 20 minutes over very low heat, stirring frequently to prevent the corn from sticking to the bottom; add milk if the mixture becomes too thick. Add the cream and stir in the paprika. Simmer for 5 to 10 minutes. Stir in the remaining 1 tablespoon butter, adjust the seasoning, and serve.

Yield: About 1 quart

Variation: For a more piquant touch, substitute a pinch of cayenne pepper for the white pepper, or eliminate white pepper and use hot paprika instead of the sweet.

Cream of Celery Soup

Cream of corn soup (page 72) and this very delicate celery soup were my mother's emergency soups that she could always put together on virtually no notice at all, since she always had all ingredients for either on hand. The celery soup is very mild in flavor and another soothing restorative for convalescents.

1½ cups diced celery	2 tablespoons sweet butter
1 to 2 tablespoons chopped celery	2 tablespoons flour
leaves	2 cups hot, scalded milk
2 cups water	White pepper to taste
Salt	

Cook the diced celery and leaves in the water with a pinch of salt for about 20 minutes, or until the celery is tender. Melt the butter in a saucepan, and when it is bubbling, stir in the flour. Add the milk all at once and bring to a simmer, beating constantly with a wire whisk until well blended and smooth. Stir into the celery and its cooking liquid. Season to taste. Cover and let steep for 20 to 30 minutes before serving, then reheat.

Yield: 1 quart

Variation: A small slice of onion can be added to the milk when it is being scalded, and removed as milk is poured into the roux (einbrenne), a touch my mother eliminated for those who were ill but sometimes added if the soup was served before a meal.

Schav

[Cold Sorrel Soup]

"White borscht" was the most common name for this piquant cold summer soup, with its sour green leaves mellowed by whipped sour cream. My father loved it with a hot boiled potato, sometimes just plain and served right in the soup, but most specially when the potato was on a separate plate, topped with onions that had been melted in butter. He would take alternate mouthfuls of soup and potato, and never cared if anything else came after the so-called first course. My mother loved to eat it as a light lunch, accompanied by a piece of dark black Russian pumpernickel spread with sweet butter. I like it all ways, and feel that when it is served with the mixed vegetable garnish, it makes an elegant and unusual soup, at least as interesting as gazpacho. The dried mushrooms were my grandmother's own touch that gave this soup its special earthy richness.

2 or 3 whole dried Polish mushrooms
   ½ cup hot water
   1 pound sorrel (sour grass or
      schav)
   7 cups water
   ¾ cup milk
   ½ cup sour cream
   2 tablespoons flour
1½ teaspoons salt, or to taste
   ¼ teaspoon white pepper, or to
      taste

2 or 3 crystals sour salt (optional)
   5 large egg yolks
      Pinch of sugar (optional)
      Lemon juice, optional and to
      taste

Garnishes: Sour cream; boiled
   potatoes with or without sautéed
   onions; or minced scallions,
   cucumbers, radishes, and hard-
   cooked eggs

Soak the mushrooms in ½ cup hot water for 30 minutes. Drain well and cut the mushrooms in small pieces.

It is very important that the stems and any heavy ribs be pulled from the leaves of the sorrel and cooked separately; otherwise they will impart an unpleasant hairy texture to the finished soup. Tear off the stems and any threadlike particles adhering to them. Wash both stems and leaves well. Place the leaves, cut-up soaked mushrooms, and 6 cups of water in a 2½-

to 3-quart saucepan, not made of iron or aluminum. Place the stems with 1 cup of water in a similar but small saucepan. Bring both to a boil, and after 15 minutes strain the liquid from the stems into the larger soup pot, rubbing through as much of the cooked greens as you can without getting the stems themselves into the larger pot. Continue cooking about 15 minutes longer, or until the leaves are completely soft and begin to disintegrate.

Combine the milk, sour cream, and flour and beat well until the flour is smoothly blended in. Bring the soup to a rapid boil, then add the cream mixture, stirring constantly with a wooden spoon or beating with a whisk. Add about 1½ teaspoons salt, ¼ teaspoon white pepper, and, for a deep, winy, sour edge, 2 or 3 crystals of sour salt. Let boil rapidly for about 5 minutes, or until the cream has blended with the soup stock and all traces of flour disappear.

Beat the egg yolks with a fork until thin. Remove the soup from the heat and, using a ladle, slowly trickle some hot soup into the yolks, beating constantly as you do so. Continue this until 3 cups of soup have been added to the yolks. Now slowly trickle the egg yolk mixture back into the soup, again beating steadily as you do so.

The next operation is one my mother claimed as unique to her family and essential for achieving a smooth, well-blended schav. Using the pot in which the soup cooked, and another pot or bowl with a good long handle, pour the soup back and forth from one receptacle to another, over and over and over again. My mother swore it was impossible to overdo this step, and felt that at least twenty backs and forths were a minimum. It is a good idea to do this over the sink, as it can get messy, and to do it carefully, so little soup will be wasted.

Finally, taste the soup and adjust the seasoning. Faint palates may prefer it less sour and so feel a pinch of sugar is needed. The strong may want an extra souring of fresh lemon juice added to the natural sourness of the sorrel and the sour salt, as I do. The juice of ¼ lemon should be enough. As the soup will be served cold, it is a good idea to taste it again after it has chilled.

To serve, ladle the soup into chilled cream-soup bowls or cups. Serve whipped sour cream on the side, or add a dollop to each serving. A boiled potato may be served in the soup or, again, on the side with a topping of onions sautéed in butter. If you prefer the last set of garnishes, chop them and pass around in relish dishes, along with sour cream.

Yield: About 2 quarts

6

Friday Night

Religion at our house was practiced more in the manner of folk customs, rather than the strict, ceremonial rituals of Orthodoxy. Nothing typified this attitude more than my mother's observance of the traditional Friday night Shabbas or Sabbath eve dinner. On that day she would begin cooking early in the morning. By afternoon the kitchen was cleaned and sparkling, the floor scrubbed, and generally (and always to the horror of my brother and myself) was covered with newspapers to keep it clean until Saturday morning, when the papers would be picked up.

To me, shuffling ankle deep through newspapers on our way from refrigerator to stove to table to sink was as much a part of Friday night as the candles burning in freshly polished brass or silver candlesticks, the choice depending on how fancy my mother felt on that particular evening and whether we were to eat in the breakfast nook or the dining room. (Silver candlesticks were for the dining room table; the heavy, and far more beautiful, gleaming brass candlesticks were relegated to the kitchen.) As the years went by and my grandmother died, and then one aunt and then another, my mother, for some reason, acquired all their pairs of brass candlesticks, and she would put candles in each. Finally there was a blaze of eight candles burning in eight golden candlesticks, all set on a big brass tray to catch the drippings. Three pairs are now mine, heavy, ornate, and gleaming like hot melted butter when newly polished. Once in a while, for the sake of nostalgia, I light them all, on whatever day of the week the idea occurs to me, and the sight of that glowing wash of light brings back the special feeling of safety and contentment we felt on Friday night.

It was most noticeable on the dark afternoons of midwinter when we came home from school and play half frozen, to be suddenly enveloped by the warm and tantalizing aromas of the day's cooking. Roasting meat, hints of garlic and onion, the almost sunny, airy scent of chicken soup, the pungency of sweet and sour cabbage, the sugary smell of a pie or coffee cake that might be baking.

Though my mother lit candles and always set out braided loaves of challah bread for Friday nights, she never said prayers when lighting those candles or cutting those loaves as my grandmother did.

Tradition here was more strictly observed in the menu, and three out of four Friday nights that meant soup and chicken until my brother and I would beg for a change. "It doesn't seem like Friday night without a plate of soup," was my mother's answer. "But at least," we said, "let's have some other kind." Variety came only by way of the garnishes in the soup— noodles, rice, matzoh balls, kreplach, or one of a dozen other choices.

Appetizers might be the expected chopped chicken livers, crunchy with the griebenes, or chicken fat cracklings, my mother added to it, or gefüllte fish or its imitator, kalechla, the chicken prepared exactly like the fish, and a trick variation that we loved. Stuffed cabbage was an appetizer, or sautéed mushrooms and onions, with or without chicken livers, on a slice of toast, or giblets and meatballs done as a spicy fricassee.

If, occasionally, the soup was not chicken, it might be mushroom and barley or borscht, both made with chunks of beef. Roast duck or turkey would replace chicken, or, if my mother was really being adventurous and forsaking poultry altogether, we would have pot roast with potato pancakes and applesauce.

Stuffed cabbage, if not an appetizer, might be a side dish served with pot roast or occasionally was the main course itself. Standard vegetables for Friday night were sweet and sour cabbage or string beans, or, if kohlrabi was in season, my mother made her version of tzimmes, a nonsweet mix of that vegetable with carrots and peas in a fragrant sauce.

Usually, no one had room for dessert, but later in the evening, when my father had had his fill of such radio programs, as "Amos 'n' Andy," Gabriel Heatter, Lowell Thomas, and H. V. Kaltenborn, we would have tea along with pie or cake my mother had made earlier in the day.

7

Soup Garnishes
and Noodles

For the most part, the only soup that was garnished was chicken soup, and if the recipe for that golden broth remained constant, its garnishes varied with my mother's whim. Unless she was serving a fancy dinner, or we were ill, I never remember having clear chicken broth without some delectable, starchy morsel added to it. Matzoh balls were far and away our favorites, and though noodles and other dough trimmings were usually purchased packaged, for special occasions my mother made her own, as my grandmother always did. Minced fresh parsley and dill are also fragrant additions.

Rice

Obviously, this was nothing more than hot, cooked rice added to soup when it was served. Allow about 1 tablespoon cooked, well-salted rice to each 8-ounce cupful of soup. Garnish with minced fresh parsley and/or dill.

Farina

Cook this cereal (or Cream of Wheat) according to the instructions on the package, but do not use the instant varieties, as they will be too pasty. Pour the cooked, well-salted cereal into a dish or pie plate to a depth of about ½ inch. Let set in the refrigerator overnight. (Breakfast leftovers are perfect for this, by the way). Remove from the refrigerator an hour before serving and cut into small cubes. Place in a plate over the simmering soup pot to warm slightly, then add to the soup when it has been ladled into individual bowls. One tablespoonful of cubed farina is about right for each cup of soup.

Knaidlach

[Matzoh Balls]

Although matzoh balls were usually served in soup, we were always happy to have leftovers, cooked and kept in the refrigerator, then sliced and fried in butter the next morning for breakfast. The result is not unlike semolina gnocchi.

3 eggs	Salt
6 tablespoons cold water	Pinch of white pepper
3 heaping tablespoons schmaltz	⅔ to ¾ cup matzoh meal
(rendered chicken fat, page 7),	2½ to 3 quarts water
solidified	

Beat the eggs lightly with cold water. Add the chicken fat and stir until the fat dissolves. Add ½ teaspoon salt and a pinch of pepper.

Gradually beat in the matzoh meal, 2 tablespoons at a time, proceeding slowly as it thickens so you do not add too much. The mixture should be as thick as light mashed potatoes, and just a little soft and spongy. Chill for 5 to 7 hours.

Half an hour before serving time, bring 2½ to 3 quarts of water to a boil. Add a handful of salt, as for pasta.

With wet hands, or two tablespoons dipped intermittently in cold water, shape the mixture into balls about 1 inch in diameter. Drop gently into the boiling water, cover the pot loosely, and let boil at a moderately brisk pace for about 25 minutes.

(continued)

When one ball tests done (cut it open and see if it is light and cooked all the way through), remove all carefully with a slotted spoon. Serve in hot chicken soup.

Yield: 10 to 12 large matzoh balls

Variation: To make fried matzoh balls, chill the cooked balls overnight. In the morning, cut into slices between ¼ and ½ inch thick and fry slowly in hot butter or margarine, turning so both sides become golden brown and the slices are thoroughly heated.

Note: For those who observe kosher dietary laws, it will be necessary either to fry the prepared matzoh balls in chicken fat or margarine, or to substitute melted and resolidified butter for the chicken fat when making the matzoh balls. If the latter is done, they can then be fried in butter, but they may not be used in chicken soup.

Eierstitch

[Royal Custard]

2 **eggs**
2 **tablespoons cold water or chicken**
    broth
Salt as needed

½ **teaspoon sweet butter or schmaltz**
    (rendered chicken fat, page 7),
    approximately

Beat the eggs with the water or broth and a dash of salt. Add more salt if you use water rather than chicken broth. Lightly grease a small ceramic or glass dish (one 4 inches square or in diameter, if round, would be perfect) and pour the egg mixture into it; the depth should be between ¼ and ½ inch. Cover tightly with foil and set in a skillet. Pour in water to come about two-thirds up the sides of the dish. Bring the water to a boil and let bubble slowly but steadily for 10 to 15 minutes, or until the custard is set and a knife blade inserted in the center comes out clean. Unmold and cut into dice. Add to soup just before serving.

Yield: Enough for 4 cups of soup

Variation: 2 teaspoons finely minced fresh parsley can be stirred into the custard mixture before it is cooked.

Einlauf

[Egg Drops]

2 eggs   **Pinch of salt**
1½ tablespoons flour

Beat the eggs with the flour until you have a smooth, lump-free liquid about the consistency of heavy sweet cream. Stir in only a tiny pinch of salt, as the soup itself will be seasoned.

Pour through a colander or a perforated spoon into simmering broth. The batter should run through in broken streams. If the streams are unbroken, the batter is too thin. If it does not run through, it is too thick. Let simmer in the soup for 2 or 3 minutes and serve, ladling the egg drops into bowls or cups along with the soup.

Yield: Enough for 4 cups of soup

Mandlen (Soup Nuts), Two Ways

At times my mother prepared these by the first method below, which resulted in a hard, chewy "nut" of crispy baked dough. Other times she prepared cream puff pastry and baked them into tiny air puffs, the version I preferred.

Mandlen I

⅔ to ¾ cup flour, as needed   1 tablespoon melted sweet butter,
    ¼ teaspoon baking powder   schmaltz (rendered chicken fat,
        Pinch of salt   page 7), or magarine
    1 extra-large egg, lightly beaten

Preheat the oven to 350 degrees.

Using butter or corn oil, thoroughly grease a shallow baking pan.

Sift ½ cup of flour with the baking powder and salt. Beat the egg with the fat and combine with the dry ingredients. Add more flour as needed until the dough is no longer sticky but is still pliable. Divide the dough in half or thirds, according to the amount you are comfortable working with. Dust hands and a pastry board with flour, then roll each portion of dough into thin rolls, about ¼ inch in diameter. With a sharp knife, cut into "nuts," each about ½ inch long. Place in the greased pan and bake for about 15 minutes, or until golden brown. Shake the pan several times so the nuts turn and brown on all sides.

These keep well if stored in an airtight container.

Yield: About 85 nuts

Mandlen II

Prepare half the recipe for cream puff pastry (page 282). Grease a shallow baking pan with butter or bland vegetable oil.

Put the cream puff dough into a pastry tube, and using a small, round nozzle, press out dough roughly the size of a large pea, or about ¼ inch in diameter. Repeat until all the dough is used up. Bake in a 375-degree oven for about 10 minutes, or until puffed and golden brown. Using a needle or skewer, prick a small hole in each soup nut and let stand in a warm but turned-off oven for about 10 minutes, so they will retain their form without collapsing.

These will keep for a week or two if stored in an airtight container.

Yield: About 75 nuts

Lokshen

[Noodles]

The first recipe is the one my grandmother followed when the noodles were meant for soup or pudding or the dough was to be made into kreplach. But when she wanted a slightly chewier, softer, eggy noodle, to be used as a side dish with goulash or pot roast, she followed the variation below, using extra egg yolks. I am partial to that second version, even for soup, but it is too soft to be used for kreplach.

3 cups unbleached flour, or as needed   2 tablespoons warm water, or as
3 extra-large eggs   needed
                                                                 1 teaspoon salt

Place the flour on a wooden pastry board and make a well in the center. Into this, drop the unbeaten eggs, water, and salt. Stir slightly, breaking the yolks but not combining them with the whites. Gradually stir the flour into the egg mixture until you have a dough that is stiff but still somewhat elastic. Add more flour if it is too soft, or a few drops of water if it is too crumbly. Knead for 10 minutes, or until the dough is smooth and elastic. Wrap in waxed paper or plastic wrap and set aside for 30 minutes.

Divide in halves or thirds, depending on how much you think you can roll out comfortably. Keep the unrolled portion wrapped. Flour the board and a heavy rolling pin, and roll each section of the dough to uniform paper thinness. The dough is thin enough when the graining of the board shows through (or, my grandmother's test, when you can read the fine print of a newspaper through it). The sheets of dough should be clothlike. Drape on a dry towel over the back of a chair or a towel rack and dry for 20 to 30 minutes, depending on the humidity and the moisture in your flour. The dough should be dry but not brittle. Roll up snugly, jelly-roll fashion, being careful not to press down as you do so. Cut in strips of desired width—very fine for soup and up to ¾ inch for noodle dishes.

Unroll the noodle strips and spread on a towel, covering with a second towel so they will stay slightly moist until they are to be cooked.

The noodles can also be dried, in which case they will keep for several weeks. Spread on a towel for several hours or overnight, or until completely dry and brittle, then store in a covered jar or tin.

Yield: Between 1 and 1½ pounds, dry

Golden Egg Noodles

Follow the above recipe using 2 whole, extra-large eggs plus 2 extra-large egg yolks. These noodles will be a little softer and stickier to roll and may require more flour on the board and rolling pin. Otherwise, handle them exactly as described above.

Noodles and . . .

Many delicious main courses and side dishes were prepared from noodles. In addition to the noodle pudding dessert on page 234, and the sautéed cabbage with noodles on page 188, two follow:

Noodles with Cottage Cheese

A main course for a light dinner . . .

For each portion allow 2 cups cooked noodles. Toss in butter and top with cottage cheese that has warmed to room temperature. Sprinkle with black pepper and, if you like, minced chives. Although my mother never served it that way, I like this dish with 2 strips of crumbled crisp bacon, and a tablespoonful or two of sour cream.

Noodles with Brown Butter

A side dish, especially good with fried fish . . .

For a portion of 2 cups of cooked noodles, melt 3 tablespoons sweet butter and let it brown slowly. Pour over the noodles and season with salt and pepper.

If you're willing to take the trouble, this is best done with clarified butter. Melt the butter, and when the foam rises to the surface, skim off, then gently pour off the clear, golden butter liquid, leaving the milky sediment at the bottom. Brown the clarified butter as described above, pour over the noodles, and toss.

Pinched Dumplings or Noodles

To make pinched dumplings, prepare noodle dough (page 82), and when it has been gathered in a ball, let it rest for 30 minutes in plastic wrap. Do not roll out. Instead, pinch off pieces of dough, each about the size of a small green pea. Scatter these pinched-off pieces on a towel and let dry, uncovered, overnight. Cook in boiling, salted water as for any pasta, allowing about 15 to 18 minutes for them to be thoroughly cooked. These are especially good with butter, or with meat and gravy dishes.

To make pinched noodles, roll out the dough as for noodles and cut into ½-inch wide strips. Then pinch off bits from each strip. Dry as above. These will cook in a little less time—about 12 to 15 minutes. Serve as above.

Yield: Between 1 and 1½ pounds, dry

Noodle Squares

"Square farfel" was the family name for this; Italians know them as *quadrettini.*

I have a special fondness for these little noodle squares that are meant to be served in soup, because whenever I was present while my grandmother made noodles, I was given the job of making the second cross-cuts that turned the strips to squares.

Follow either recipe for noodles on page 82. Dry, roll, and cut into strips about ¼ to ⅓ inch in width. Do not unroll the strips, but make cross-cuts in them, each again about ¼ to ⅓ inch in width, to form squares. Make thinner cross-cuts at each end, as the end pieces will unfold to double the width cut. If for any reason you want larger squares, simply cut the strips wider, then make cross-cuts of matching width.

Yield: Between 1 and 1½ pounds, dry

Riebele

[Grated Noodles]

Prepare one-third the amount of noodle dough according to the recipe on page 82, using whole egg and eliminating the water. When the dough is gathered into a ball, cut the ball in four parts and let each dry, uncovered, for about 1 hour. This time will vary depending on the humidity. When the dough feels firm and almost powdery to the touch, grate on the fine side of a grater, letting the pieces fall wide apart onto a platter or a sheet of waxed paper. If they cluster, they will stick together. Drop into boiling, salted water and cook for about 15 minutes, or until tender. Serve in soup.

These too can be allowed to dry and can be stored in a covered jar or canister.

Grated noodles are good in chicken soup, beef broth, or split-pea soup.

Yield: About 6 ounces, dry

Variation: Riebele can also be made in a larger size by using the coarse side of the grater, in which case they can be used as egg barley, described below.

Farfel

[Egg Barley]

Plain or toasted egg barley of very good quality can be bought in packages. The Goodman brand is the one I use when I can find it. If you can only find plain egg barley, you can toast it yourself (for added flavor and color) by spreading a single layer on a baking pan and baking it in a 350-degree oven for about 20 minutes, shaking the pan several times so the pieces brown evenly.

To make your own, follow the basic noodle recipe on page 82, making one-third the amount of dough (basic proportions 1 cup flour, 1 egg, 2 teaspoons water) and using a little extra flour to get a slightly stiffer dough (an extra ¼ cup should be enough). Gather into a ball, then press flat into a disk. Let dry for 1 hour. Working on a cutting board or in a wooden bowl, chop the dough into fine, barleylike bits. Spread out to dry. Use plain for soup or toast as described above. This will make about 2 cups, uncooked.

Toasted or plain, egg barley for a side dish should be boiled 15 to 20 minutes in well-salted water, until tender. Drain well and mix with ½ medium onion, finely chopped and sautéed in 3 tablespoons butter, schmaltz (rendered chicken fat), or margarine. Season well with salt and pepper. Sautéed mushrooms can also be added. The barley may be served with meat main courses this way, but my mother preferred to bake it so the top would be slightly crisp. To do this, place the egg barley, already tossed with onions and fat, in a baking dish, allowing the barley to come to a depth of about 1½ inches. Bake at 350 degrees for 30 to 45 minutes, or until the top and sides are light golden brown. My father liked this very dry, so my mother would stir it several times during baking so the underside would brown as well.

Baked or not, egg barley is especially good with roast poultry (most of all duck) and with dishes such as goulash and pot roasts that have rich, paprika-flavored gravies. It can also be used in split-pea soup, as well as in chicken or beef broth.

Kreplach

1 pound of beef flanken or lean chuck, for boiling (see note below)
1 carrot, scraped
3 onions, peeled
1 stalk celery with leaves
2 sprigs parsley
Salt
3 tablespoons schmaltz (rendered chicken fat, page 7) or margarine

Pepper to taste
1½ tablespoons finely chopped parsley
2 egg whites
1 recipe basic noodle dough (see page 82)
3 quarts water

Boil the beef in water to cover along with the carrot, 1 peeled onion, celery, parsley sprigs, and ½ teaspoon salt. Boil for about 1 hour, or until half tender. Cool the meat and chop or grind very fine (do not use a food processor), reserving the broth for other purposes. The meat may be cooked a day in advance.

Melt the fat, and in it sauté the remaining onions, finely chopped, until soft and yellow. Do not brown. Add the sautéed onion and all the fat remaining in the pan to the chopped beef. Add salt and pepper and the finely chopped parsley. Add the egg whites.

Prepare the noodle dough, but do not dry out the sheets. Keep in a ball, wrapped in plastic or waxed paper until the filling is prepared, or for at least 30 minutes.

Roll out the dough to just a little less than ¼ inch thickness; it should be a bit thicker than for noodles. Cut into 2- to 2½-inch squares.

To fill the dough, turn a point of each square toward you, in a diamond shape. Place a generous teaspoonful of filling on one side, then fold the square in half to form a triangle, pressing the top points firmly in place. Then pinch the sides tightly closed. If the dough is moist, the seams should close tightly enough, but if it seems dry, moisten the edges with a little cold water and then pinch shut. It is important that they remain closed during boiling.

When the seams are closed, bring the two bottom points of each triangle together to form a ring and press firmly closed. Let the kreplach sit at room temperature for 15 to 30 minutes before cooking.

Bring the 3 quarts of water to a rapid boil and add a handful of salt. Adding 1 dozen kreplach at a time, cover and cook each batch for about 20 minutes, or until done.

Drain well and add to chicken soup, allowing 4 to 5 per portion. Leftover cooked kreplach can be kept for a few days in the refrigerator and can be reheated in soup, or fried as below.

Yield: About 48 kreplach

Note: If you want to make kreplach in a hurry and do not have boiled beef, use 1 pound lean chopped meat and sauté it with the onions only until the meat loses its red color. Add the seasonings and eggs as described above. This is not quite as good a method, but it is an acceptable one.

Variation: Unboiled kreplach can be fried slowly in deep fat (corn oil) for about 10 minutes. They will be crisp, and very good as hot hors d'oeuvres. Once boiled, they can be fried in shallow fat (butter, chicken fat or margarine) until browned, to be served as a side dish.

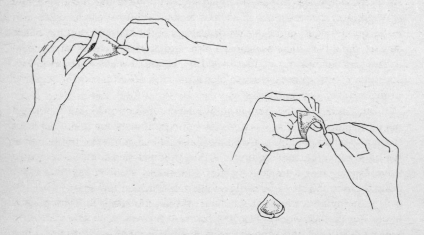

8

Breakfasts

As in most families, Sunday morning breakfasts were the most elaborate and special of the week, and in addition to standard American favorites such as bacon and eggs, griddle cakes or waffles, ours often included the classic Jewish stand-bys such as smoked fish and salmon, bagels and cream cheese. Sometimes my mother would fry blintzes, which we topped with sour cream, or she prepared scrambled eggs with smoked salmon and onions, or matzoh brei, or French toast.

But beside Sunday there were two other types of breakfasts that stand out in memory. The first was a feature during summers spent at a big field-stone-and-wood country house in the Catskill Mountains. The house was at the edge of an icy, running brook. Although it was illegal, my father would leave fishing poles with eight or ten baited hooks in the stream overnight, fixing them to the shore by wedging the rods between rocks.

In the morning we invariably had a silvery, red-speckled trout on each hook. My mother would clean the fish, roll them in flour that had been seasoned with salt and pepper, and fry them quickly in hot butter, in a thin black iron skillet. She cooked on an old black iron coal stove, and the warming scents of freshly burning wood used to get the stove going, the sizzling fish, the big crusty rolls heating on the back of the stove, and the strong, perking coffee gave us a start that would see us through even the most exasperating day. Such breakfasts were usually finished off with bowls of wild strawberries, raspberries, or blackberries, which we had picked the evening before. They were served with brown sugar and a pitcher of sweet cream or a bowl of thick sour cream.

The other breakfasts I remember fondly were those on freezing cold mornings in winter.

"It's a hot cereal morning," my mother would whisper, half aloud, half to herself, as she routed us out of bed on the coldest, darkest school mornings in midwinter. It was an announcement that told us more than merely what we were having for breakfast; it was a weather report as well. A firm believer in children eating a solid breakfast before going to school, and a hot one whenever possible, my mother would no more let us out the door without hot cereal on the frostiest mornings than she would let us leave without coats and scarves, boots and mittens.

On hot cereal mornings, it was difficult to inch ourselves out of sleep-warm beds piled high and heavy with layers of blankets and, almost certainly, with a pillow my mother would have placed over our feet in the middle of the freezing cold nights. On such mornings, windows would always be etched with a frosty pattern of lacework, and the milk left at the back door around five A.M. by the milkman would have frozen and expanded up and out the top of each long, narrow-necked glass bottle, forming a white top hat, rakishly askew.

Before my mother could cut the frozen cream into a bowl, where it would thaw and be poured back into the unhomogenized milk, we would sneak several spoonfuls—a delectable icy treat unmatched in memory by even the richest ice cream.

If the rest of the world presented a frost-white picture, the kitchen at least was a fragrant, steaming, and lively center of warmth and well-being.

Coffee would be perking for grownups, perhaps cocoa simmering for children, cinnamon toast might be gilding under the broiler, and the sharp, tropical scent of freshly sliced oranges would add their reminders of sunshine. A peek into the bubbling pot told us which cereal was on the daily menu, and if memory serves correctly, my mother kept a regular store of half a dozen varieties.

In addition to creamy, grainy oatmeal and sun-gold cornmeal, there were what we call the brown cereals and the white. Brown cereals included

Wheatena, Ralston, and Maltex. White cereals meant Cream of Wheat, Farina, and, on miserable mornings, the starchy, gluey Cream of Rice I detested then as now.

To many, I know, the very mention of hot cereal summons up memories of gray and pasty gruels. To me it recalls an incomparable sense of being loved and cared for.

At our house cereal was smooth and free of lumps, but it was thick— too thick to run in the bowl, thick enough to hold a spoon upright in the pot. We thinned it ourselves first with generous knobs of butter and then with just the thinnest trickle of heavy sweet cream, or occasionally with hot milk. Never having had much of a taste for sugar, I preferred cereals as I do now, salted and liberally sprinkled with pepper, an idea that always convinced my mother she was raising at least one crazy child.

The cereal I liked best, primarily for its toasty, nutty smell, was Wheatena. Neither Ralson or Maltex came close and I could never understand why if we were having "brown" cereal we bothered with any other. Thick, creamy oatmeal and fine cornmeal were tied for second place, and as for the "white" cereals, I could take them or leave them as long as the slippery Cream of Rice was not presented.

My mother gave us peeled and sliced oranges with hot cereal breakfasts because she felt juice would make the whole meal too liquid, what with the wind-up of cocoa or milk.

As much as I loved the cereals the day they were cooked, I adored them even more the second day, when leftover chilled mush was cut into squares and slowly fried in butter until both sides were golden brown and the insides were hot; fried Wheatena and cornmeal were especially good topped with crisp slices of bacon.

They still are, as I discovered one morning recently as I worked my way through almost twenty cereals to see if my ideas about them had changed. Miraculously, all of the brands I remembered still exist, though many are now also made in quick or instant forms. Considering that most old-fashioned regular cereals cook in five to fifteen minutes, it is hard to understand the necessity for those that cook in three to five minutes (or even less time), especially because the treatment grain gets to become "quick" cooking sacrifices much in the way of both texture and flavor.

Wheatena still edges into first place, fried or freshly cooked, but my tastes in oatmeal have altered slightly. For while the rolled old-fashioned oats packed by Quaker still satisfy, they have far less character and flavor than the steel-cut Irish oats packed by John McCann. Maltex with its dosing of barley malt syrup seems syrupy sweet, although I did not remember it that way, and Ralston proved totally bland and tasted more of the box in which it was packed than of anything else.

Quaker's cornmeal was still pleasant enough, but the stone-ground variety by Indian Head, a whole-grain cornmeal, not degerminated, was light years ahead of the more refined meal.

The big surprise was how much better Cream of Wheat and Farina were than I remembered, both of them subtle, soothing, and gentle with their melting pools of butter and salt and pepper seasonings. And white cornmeal hominy grits, a taste developed in adulthood, I now list among my favorites.

For my taste, all cooking instructions on commercial cereal boxes call for too much water. I reduce this ingredient by one-fourth to one-third. The only tricky step in cooking cereals comes at the point when the grain is poured into the boiling water, for it is then that irreducible nasty lumps can form. Grain should be poured so slowly that the water never stops boiling, and it is important to stir as you pour. If cereal is too thick it can easily be thinned with a little boiling water; if it is too thin, it will thicken if left to cook uncovered until the desired consistency is reached.

It is best to cook cereal in a heavy pot so it does not scorch. For easy cleaning, soak the empty pot in cold water until the leftover cereal forms a skin that slides out. All cereals develop extra flavor if they are allowed to stand covered, off the heat, for 5 to 8 minutes after they have finished cooking.

Cereals are perishable, so it is possible to buy them stale. Stale cereal will have a musty, moldy odor and may develop tiny white threadlike bugs that cause the grains to lump or string together. Fresh cereal has a bright, clean look; if stale it will look dull and dusty. Because grains contain oils that can turn rancid, it is best to store cereals in the refrigerator.

9

Eggs, Pancakes,
and Crêpes

Fried Eggs

If it seems strange to include a recipe for so common a dish, it is only because fried eggs were perhaps my favorite of all foods and what I always asked for when I was recuperating from an illness, or when I couldn't think of anything else to have, or what I fixed for myself as a sandwich, as I still do. But I was (and am) very particular about the way they are done, and the rim of dark brown crispness I love around them probably is considered heresy by more effete gastronomes.

1 tablespoon sweet butter	Kosher (coarse) salt
2 eggs	Freshly ground black pepper

I loathe eggs fried in brown or blackened butter, and if that happens I throw the whole thing away and start over. This means a heavy skillet is

93

needed and the cooking must be done over low heat.

The best-sized pan for 2 eggs is one that is 5 inches in diameter. Heat the butter in it, and when frothy and bubbling all over, break the eggs into it gently. Fry over low heat for about 5 minutes. When the eggs are set, sprinkle with coarse salt. Baste frequently with hot butter from the pan so the tops of the eggs cook. When almost done (about 7 minutes in all), very carefully remove the membrane from the top of the yolks. Do this with a teaspoon, carefully nudging the membrane back and tipping the pan so the membrane will slide to the edge of the pan, where it will cook. I do this only because I am finicky about the membrane. The same effect can be achieved by covering the pan, but the result is a white film covering the yolk.

Fry slowly until the eggs develop a very thin line of brown crispness around the edge.

Serve sprinkled with black pepper.

Yield: 1 serving

Variation: On certain occasions I turn the eggs over and lightly brown the second side. When the egg has finished cooking on the first side, I flip it over carefully with a wide spatula, so as not to break the yolk, and fry on the second side for about 2 minutes.

Fried Egg Sandwich

This is perhaps the only thing I like made with American white bread; Pepperidge Farm, the least horrible, is the one I use. If the bread is kept in the refrigerator, let 2 slices stand at room temperature a few minutes so they will not be cold. Prepare 2 fried eggs, turned over, as described above, and place on one of the slices of bread. Drizzle over it any melted butter left in the pan and sprinkle with ground black pepper. Top with the second slice of bread. Try to cut in half between the egg yolks so they will not break, something to plan for when you place the eggs on the bread. If the yolks are too close, do not cut the sandwich.

Fried egg sandwiches are marvelous with champagne, coffee, or beer, in that order.

Yield: 1 sandwich

Fried Egg and Bacon Sandwich

This was something my mother would prepare as a picnic breakfast to be eaten in the car when we drove to and from our country house in the Catskills. We always got a head start on the day by leaving just before sunrise—usually at five or perhaps a little earlier. Somwhere along the route, we ate these sandwiches, which were still ever so gently warm and lusciously soggy and fragrant. Although it was rare for my brother and me to drink anything but milk, on these occasions we all had steaming sugared coffee with scalded milk that had been kept hot in a big thermos bottle. The best accompaniment to this sandwich, in addition to coffee, is a country road when the sun comes up behind a veil of rising dew. Follow it by a big yawn and stretch in the open air and a five-minute walk along the road. Then head back to the car for a catnap that, with luck, lasts the rest of the journey.

The sandwich is prepared very much like the fried egg sandwich above, with the following exception. For each sandwich fry 2 slices of bacon that have been cut in half. Drain on paper towels. Fry eggs as above in butter, but when you lift the eggs to turn them over, place the fried bacon half-slices in the pan and turn the eggs over on them, so that the bacon fuses with the eggs. Fry about 3 minutes, or until the yolks are thoroughly firm and no longer runny, then place on bread, sprinkle with pepper, wrap snugly in waxed paper, and put the sandwich in a box.

Scrambled Eggs

These were prepared the standard way, without milk or water being added to the mix, and cooked in lots of butter. But the unusual touches came by way of things my mother added to them—diced Cheddar cheese, caraway seeds, minced dill or parsley, sautéed (but not browned) onion, flecks of sautéed green pepper, or, oddly enough, small square croutons, which she made out of leftover bread. The following was a similar dish that we loved at Passover time.

Scrambled Eggs with Matzohs

If matzoh brei can be described as matzohs soaked in eggs, this recipe is the reverse—eggs with just a slight crunch of matzoh mixed in.

4 eggs, lightly beaten	Pinch each of salt and black pepper
½ matzoh square, broken in approximately 1-inch pieces	3 tablespoons sweet butter

Combine the eggs, matzoh pieces, salt, and pepper and stir so the matzoh pieces are enveloped in egg.

Heat the butter in an 8-inch skillet. When hot and bubbling, add the eggs and cook as regular scrambled eggs to desired degree of doneness—just set but creamy being best with the matzoh pieces.

Yield: 2 to 3 servings

Eggs with Smoked Salmon and Onions

Known best simply as "lox and eggs," this was sometimes made with true lox—brine-cured Pacific salmon—or with smoked Nova Scotia salmon, which I much prefer. When my mother used lox, she soaked it overnight; Nova Scotia needed soaking for only half an hour. Even if the salmon does not taste very salty, remember that cooking will bring out the salt flavor, so it is probably safest to soak it briefly, in any case.

¼ pound lox or Nova Scotia salmon in slices just a little less than ¼ inch thick	3 or 4 tablespoons sweet butter, or as needed
⅓ cup chopped onion	6 large eggs, lightly beaten
	Salt, if needed
	Black pepper

If using lox, soak overnight in a bowlful of very cold water, in the refrigerator. If using Nova Scotia, soak 30 minutes at room temperature. Remove the salmon from the soaking water and dry on paper towels. Chop or cut up coarsely.

Heat 2 tablespoons butter in a 7-inch skillet, and when bubbling add the onion. Sauté slowly over low heat, stirring frequently until the onion softens and becomes bright yellow. Do not let it brown. Stir in the salmon and sauté for a minute or two until hot. Add 1 or 2 tablespoons butter, depending on how much is left in the pan. Pour in the eggs and cook as for scrambled eggs. Taste when the eggs are almost as firm as you want them and add a little salt if needed, and pepper to taste. Serve at once on heated plates.

Yield: 3 to 4 servings

Variation: In fairness it must be stated that many prefer this dish made with onions that have browned slightly, so try it both ways and decide for yourself. Dairy restaurants also feature a version known as a "Jewish Western omelet." To prepare it they sauté the onion with ¼ cup finely chopped seeded green pepper, then add the salmon and then the beaten eggs. The omelet is cooked pancake style, which means it is turned over when the first side has browned slightly. Green pepper can also be added to the scrambled version, but it tends to overpower the flavor of the salmon.

Scrambled Eggs with Chicken Livers

The only special touch my mother gave this standard dish was to scramble the eggs directly in the pan in which the livers had been sautèed, thereby scraping in the lovely brown and crusty bits of flour and liver that remained. We liked these best with toasted English muffins and cottage cheese. It is equally good for Sunday breakfast or a light dinner.

1 **pound chicken livers, at room** **temperature**	6 to 8 **tablespoons sweet butter, or as** **needed**
Salt and black pepper	5 **extra-large eggs, lightly beaten**
Flour for dredging	**with a pinch of salt**

Clean the chicken livers, removing connective tissue and bits of fat and discarding any livers showing green gall spots. Pat dry with paper towels. Sprinkle lightly with salt and pepper, then dredge lightly with flour. Heat 4 tablespoons butter in a heavy 10-inch skillet. When hot but not brown, add the livers and sauté slowly, turning frequently so they brown on all sides and adding more butter if needed during sautéing. In about 12 minutes the livers should be done. Remove and keep warm.

Add 2 tablespoons butter to the pan and, as it melts, scrape in coagulated bits from the pan, using a wooden spatula. When the butter foams, add the beaten eggs and cook as for scrambled eggs. Serve on a heated platter with the livers.

Yield: 3 to 4 servings

Scrambled Eggs with Calf's Brains and Onions

This also is a lovely dish for Sunday breakfast or a light dinner. We were fond of it with either toasted bagel halves or dark pumpernickel. If serving it for lunch or dinner, add a cucumber salad (page 200).

1 **pair of calf's brains**	4 **extra-large eggs, lightly beaten with**
6 to 7 **tablespoons sweet butter, or as**	**a pinch of salt**
needed	1 **small onion, finely chopped**
Salt and black pepper	

The calf's brains should be soaked, parboiled, and trimmed as described for sweetbreads on page 179. For this recipe it is not necessary to add celery and onion to the water during parboiling, nor is it necessary to flatten the brains.

When they have been trimmed and cooled and are firm, the brains can be diced or separated into small clumps. Heat 4 tablespoons butter in an 8- or 9-inch skillet, and when the foam subsides add the brains, sprinkling with a little salt and pepper. Sauté slowly, turning, until the brains are pale golden brown. Remove and keep warm.

Add the onion to the pan, with a little more butter if needed, and sauté slowly until soft and yellow but only very faintly edged with brown. Return the brains to the pan, add 2 tablespoons butter, and stir in the beaten eggs. Cook as for scrambled eggs. Serve on a heated platter.

Yield: 2 to 3 servings

Omelet with Tongue, Salami, or Bologna

More commonly known as "tongue (or salami or bologna) and eggs," this golden-brown pancake omelet was a favorite Sunday night supper, served with rye bread, cole slaw, and lots of hot mustard. We made it with butter, not with chicken fat, the usual kosher frying fat. I hate the combination of chicken fat and eggs used in this way and suggest margarine as an alternative. Corned beef or pastrami and eggs were also popular, but not at our house.

For each omelet:

2 tablespoons sweet butter,
    margarine, or schmaltz (rendered
    chicken fat, page 7), or as needed
  About 6 quarter-inch-thick slices
    smoked or pickled tongue, or

somewhat thinner slices of salami
  or bologna
2 extra-large eggs, lightly beaten with
  a pinch of salt

Heat 1 tablespoon fat in a 7-inch skillet, and when it is hot add the slices of meat. There should be enough to cover the surface of the pan with some overlapping. Fry slowly, turning once or twice so the slices become hot and faintly golden brown around the edges. Add 1 tablespoon fat to the pan. Pour the beaten eggs over the slices. Cook as you would an omelet, pulling the cooked edges of the egg away to let the unset portion run onto the pan. I prefer this with a soft top and brown bottom, but many prefer both sides browned. If you prefer the latter, turn the omelet and brown the second side.

Yield: 1 generous serving

Note: If you want to make several portions at once, use a much larger skillet and cut the finished omelet into wedge-shaped portions. It is not a good idea to make more than four portions at a time. Increase the ingredients proportionally for each serving.

Soufflé Omelet

This elegant-looking omelet never ceased to delight me when I was a child. It was added to the family repertory by a baby nurse who took care of my brother and who was with us for a year. It was her special treat for me when my parents went out and she fixed dinner, as were the noodles with brown butter on page 84. She did this either "sweet" or "salty," depending on her mood and ours. The salty version might be plain or seasoned with cheese or chives.

(continued)

2 extra-large or jumbo eggs, separated	1 tablespoon grated Cheddar or Parmesan cheese or minced chives (optional)
Salt	
Generous pinch of white pepper	1 generous tablespoon sweet butter

Preheat the oven to 450 degrees. Beat the egg yolks until foamy along with ¼ teaspoon salt and the pepper and cheese or chives if you use either (or both).

Beat the whites with a pinch of salt until they stand in stiff and shiny peaks.

Fold the whites and yolks together quickly but thoroughly, using a rubber spatula. Heat the butter in a heavy 5- to 6-inch skillet and turn the egg mixture into it. This looks best if the top mounds in peaks rather than being smooth and level. Cover the pan. A high lid is all right for this, but a deep pot turned upside down that fits the rim of the skillet is preferable if you have one. Let the egg cook slowly for 7 or 8 minutes. Once or twice during the cooking, poke holes right through the omelet to the bottom of the pan so the crust will be broken and heat can rise through the egg mixture. Be sure the heat is low or the bottom of the omelet will become overdone and leathery. When the omelet has risen a little way above the pan and is set most of the way through, uncover the pan and slide into the upper third of the preheated oven.

Bake for 5 to 7 minutes, or until the top is set and a light golden brown.

Slide the omelet out of the pan onto a heated dinner plate. (If the plate is cold, the omelet will fall even faster than it will if the plate is warm.) It may fall after 3 or 4 minutes, but it will not flatten completely and should retain a puffy appearance.

Yield: 1 serving as a main course

Sweet Soufflé Omelet

Prepare as above, with the following exceptions. Add only a tiny pinch of salt to the egg yolks and omit the pepper. Add 2 teaspoons sugar and ½ teaspoon vanilla and beat in. Add a pinch of salt and 1 teaspoon sugar to egg whites when they begin to get foamy as you beat them. Fold together and cook and bake as directed above. If you like, a little granulated sugar can be sprinkled on top of the soufflé just before it is slid into the oven. Serve plain or with preserves or warm cooked fruit or applesauce, or with crushed strawberries or raspberries.

Yield: 2 servings as a dessert

Egg Salad with Green Peppers

This develops flavor if it is allowed to sit in the refrigerator for 1 to 2 hours after it has been prepared. But because it contains green pepper, which can become watery, do not keep it more than 3 hours, and always refrigerate.

> 2 extra-large or jumbo eggs,
>   hard cooked
> 1½ tablespoons seeded, finely
>   minced green pepper
>
> 1½ to 2 tablespoons mayonnaise
>   Salt and white pepper to
>   taste

Peel the eggs and chop to a moderately coarse texture. Combine with the minced green pepper. Using a fork, toss in the mayonnaise. Do not stir vigorously, or the eggs will disintegrate and the salad will be mushy. Pieces of egg should be discernible. Season with salt and pepper. Store, covered, in a bowl in the refrigerator for 1 to 2 hours.

Serve on a salad plate or in a sandwich. This is especially good with Boston lettuce on a poppy-seed roll or on pumpernickel.

Yield: 1 serving as a main-course salad; filling for 2 generous sandwiches

Buttermilk Buckwheat Pancakes

Although we generally used the old reliable Aunt Jemima pancake mix, my mother occasionally made the following recipe from scratch, and they spoiled me for the store-bought mix. I prefer pancakes just with butter; the rest of the family (and the world apparently) seems to like syrup of some sort.

> ¾ cup buckwheat flour
> ¾ cup unbleached flour
> 2½ tablespoons sugar
> 1 teaspoon baking soda
> ½ teaspoon salt
> 2 large or extra-large eggs
>
> 1½ cups buttermilk
> 1½ tablespoons melted sweet butter,
>   plus butter for frying
>
> *Garnish:* Butter, and honey or maple
>   syrup (optional)

Sift together the two flours with the sugar, baking soda, and salt. Beat the eggs with the buttermilk, then beat in the melted butter. Add the liquids to the dry ingredients slowly, stirring as you do so. The mixture should be blended but not overmixed.

(continued)

Heat a griddle until a droplet of water sizzles on it. Brush lightly with butter. Using a ladle or measuring cup, pour the batter onto the griddle, allowing about 2 tablespoonfuls per pancake. When the edges of the pancakes are dry and the tops are all bubbly, turn and brown the second side. Continue until all the batter has been used. Brush the griddle with butter between batches if it seems dry. Serve in stacks of three with a small pat of butter on top of each pancake. Honey or syrup can be poured on at the table by those who like it. Garnish with bacon, fried ham or sausages.

Yield: About 16 pancakes

Matzoh Brei

A favorite Passover breakfast treat, this is really a first cousin to French toast. It is one dish in which preground black pepper tastes better—or perhaps more comfortably familiar—than the freshly ground variety. In some families, matzoh brei is served sweet, sprinkled with sugar; ours was always well salted and peppered and served with cottage cheese.

8 matzohs	¼ to ½ teaspoon black pepper
3 to 4 cups boiling water	½ cup (¼ pound) sweet butter
4 extra-large eggs, lightly beaten	Cottage cheese, as accompaniment
1 teaspoon salt, or to taste	

Break the matzohs into 1½- to 2-inch squares. Place in a large bowl, preferably with a handle, or in a large saucepan, so draining will be easy.

Bring the water to a boil and pour over the matzohs. Drain immediately through a sieve or colander. Do not stir the matzoh pieces through the water, or let them stand. They should be only very slightly moistened, not soggy, so they will absorb the egg. Drain very thoroughly and return to the bowl or saucepan.

Add the beaten eggs, salt, and pepper. Toss lightly with a fork until all the matzoh pieces are well coated with egg and the seasonings are distributed evenly. Do not mix or stir vigorously, as the matzohs should not be broken up any more than necessary. Matzohs have a bland flavor, so plenty of salt and pepper will be needed.

Heat the butter until hot and bubbling (but not brown) in a heavy 10- to 12-inch skillet, preferably of black iron. Turn the matzoh mixture into the butter and fry over moderate heat. When the underside begins to brown, turn in sections with a spatula.

Keep turning until all sides are light golden brown. It is not necessary, or even desirable, to keep a pancake shape. A jumble of pieces, golden brown contrasted to some that are slightly golden and tender, is the ideal. Check the seasoning once during the frying and adjust as needed. The total frying time should be about 10 minutes. Serve on a heated platter or individual plates, with cottage cheese on the side.

Yield: 4 servings

Matzoh Meal Pancakes

My mother served these for Sunday breakfasts, not only during Passover but the rest of the year as well. They are very good with some warm applesauce (page 227) on the side, or simply sprinkled with cinnamon sugar or sugar alone.

3 **eggs, separated**	⅔ **cup matzoh meal**
½ **teaspoon salt**	**Sweet butter and corn oil, for frying**
½ **cup cold water**	**Sugar or cinnamon sugar, for**
1 **teaspoon grated lemon rind**	**topping**

Combine the egg yolks, salt, and water and beat until foamy and well blended. Stir in the lemon rind and matzoh meal. Beat the egg whites until stiff and shiny and fold gently but thoroughly into the yolk mixture.

Heat a 1-inch depth of half butter and half corn oil in a large, heavy skillet. The fat should be very hot—about 375 degrees. Drop the batter by rounded tablespoonfuls into the hot fat, but do not crowd too many into the pan at a time. Let fry slowly until the first sides are golden brown, then turn and brown the second sides. Total frying time per batch should be about 8 minutes, and the pancakes should not be turned more than once. Drain on paper toweling and keep warm until all are fried. Serve at once, with sugar or cinnamon sugar on the side.

Yield: About 12 pancakes, or 4 servings

Note: These can also be fried in about a ¼-inch depth of butter alone, but it is difficult to keep butter from burning, and pancakes stay puffed up longer when fried in the deeper fat.

Cheese Blintzes

Cheese was the only filling we ever had in blintzes at home, and they were served as desserts, as accompaniments to afternoon or evening coffee, as breakfast, or as a main part of a light dinner. They freeze very well and should be fried without having first been thawed. The optional touch of wheat germ is my own.

CRÊPE BATTER:

2 extra-large eggs
⅔ cup milk
⅓ cup water, or as needed

Pinch of salt
6 to 7 heaping tablespoons flour
(1 scant cup)

CHEESE FILLING:

½ pound dry (uncreamed) pot cheese
plus ½ pound farmer cheese, or
1 pound farmer cheese
1 extra-large or jumbo egg
1½ tablespoons sugar, or to taste
½ teaspoon cinnamon, or to taste

1 teaspoon vanilla, or to taste
Pinch of salt
2 heaping tablespoons toasted
wheat germ (optional)
Sweet butter, for frying
Sour cream, as accompaniment

Beat the eggs lightly with a fork. Using a rotary beater, beat in the milk and water and a pinch of salt. Gradually beat in the flour, 1 heaping table-spoonful at a time. Be sure each addition is thoroughly absorbed before adding the next. Stop when the batter is the consistency of heavy cream. If there are air bubbles, stir in a little water and hit the bottom of the bowl against the counter top so the bubbles will rise to the surface. Bubbles will become holes in finished crêpes. If the batter has lumps of flour, pour through a fine sieve, rubbing undissolved flour through. Let the batter stand for 30 minutes before frying. Stir before frying.

Prepare the cheese filling by carefully mashing the pot cheese (if you use it) and farmer cheese together. For finest results, both can be rubbed through a sieve. Mix in the egg, sugar, cinnamon, vanilla, salt, and wheat germ, if you use it. Mash together well and adjust the seasoning.

To fry crêpes, it is best to have a traditional crêpe pan or a 6½-inch skillet. Have on hand 4 or 5 tablespoons of melted sweet butter. Batter is most convenient to pour if it is in a pitcher or a bowl with a lip. Add 1 table-spoon melted butter to the batter. Stir the batter between pourings; do not beat.

Spread a thin film of butter on the skillet and heat until a drop of water froths but does not jump or sizzle. Pour in just enough batter to cover the pan. After pouring, tip and rotate the pan so the batter covers the bottom, then quickly pour excess batter back into the bowl. If the batter sets in ripples as it is poured, the pan is too hot; if it slides around without setting, the pan is not hot enough. Work very quickly so excess is poured off before it sets and the crêpe becomes too thick. When the crêpe looks dry around the edges and begins to curl from the pan, invert the pan over a clean towel and drop the crêpe out. Rebutter the pan every 2 or 3 crêpes. Crêpes should not be brown, but a pale golden glaze is acceptable. Ideally, they should be the color of boiled noodles. Be sure you keep the cooked sides up on the towel. Continue until all the crêpes are made; you should have about 14.

The lip or "tab" formed when excess batter is poured back will be convenient for filling the crêpe.

With the tab toward you, on the cooked side of each crêpe place a rounded tablespoonful of cheese filling. Turn tab with filling over once, fold over the side of the crêpes, then continue folding to form a small rectangle, as shown here. Fill all crêpes before folding, so the amount of filling in each can be adjusted to fill all crêpes evenly.

Place fold side down on a platter and store in the refrigerator until just before serving. Or wrap the blintzes in foil, two to a packet, and freeze.

To fry blintzes, heat enough butter in a frying pan to enable the blintzes to swim slightly. Fry slowly over moderate heat until the first side is golden brown. Turn and fry the second side. If the blintzes are frozen, keep the heat very low and cover the pan for the first 7 or 8 minutes.

(continued)

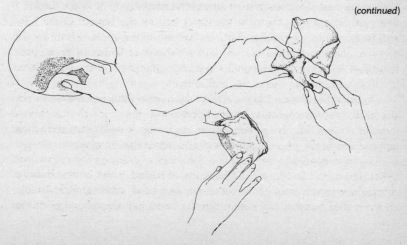

By the time the blintzes are golden brown and crisp on both sides, the filling should be thoroughly hot all the way through, so adjust the frying time accordingly.

Serve immediately with beaten sour cream, to be spooned on at the table.

Yield: About 14 blintzes; 2 to 4 blintzes per serving

French Toast

There is no bread quite like challah for making superb French toast, and because that beautiful braided loaf was always part of Friday night dinner, Saturday or Sunday mornings were the times we were most likely to have this at breakfast. Although French toast can be made from any white bread, it is best to buy a loaf unsliced so you can cut it into slices at least ¾ inch thick. Brioche also makes excellent French toast, but to get large slices you will have to make or buy a large round brioche; the individual size is too small. You can, of course, use French bread, but the texture and absorption will not be as good. The bread should be slightly stale. I prefer French toast with either of the sugars indicated below; syrup or honey makes it too soggy.

8 slices bread, preferably challah (page 247), ¾ to 1 inch thick	Tiny pinch of salt Sweet butter, for frying and garnish
2 to 3 extra-large eggs ¾ to 1 cup milk ½ teaspoon vanilla extract	*Garnish:* Cinnamon sugar or confectioners sugar, or maple syrup or honey

For best results, use bread that is slightly stale, or let slices of bread dry on a rack at room temperature for an hour or two.

Beat 2 eggs with ¾ cup milk, reserving the extra egg and milk in case more is needed for dipping. Stir in the salt and vanilla. Start melting butter in a large, heavy frying pan.

Dip the bread slices, one at a time, into the batter, turning so both sides are well coated and some of the batter is absorbed. Do not let the bread get so mushy that it cannot be handled. Let excess batter drip off and place the dipped slice in the hot butter at once. Add other slices as they are dipped. Do not crowd the slices in the pan. Fry slowly until the first side turns golden brown—about 5 to 7 minutes—then turn and brown the second side for the same amount of time. By the time both sides are golden brown, the inside of the bread slice should be moist and almost custardlike. If you fry the slices too rapidly, the inside will be uncooked and wet.

Serve on heated plates. Place a dab of butter on each slice and sprinkle with either of the sugars, unless syrup or honey are to be used.

Crisp slices of bacon are perfect accompaniments.

Yield: 4 to 8 servings

French-Toasted Cottage Cheese Sandwich

For each sandwich:

2 slices bread, preferably challah,
   cut ½ inch thick
1 egg
¾ cup milk
   Pinch of salt
2 tablespoons well-drained small-
   curd cottage cheese or mashed
   farmer cheese

Pinch each salt and cinnamon
½ teaspoon sugar
2 or 3 drops vanilla extract
   Sweet butter, for frying
   Sour cream, as
      accompaniment (optional)

Cut each slice of bread in half. Beat the egg with the milk and salt. Mash the cheese with salt, cinnamon, sugar, and vanilla. Spread half of the cheese onto each of two bread halves. Top with the remaining half slices of bread to form half sandwiches. Carefully dip into the egg-milk mixture, turning so both slices of bread absorb the liquid. Let excess drip off, then fry slowly in butter. When the first side is golden brown, turn the sandwich and brown the second side. Serve at once. Sour cream can be added at the table.

Yield: 1 serving

10

Summer

Summer was always my favorite season, not only because I loved heat, but because school was closed and I was free.

Flatbush was beautiful in summer, and a visit there only a short while ago proved that it still is. The small streets with their amply spreading maple trees are dappled with sun and shade, and the somewhat unprepossessing builders' houses are set in velvety lawns and flowery borders. And occasionally, one still hears the giggles of children in bathing suits running under hissing lawn sprinklers in backyards.

Our house was cool and dark in summer, and the faint, exotic aromas of camphor and tar paper hung in the air, adding to the out-of-season relaxed feeling, though I suppose some people might find those odors stifling. All the furniture was covered with the same slipcover fabric, a teal-blue and natural striped Belgian linen, fine, heavy, and glossy, piped in orange. Even the upright piano and its bench wore their shrouds from early June to late September. Oriental rugs were rolled on poles and wrapped in tar paper and slid up to the attic, to be replaced by white and flowered Indian druggets that stank to high heaven on damp days.

Most of our time was spent at the Brooklyn beaches, Manhattan and Oriental, which were then private, and where the name bands of the late

thirties—Benny Goodman, the Dorsey Brothers, Glenn Miller, and more—
played every afternoon on week-long engagements.

We took wonderful sandwiches to those beaches—big, squashy and
crisp poppy-seed rolls or sliced rye bread piled with egg salad made with
minced green pepper; salmon or tuna salad with celery and parsley; thick
slices of home cooked pickled tongue with fiery mustard; rare roast beef
with both mustard and butter; tomato herring with slices of Bermuda onion
and butter; and others. I say wonderful now, but I remember the embarrass-
ment I felt at the rye bread sandwiches and how I wished for neat, squared-
off sandwiches on packaged white bread, which I considered more American and, therefore, classier.

The problem with the rye bread was its shape—the standard loaf that
tapered toward both ends. My mother cut it on the diagonal to make larger
slices, and because the loaf tapered, no two slices were the same size, so the
edges of my sandwiches did not "match." They were, I thought, sloppy
Jewish sandwiches, and what wouldn't I do to be eating one even as I write?

In addition to our own, we ate other food sold at the beach. Not only
hot dogs and ice cream, but the local specialty—hot, freshly made waffles,
which we sprinkled with lots of vanilla-scented confectioner's sugar as we
held them between sheets of glassine paper.

There were marvelous summer dinners, too—fried chicken at room
temperature, assortments of salads, perhaps an all-dairy dinner with blintzes
and sour cream as a combination main course and dessert, or sour cream
and pot cheese mixed with chopped radishes, scallions, and cucumbers,
slices of cold roast beef with homemade pepper slaw and potato salad. But
one summer dinner stands for all others in my memory.

It took place when I was very young—about nine or so—and had spent
the day with a friend seeing the movie *It Happened One Night,* with Clark
Gable and Claudette Colbert. One look at Gable sans undershirt (the
famous scene that sent undershirt sales plummeting), and even at nine I was
hooked.

We ate in the dining room that very hot night because it was cooler
than the kitchen. There were only three of us (my brother was too young to
eat with us and was already asleep), and the table was huge, so my mother
set only half of it, drawing the ivory-colored crocheted lace cloth back and
placing a pad and white damask cloth over the half at which we sat.

The menu was cold beet borscht with sour cream and hot boiled potatoes, cold fried flounder with just hints of cinnamon and hot paprika in its
crisp breading, hot buttered corn, pepper slaw, a fresh peach kuchen in a
deep dish bathed with thick, heavy unwhipped sweet cream, and a pitcher

of iced tea with lemon slices and sprigs of mint from the back yard.

As my father, mother, and I sat down, I announced that I knew who I would marry.

"Really? Who?" asked my mother.

"Clark Gable," I answered emphatically.

"Over my dead body," my mother said with shock and a disturbing firmness in her voice.

"Why not?" I asked, amazed that such a simple announcement should touch off such an obvious wellspring of disapproval.

"Because he's not Jewish, and Jewish girls marry Jewish boys," she answered.

"Then I won't be Jewish. I think that's stupid," I answered, and the argument was on.

Midway through dinner my father, whose temper was shorter than usual in hot weather, shouted "Quiet! Quiet!" and to me, "Look, if you want to marry Clark Gable, marry Clark Gable. I'll pay for the wedding."

This was more than my mother could stand, and she flared up at him, yelling, "Sure, you give her ideas—go ahead, go ahead, encourage her. Very nice for a rabbi's granddaughter!"

This time my father blew up, banging for quiet on the table with such force that his borscht flew up out of his bowl on to the white cotton cloth. As the argument continued I watched the slow, inevitable spread of the pink stain as it bled out on the cloth.

"You're crazier than she is," he said to my mother. "Imagine arguing with a nine-year old child because she wants to marry one of the country's top movie stars. She'll never even meet him," he said.

He was wrong, for about twenty-five years later I did meet Clark Gable. It was on a movie set in Rome, where I worked for a few minutes as an extra. We talked for a while, he complaining about having had all of his guns stolen during a recent hunting trip in Austria, and I noting that even though he was obviously aging and that his thick figure was stiffly corseted, the King was still King. I like to think that the possibility of our marriage was not quite as remote as my father had thought it to be.

11

Fish and Seafood

Because we lived so close to Sheepshead Bay, where so many fishing boats brought their catches directly into local markets, my mother preferred shopping for her fish there. She was adamant about the freshness of the fish she bought, and though as a child I found her performance embarrassing, it's one I imitate now for the same reason she did. The first clue as to the freshness of a fish is its eye, which should be dark, clear, and high in the socket. If the eyes are faded or sunken, there is no need to continue the examination. The skin of the fish should be bright and clear, and when you press the body of the fish with your forefinger, no indentation should remain. The gills should be bright blood-red, not dark and brownish, and the whole fish should smell only very faintly of the sea. It should never smell acrid or typically "fishy." To judge precut fillets or slices, look for a moist shiny exterior and a fine grain. Lobsters and crabs should always be purchased live, clams and oysters should be tightly shut, and shrimp should be very clear and shiny. If shells are dried, crackled, or pink, shrimp are inferior. Scallops should be the palest cream or pink color and should be translucent; if they are snow white and opaque they have been soaked in water to add weight. All recipes in this book are based on fresh fish. If that is not available, I cannot really recommend making these dishes, but if you do use frozen fish, always thaw it before proceeding with the recipe.

If shellfish tastes of iodine after it has been cooked, it is not fresh and should be returned to the market. Some fish take on the flavor of petroleum oil from the waters in which they were caught. To ascertain this in advance, slip your finger under the fish gill and extract a little of the bloody matter there. Rub it on the back of one hand and then sniff. If oil is present, you will smell it.

One of the great triumphs of my mother's life was reporting a fish market to the Department of Health because she felt fish she had bought there was contaminated. The health inspector agreed with her and poured kerosene over the fishmonger's entire stock. "Good for him," my mother said as she told us what had happened. "They should have poured it on him, too, for selling people fish that stinks."

Smoked Fish

Thick, moistly fatty smoked whitefish, their skins as golden and thinly crackling as gold leaf; gilt-edged alabaster slices of sturgeon; pearly, satiny sable (the smoked cod that is known as poor man's sturgeon); brine-cured salmon that is lox and the firmer, more elegant smoked Nova Scotia salmon, or Novy, made up the platters that graced Sunday breakfast tables or that were served for late-night suppers after card parties.

These were, of course, purchased in appetizer stores, never homemade, although my mother and grandmother generally made the unsmoked, paprika-baked carp and pickled herring that were also sold in such stores.

My mother disliked the smaller whitefish known as "chubs" because they were bony and not meaty. Even when she wanted a small amount, she preferred buying a piece of a larger fish.

When buying any of these fish that are sold sliced, it is best if they are sliced to order. Preslicing results in dry fish, and if the store itself buys it presliced, usually packed with oil to prevent drying, forget the whole thing; the results can only be disastrous. Smoked salmon or lox is usually sliced differently when it is to be served on bagels than when it is to be eaten from plates. When sliced for bagels, salmon is usually cut straight down in thin narrow strips. When meant to be eaten on a plate, the salmon is cut in wide, thin, palm-shaped slices, the knife being held almost parallel to the cutting surface. I prefer the latter cut even for bagels, for the thinner wide slices, folded on themselves, make better sandwiches.

When buying Nova Scotia salmon, look for a silky sheen and fine grain as well as a back skin that is silvery and supple. A good slicer will not include bones or smoked skin along the edges of the slices, and he will pack the salmon flat, with sheets of waxed or glassine paper between layers of fish.

If you are buying lox or Nova Scotia to be mixed with scrambled eggs (page 95), you can save money by buying the wing tips and chunks, usually sold inexpensively. The bits of salmon you cut out of them will be just right for the eggs.

Sturgeon, too, should be moist, fine grained, and shiny. My preference, however, is for the far less expensive and unctuously dewy sable.

Platters of sliced tomatoes and Bermuda onion dotted with the salty, oily, wrinkled black musselines olives always accompanied the fish platter, together with baskets of bagels, bialys, onion rolls, onion breads, and pumpernickels, and cream cheese (sometimes with chives mixed in), butter, and slices of Muenster and imported Swiss cheese. I can almost smell the coffee brewing now.

Scharfe Fish

[Pickled Jellied Fish]

A wonderful appetizer or hot-weather lunch entrée . . .

3 pounds pike, carp, or pickerel, alone or in combination	1 bay leaf
Salt	1 tablespoon mixed pickling spices, tied in cheesecloth
3½ cups water	⅓ to ½ cup vinegar, as needed
2 onions, peeled and sliced	1 teaspoon sugar, or to taste
2 carrots, scraped and cut into 1-inch slices	

Cut the fish into 2-inch slices. Do not remove bones or skin. Sprinkle with salt and place in the refrigerator for 1½ hours.

Remove the fish from the refrigerator and rinse quickly under cold running water.

Combine the water, onions, carrots, bay leaf, spices, and ⅓ cup vinegar. Bring to a boil and simmer for 15 minutes. Add the fish and 1 teaspoon sugar. Reduce the heat, cover the pan, and simmer gently for about 20 to 30 minutes, or until the fish is done but still retains its shape. Using a slotted spoon, remove the fish to a ceramic or glass bowl or jar. Season the stock to taste, adding salt, sugar, and vinegar as needed. Remove the cheesecloth sack of spices and pour the stock, with the vegetables, over the fish. Cover and chill for at least 48 hours.

Serve the fish cold in its own jelly; use the sliced carrots and onions as garnish.

Yield: 4 to 6 servings

Fish in Aspic

It is convenient and refreshing to have a jar of this mild and flavorful fish on hand in summer for a first course or a light dinner. It is much gentler and more subtle than the pickled versions. Fish cooked this way can also be served hot, but more flavor develops as it stands in the refrigerator. It is most interesting made with a combination of freshwater fish, most especially of pike and whitefish.

4 pounds freshwater fish such as pike, whitefish, or carp with miltz or roe, alone or in combination
Kosher (coarse) salt
3 large onions, peeled and sliced
¼ inch peeled knob celery root, if available, or 1 small stalk celery with a few leaves

2 sprigs parsley
1 large bay leaf
6 to 8 peppercorns
4 cups water, approximately
2 medium carrots, scraped and sliced in rounds
3 lemon slices
Pinch of sugar, if needed

Have the fish cut in slices about 1 inch thick. Sprinkle the slices, as well as head and tail pieces, with coarse salt and let stand in the refrigerator for 4 or 5 hours. Rinse. Set the miltz and roe aside. Place the head and tail pieces of the fish, the onion slices, salt, celery root or celery, parsley, bay leaf, and peppercorns in a pot with about 4 cups of water. Bring to a boil, reduce the heat, and simmer for 20 minutes.

Remove the celery, parsley, bay leaf, peppercorns, and as much of the tail and head bones as possible. Strain the broth, rubbing the onions through the sieve into the broth. Return the broth to the pot and add the fish slices, miltz or roe, and carrots and lemon slices. Simmer slowly but steadily for about 20 minutes, or until the fish flakes when tested with a fork. Do not overcook. Lift the fish from the stock with a slotted spoon and place in a deep glass or ceramic baking dish or platter. Arrange the carrots and lemon slices on top of the fish and pour the broth over all. Season the broth to taste, adding sugar if necessary. Chill in the refrigerator at least several hours and preferably overnight before serving.

Yield: 6 servings

Variation: My own preference here is for ½ cup of white Rhine or Moselle wine to be substituted for that same amount of water in making the stock, along with a tiny pinch of powdered allspice to be added with the other seasonings.

Carp, in General

Throughout this chapter there are a number of recipes calling for carp, alone or mixed with other freshwater fish. This is a meaty fish that can add interesting texture and flavor to a dish, but it can also ruin it because carp is a bottom fish that often develops a musty, muddy flavor that is described as *dumpfig* or *verdumpfen* in German and *verdimpen* in Yiddish. Carp is least likely to have these undesirable characteristics in late fall and winter when the water is cold, and most likely to have them in spring and summer. For this reason my mother never served carp in the warmer seasons and eliminated it from her gefüllte fish mixture as well. Although fish markets sometimes have carp ranging from 3 to 4 pounds in size, the huge fish are better because they have fewer, less densely distributed bones.

Buffalo fish, more commonly known as "buffle," is a freshwater fish similar to the cod and the largest varieties of this fish are good substitutes for carp.

Baked Paprika Carp

Although this is sold prepared in appetizer stores, it is usually very hard and dry. When made at home, it can be well basted with butter and not overcooked so the final result is firm, but not chokingly dry. A carp is a very large fish, and in fish markets it is split in half before being cut in slices. The backbone remains on one side of the split fish, and that is the half from which to have your slices cut. The bone keeps the fish intact and moist while it bakes and adds flavor, and the cooked fish is easily cut away from the bone for serving.

4 pounds carp, cut from the side of the fish that has the backbone in Kosher (coarse) salt	3 tablespoons sweet paprika, approximately
1 teaspoon black pepper, approximately	2 or 3 cloves garlic, very finely minced (optional)
	6 to 8 tablespoons sweet butter, softened

The carp should be cut into slices 1½ inches thick, with the bone in. Sprinkle the slices with coarse salt and let stand in the refrigerator for several hours or overnight. Rinse.

Preheat the oven to 425 degrees.

Combine the black pepper and paprika and, if you are using it, the finely minced garlic. Rub this mixture lightly over both sides of each slice of fish. Spread a layer of half the soft butter over the bottom of a baking dish large enough to hold the fish slices in a single layer. Lay the fish in, then dot the tops of the slices with the remaining butter.

Bake in the preheated oven, basting with butter several times, until the fish flakes when tested with a fork—about 25 minutes. Lift the fish from the pan, drizzle the pan juice over, and chill for several hours or overnight. Serve at room temperature.

Yield: 8 to 10 servings

Note: Carp and buffalo fish are both delicious when prepared according to the recipe for Hungarian baked fish and vegetables, paprikash (page 120).

Kippers and Eggs

Plump, pungent, smoke-flavored kippers gently sautéed in butter were served often for Sunday breakfast. Although scrambled eggs are the usual accompaniment, we all preferred fried eggs laid on top of the kippers because we loved to mix the runny yolks with the fish. When buying kippers, look for those that are thick and soft to the touch; if thin, leathery, and dried out, there will be little edible flesh on them.

4 tablespoons sweet butter,   Sweet butter, for frying
   approximately   Salt, if needed
4 large, plump kippered herrings   Freshly ground black pepper
8 eggs

Heat the butter in a large, heavy skillet (or two if needed because of the size of the herrings). Add the kippers, flesh side down, then cover the pan loosely and let fry very gently for about 5 minutes, or until the herrings begin to soften. Turn and fry the herrings, skin side down, for 8 to 10 minutes more, or until the fish are soft and thoroughly heated through. Uncover the pan for the last 2 or 3 minutes.

Fry eggs in a separate pan (see page 93). Serve the kippers flesh side up and top with the fried eggs. Because the fish are salty, each eater should decide whether or not to salt the eggs. Freshly ground pepper should be sprinkled over the eggs at the table.

Yield: 4 servings

Sweet and Sour Salmon

Served cold as an appetizer or as part of a cold dairy lunch or dinner, this salmon was a particular favorite in summer. The same recipe is also very good with carp.

1½ large onions   6 to 8 cloves
⅓ cup brown sugar   4½ cups water, or as needed
⅓ cup lemon juice   3½ to 4 pounds fresh salmon, in 4
⅓ cup golden raisins   thick slices
2 bay leaves   2 lemons, cut in paper-thin
3 or 4 pieces of cracked ginger   slices
2½ teaspoons salt

Peel the onions and cut into thin, round slices; separate into rings. Combine with the sugar, lemon juice, raisins, bay leaves, ginger, salt, cloves, and water and simmer for 10 minutes, or until the onions are fairly soft. Add the fish and poach gently for 15 to 20 minutes, or until done enough to flake when tested with a fork. Do not overcook, as the fish should not fall apart. Remove the fish to a deep dish in which all the pieces can lie in a single layer. Strew paper-thin lemon slices over the top and pour the cooking liquid, with all the spices and onion, over the fish; the liquid should barely cover it. Chill for at least 8 hours before serving. Serve cold.

Yield: 8 to 10 servings

Variations: 1. A touch I like but of which my mother disapproved is the substitution of 1 cup of dry white wine for part of the water used in cooking. Rhine and Moselle wines are especially well suited to this because of their fruity bouquet.

2. Carp, cut in thick slices, can be substituted for the salmon, but will require slightly longer cooking time.

Creamed Finnan Haddie

Served as Sunday breakfast or as a light dinner, this was a favorite of my father's. Real finnan haddie (smoked haddock) is not easy to find these days, but it is worth searching out for this gentle and subtle dish.

2 pounds finnan haddie
6 tablespoons sweet butter
5 tablespoons flour
2 cups half-and-half milk and cream, scalded and hot

Salt to taste
Pinch of cayenne pepper or to taste

Garnishes: 4 hard-cooked eggs, peeled and sliced, and hot paprika

Place the finnan haddie in a deep skillet or casserole and pour in enough water to barely cover. Bring to a boil, reduce the heat, cover the pan, and simmer very gently for 15 minutes. Lift the fish out of poaching liquid and set aside to cool. Reserve and keep hot 1 cup of poaching liquid.

When the fish is cool, flake coarsely into fork-sized chunks, removing the bones as you do so.

Melt the butter, and when it is bubbling hot, stir in the flour. Let sauté for 3 or 4 minutes, then stir in, all at once, the hot reserved poaching liquid and the hot, scalded half-and-half. Beat with a wire whisk over low heat until the sauce is smooth and thick; season with salt and cayenne to taste.

Turn the fish into the sauce and reheat together for about 10 minutes. Serve on individual heated plates, garnishing each portion with slices of hard-boiled egg and paprika. Serve with boiled potatoes, or on toast.

Yield: 4 servings

Halibut Salad with Dill

My mother liked to serve this as a main course at luncheons. "They all thought it was crab meat," she would boast if it had been particularly successful. While no one could quite make that mistake, if the fish is firm and not finely minced it does have a meaty texture that can let it pass as mock crab meat for those who are kosher and cannot eat shellfish. Generally it was prepared as it is described here, but sometimes my mother added shrimp for a touch of additional flavor. The same recipe works well for a salad made only of shrimp, crab meat, or lobster meat. It was also a favorite sandwich filling on toast or thinly sliced pumpernickel.

1 quart water	in a thick steak or chunk
1 large stalk celery with a few	with center bone in
leaves	2 or 3 teaspoons lemon juice
1 thick slice lemon	¼ to ½ teaspoon white pepper
5 or 6 peppercorns	2 tablespoons minced fresh dill
Salt	¾ cup mayonnaise, as needed
3 pounds halibut, preferably cut	Boston or romaine lettuce

Bring 1 quart of water to boil with the celery, lemon slice, peppercorns, and 2 tablespoons salt. Gently lower the fish into the boiling water, then cover the pan and reduce the heat until the water is at a barely perceptible simmer. Poach the halibut for 10 to 12 minutes, depending on thickness, until firm and white through to the bone; do not let it fall apart, but be sure there are no traces of blood close to the bone. Remove from the liquid and drain. Let stand until cool.

Trim off the skin and break the fish away from the bone. Remove all small bones from the edges if there are any. Working with two forks or your fingers, break the cooled fish into small clumps or pieces. Try not to shred or mash it. Sprinkle with 2 teaspoons lemon juice, a pinch of salt, and white pepper. Add the dill and toss lightly with a fork to distribute the seasonings. Add the mayonnaise and fold it in gently with a wooden spoon, being careful not to break the fish any more than you have to. There should be enough mayonnaise to bind the mixture, but it should not be a creamy excess. Check the seasoning. Chill thoroughly, preferably 5 to 7 hours. Serve on cold, crisp, washed leaves of Boston or romaine lettuce.

Yield: 6 servings

Halibut and Shrimp Salad

Follow the above recipe, using 2 pounds of halibut and 1½ pounds shrimp as purchased in the shell. Cook the shrimp and halibut separately, each with some celery, onion, and a lemon slice in the water. Let the shrimp cool, then peel and devein before combining with the cooled boned and skinned fish.

Shrimp, Crab Meat, or Lobster Salad with Dill

For shrimp, follow the above recipe, using 3½ pounds shrimp as purchased in the shell.

If using crab meat, 2½ pounds will do, as will the same amount of cooked, shelled lobster meat. If you want to do the lobster from scratch, you will need 4 pounds in the shell to get about 2½ pounds cooked, shelled meat.

Hungarian Baked Fish and Vegetables, Paprikash

With some steamed rice or boiled new potatoes, this becomes a complete and tempting entrée. It is also good served cold or at room temperature as an appetizer or a summer entrée. Bass, pike, pickerel, halibut, and sea or lake trout are good prepared this way.

½ cup (¼ pound) sweet butter
1 large green pepper, seeded and
    sliced into strips
1 large onion, peeled and sliced
3 stalks celery, sliced
1 clove garlic

1 tablespoon paprika
1 can (20 ounces) peeled whole
    tomatoes, drained and cut up
3 pounds fish, cut in steaks 1 to 1¼
    inches thick

Preheat the oven to 375 degrees. Heat 4 tablespoons butter and in it sauté the green pepper, onion, and celery until they begin to wilt. Do not brown. Add the garlic and paprika and sauté for a minute or two longer. Add the drained, cut-up tomatoes and cook over high heat until the liquid almost evaporates. Turn half of the vegetable mixture into a baking pan. Top with the fish. Cover with the remaining vegetables and dot with the remaining 4 tablespoons butter. Cover the pan with aluminum foil and bake in the preheated oven for about 15 minutes. Remove the foil and bake for 15 to 20 minutes longer, until the fish is done and flakes when tested with a fork.

Yield: 4 to 6 servings

Variation: A whole whitefish, weighing 2½ to 3 pounds, is especially good this way. The fish should be left whole and will have more flavor if the center bone is left in, but that may be removed if you find it much easier for serving. Follow the recipe above exactly, but spoon a little of the vegetable mixture inside the fish as well over the top.

Fried Fish

I have never had better fried fish than my mother made. It was delicious hot from the pan, but an even more special treat was when it was cold—really room temperature—as the main course for a summer dinner. My mother would season it with cinnamon and paprika, then fry it at three or four in the afternoon and let it cool on its fragrant bed of dill until dinnertime, which was at six. Potato salad (page 216), cole slaw (page 199), and tartar sauce (page 13) rounded it out. We might begin with schav (page 74) or cold beet borscht (page 62), in which case we had some kind of fruit pie for dessert. If these soups, which were served with sour cream, were not on the menu, we had cheese blintzes (page 104) topped with sour cream for dessert.

Fluke, flounder, or whiting are all good for this recipe, and though it can be prepared with fillets, there is more flavor in the fish if it is fried in cross-cut slices, bones in.

About 5 pounds of fish—about 4 large fluke or flounder, or 6 large whitings
Kosher (coarse) salt
1 cup flour, approximately
½ teaspoon powdered cinnamon
½ teaspoon white pepper

3 eggs
2 tablespoons lemon juice
2 cups dry bread crumbs, approximately
1 tablespoon sweet paprika
Corn oil, for frying
Large bunch of fresh dill

Whichever fish you use, it should be cut in fairly thick crosswise slices, each about 2 inches wide. This will usually mean you will get three, or at the most four slices per fish, eliminating the head but using the trimmed tail piece. Sprinkle with coarse salt and let stand for 2 to 3 hours in the refrigerator.

Rinse and dry well. Place the flour on a sheet of waxed paper and mix the cinnamon and white pepper into it. Beat the eggs lightly with the lemon juice in a wide bowl. Arrange the bread crumbs on another sheet of waxed paper and mix the paprika into them evenly.

Dredge each piece of fish in flour, tapping off excess; then dip into egg, letting excess drip off; finally, dredge well with bread crumbs. Arrange the breaded pieces on a rack suspended over a pan or platter and let set for 30 minutes at room temperature before frying. Meanwhile, wash and dry the dill and arrange in a bed on a serving platter.

Pour a 1-inch depth of corn oil into a large, heavy skillet, and when it is hot add the fish, in a single layer and without crowding. Fry slowly but steadily. When the first side is rich golden brown, turn the pieces and fry the other side. Total frying time varies with the fish. Whiting will take about 10 to 12 minutes and should also be turned so the end sides brown. Fluke and flounder may take a little less time.

Drain quickly on paper towels, then arrange on the dill. Serve hot or let stand at room temperature until serving time. Leftovers can be refrigerated and eaten cold later, an out-of-hand treat we always looked forward to.

Yield: 4 to 6 servings

Fried Herring

Salt herring are much better for this dish than schmaltz herrings, because of their firmer texture. This was a favorite dish at Sunday breakfasts, especially when we were in the country on summer vacations.

4 salt herrings, soaked as for pickled
    herring (page 25)
1 cup flour, or as needed
1 teaspoon black pepper, or as
    needed
2 large eggs, beaten with 2
    tablespoons cold water

1 large yellow onion, peeled, sliced,
    and separated into rings
½ cup (¼ pound) sweet butter,
    approximately
Boiled or baked potato, as
    accompaniment (optional)

Soak the herrings as directed for between 3 and 5 days. They may be filleted as described for pickled herring, or fried whole, as we preferred them.

Dry the herrings or fillets on paper towels. Toss 1 cup flour with 1 teaspoon black pepper. Have the flour spread on a sheet of waxed paper and the beaten egg in a wide bowl so the herring can be dipped into it.

Melt about 4 tablespoons butter in a large skillet, and in it sauté the onions until they begin to turn light golden brown. Remove and reserve both the onions and the butter left in the frying pan.

Dredge each herring lightly in flour; then dip in egg, letting excess drip off; then dredge again in flour. Add another 4 tablespoons butter to the pan, and when it is hot and bubbling, fry the herrings very slowly, turning several times so they become crisp and golden brown on both sides. Be sure to do this slowly, so the insides of the fish will cook without having the outsides burn. The total frying time should be about 15 minutes. When the herrings are almost done, and a nice golden brown, return the onions to the pan and, with a wooden spatula, gently turn them between the herrings. Fry together for the last 5 minutes.

Serve with boiled or baked potatoes and butter. One herring is usually an adequate portion, and often half will do, especially if you serve fillets.

Yield: 4 to 8 portions

Codfish Cakes

Generally, dried salt codfish is used for this, but my mother made it with fresh codfish. I have a slight preference for the salt cod, as it has more flavor and texture, but hers was also delicious. The usual proportion of half fish, half potatoes seemed to her overly heavy on potato, so she used the following proportions:

2 to 2½ pounds fresh codfish, in one
      chunk
      Kosher (coarse) salt
      Juice of 1 lemon
   1 large stalk celery with leaves
   1 small onion, peeled and
      sliced
6 to 8 peppercorns
   4 medium boiling potatoes
      (about 1½ pounds), peeled
   5 tablespoons sweet butter

1 extra-large or jumbo egg, lightly
      beaten
3 tablespoons heavy cream
1 teaspoon salt, or to taste
½ teaspoon white pepper, or to taste
      Pinch of mace or cayenne
      (optional)
      Corn oil, for frying
      Tartar sauce (page 13) or tomato
      sauce (page 10), as
      accompaniment

Sprinkle the codfish liberally with coarse salt and let stand overnight (or 5 to 7 hours) in the refrigerator. Rinse. Place in an enameled or stainless-steel pot with cold water to cover. Add the lemon juice, celery, onion, and peppercorns. Bring to a boil, cover, reduce to an almost imperceptible simmer, and cook for about 30 minutes, or until the fish flakes when tested with a fork. If there is a bone in the fish, be sure there are no traces of blood close to it.

Remove the fish from the cooking liquid and drain. Cool thoroughly. Trim off the skin and bones and with a fork (or two forks, if it is easier) flake the fish. Do not chop or mash it.

While the fish is cooking, boil the potatoes; when they are done, drain thoroughly and return to the dry, empty, hot pot. Place over very low heat and shake the pot back and forth over the heat until the surface of the potatoes is dry and mealy. Mash fine or, better yet, press through a ricer.

Combine the potatoes and flaked fish and beat in 3 tablespoons butter with a wooden spoon. When the butter has melted and is evenly distributed through the fish mixture, stir in the cream and seasonings to taste. (This mixture is cooked, and it is therefore safe to taste it.) Shape into 10 to 12 round cakes, each about 1 inch high and 3 inches in diameter. Lay the cakes out on waxed paper.

Pour a 1-inch depth of corn oil into a large, heavy skillet and add 2 tablespoons of butter for flavor. When the fat is hot (about 375 degrees), place the fish cakes in it, allowing a little space around each one. Fry slowly, allowing about 7 to 8 minutes for the first sides to become golden brown; turn and brown the second sides (about 5 minutes). Be sure the insides of the fish cakes are piping hot; if the outsides brown and the insides are too cool, the cakes were fried too rapidly.

Serve with the sauce of your choice, tartar or tomato, but see note below.

Yield: 4 to 6 servings

Note: Although we sometimes had these with tomato sauce, I always preferred tartar sauce, never having cared for a liquid sauce on something that was crisp.

Variation: To make codfish cakes with dried salt codfish, buy 3 pounds of the dried salt cod and soak in several changes of water for 24 hours. Cut in convenient pieces and cook as described for fresh codfish above. Cool and flake, removing bones as you do so. Proceed with the recipe as above, but taste before adding salt, as none, or very little, may be required.

Salt codfish (*bacalao*) is generally available in fish markets in Italian or Hispanic neighborhoods. It is sometimes presoaked, but it is safer to resoak it as above.

Steamed Clams

My father usually brought steamers (soft-shelled clams) home as a surprise on weekends. He would drive to Lundy's, the famous and enormous sea-food restaurant in Sheepshead Bay and bring back baskets of soft-shelled clams. We might eat them as a between-meal snack, or my mother would adjust the dinner menu so that they served as a first course. They were always part of a lobster dinner.

Steamers are available almost exclusively in the Northeast, and though other clams can be prepared this way, they are really too tough to be enjoyable. Steamers are sold by the pound or by the pint. They are small, so allow at least 24 clams per person. Discard clams that are opened wide. Let the others soak in cold water for 20 minutes. Scrub both sides of each clam with a stiff brush under cold running water to remove any sand; otherwise it will get inside the clams when they steam open. There may also be sand inside the shells. You cannot do anything about this, so for that reason do not use clams that feel much heavier than they look. Grittiness in steamers can ruin the experience of eating them.

Place the scrubbed shells in a large kettle or Dutch oven (or a clam steamer) and add water to a level of 1 scant inch. Cover the pan tightly, bring to a boil, and let steam for 8 to 10 minutes, or until all shells are open. If the bottom clams open and those on top are closed, use a wooden spoon to gently turn the clams over so those on top slide to the bottom.

Lift the clams out of the pot with a slotted spoon and place in a big serving bowl or individual bowls. Let the cooking liquid settle, then ladle into cups, trying not to stir up any sand that might have settled to the bottom of the pot.

Serve a warmed ramekin of hot melted butter, a wedge of lemon, and a cup of clam broth with each portion of clams. If the clams are still a little sandy, they can be swirled in broth before being dipped into butter. In that case, be sure the clam broth settles before you attempt to drink any. A dash of lemon juice can be added to the broth.

To eat steamers, hold by the neck and bite off at the point where the clam meets the neck. Some pull off the neck covering and eat the entire clam.

Fried Oysters

Fried oysters were my mother's idea of a fine quick meal. We thought so too, especially when served with mashed potatoes and cole slaw. Oysters must be freshly shucked and in their own liquor, and should never be washed.

24 oysters, shucked and drained, but
    not washed
  Black pepper
1 cup matzoh meal, or as needed
  Corn oil for frying

2 tablespoons sweet butter
  Lemon wedges, for garnish
  Tartar sauce (page 13), as
    accompaniment
  Fried bacon, for garnish (optional)

Drain off the liquid from the oysters, but do not dry them. Sprinkle a little black pepper on both sides of each oyster. Arrange the matzoh meal on a plate or sheet of waxed paper. Dredge the oysters with meal. Heat a 1-inch depth of oil plus the butter in a large skillet and add the oysters when it is hot. (The oysters should begin to fry as soon as they are dropped in, but there should be no great hiss of steam; this will be at about 365 to 370 degrees on a deep-frying thermometer.) Ideally, all should fit at once in a single layer without being crammed in. This can be accomplished if you have a 12-inch skillet. If not, fry in batches but keep the fried oysters hot while the remainder fry. Brown one side, then turn and brown the second side. Total frying time should be about 5 to 7 minutes per batch. Drain for a few seconds on paper towels and serve with lemon wedges and with tartar sauce on the side.

Mashed potatoes (page 211) and cole slaw (page 199) are perfect with this. Fried oysters are also good on hot buttered toast, topped with slices of bacon.

Yield: 3 to 4 servings depending on the size of the oysters

Note: Oysters are usually salty in themselves and so need no salt added. If you do want to salt them, do so after they are fried.

Baked Lobster

Sometimes my mother planned to have lobster for dinner, but more often it was one of my father's Sheepshead Bay surprises, which she prepared either boiled or split, buttered, and broiled. Neither was in any way a unique recipe, but both were delicious. Our preference was for hot boiled lobster with lots of melted butter. Once in a while, however, my mother made this baked lobster variation, and the delicate center portion, where the gray-green liver (tomalley) and red roe (coral) are, was protected against drying out by the buttered cracker-crumb topping.

For each serving:

1 live lobster of any size you wish
  Melted sweet butter
3 or 4 coarsely crumbled unsalted
  soda crackers, such as pilot

crackers, Bremen wafers, or
Uneeda biscuits (about ⅔
cup)

Preheat the oven to 425 degrees.

To split the lobster, turn it on its back, legs up. Stick the sharp point of heavy, sharp knife into the soft spot between the lobster's eyes, then cut straight down through the center of the body, severing it all the way through the back shell. Pull out the soft spongy material under the eyes and remove the black vein that runs down the center of the lobster. Lay the lobster, flesh side up, in a baking pan. Drizzle a little melted butter over the flesh and pour a little melted butter over the green tomalley and coral, if there is any. Stir the crumbled cracker crumbs in melted butter until they absorb some and fill the cavity loosely with the crumbs. Put an extra layer over the center top cavity. Pour a little more butter over the top and bake for about 20 minutes, or until the meat is done and the cracker topping is puffy dry and pale golden.

Yield: 1 serving

Note: Lobsters should always be purchased alive and moving. If you are going to broil or bake them and are squeamish about cutting them open while still alive, your fishman can do it for you; but do this only if you plan to cook them within 2 hours. Be sure he retains the tomalley and coral, if any, when he cleans them. The black intestinal vein and the spongy sac near the head are all that need to be removed.

Seafood Newburg

This was a midnight supper or luncheon dish that my mother considered the height of elegance. Results are best when raw shellfish is used, as sautéing it in the butter on which the sauce is based produces the richest and sprightliest flavor. Cooked shellfish should be reheated in the butter. The only shellfish that is acceptable if purchased ready-cooked is canned (not frozen) fresh lump crab meat, preferably from Chesapeake Bay or Florida.

1 pound raw, peeled shrimp (1½ pounds as purchased in the shell), or raw meat from a 1½-pound live lobster, or 1 pound raw or cooked crab meat

6 tablespoons sweet butter

1½ tablespoons flour

Generous pinch of paprika

Pinch of cayenne pepper

2½ cups heavy sweet cream, scalded and hot

Salt and white pepper to taste

3 egg yolks

3 to 5 tablespoons dry sherry, or to taste

Freshly made toast or hot, cooked white rice

Be sure all shellfish is carefully picked over and is deveined or free of shell and spiny fragments. Heat 3 tablespoons butter in a small, heavy skillet, and in it gently sauté the raw seafood for a minute or two; cover the pan, remove from the heat, and let stand for 10 minutes. If you are using cooked crab meat or other shellfish do not sauté; merely add it to the hot butter, cover the pan, and let the seafood warm in the butter for 10 minutes.

Follow the instructions for basic cream sauce (page 10), using the remaining butter, all of the flour, the paprika, cayenne pepper, and hot, scalded cream. Simmer for 3 or 4 minutes, or until smooth. Season with salt and white pepper.

Beat the egg yolks with a fork until thin and watery. Gradually ladle a little of the hot cream sauce into the yolks, beating constantly as you do so. When 1 cup of sauce has been added, pour the egg yolk mixture slowly back into the remaining cream sauce, beating constantly. Cook over very low heat, stirring all the time, until the sauce is thick enough to coat a spoon. Do not let it boil or the egg will curdle. Stir in the sherry and the seafood and heat thoroughly but do not boil. Adjust the seasoning. Serve on freshly made toast or rice.

Yield: 4 appetizer servings; 2 to 3 main-course servings

Shrimp au Gratin

1½ cups water
1 stalk celery with leaves
8 peppercorns
1 slice lemon
  Pinch of salt
2 pounds raw shrimp, in the shell
  as purchased
4 tablespoons sweet butter

¼ cup flour
1¼ cups half-and-half milk and
  cream, hot and scalded
Pinch of mace
Salt and white pepper to taste
¾ cup freshly grated Parmesan
  cheese
½ cup buttered bread crumbs

Bring the water to a boil with the celery, peppercorns, lemon, and a pinch of salt, and simmer 5 minutes. Add the shrimp, cover the pot, and let stand for 6 or 7 minutes. Drain, reserving the cooking liquid. Rinse the shrimp under very cold water, peel, and devein.

Preheat the oven to 400 degrees. Melt the butter in a saucepan and stir in the flour. Simmer for 3 or 4 minutes, but do not let the flour brown. Add ¾ cup hot shrimp stock and 1¼ cups hot, scalded half-and-half. Whisk until smooth and simmer for 5 minutes, or until thick. Season with mace, salt, and pepper. Turn the shrimp into the sauce. Divide the mixture between 6 individual gratin dishes or pour into a 6-cup shallow baking dish. Sprinkle with the grated cheese and bread crumbs. Bake in the preheated oven until the mixture is hot and bubbling and the top has a golden brown crust—about 10 minutes.

Yield: 6 servings

Crab Meat au Gratin

Using 1 pound of fresh lump crab meat, pick over carefully to remove cartilage. Heat in a little butter as described under seafood Newburg (page 128). Make a cream sauce with 3 tablespoons butter, 3 tablespoons flour, and 1½ cup hot heavy sweet cream. Season with salt, pepper, nutmeg, and mace. Fold the crab meat into the sauce, then turn into a baking dish. Top with cheese and crumbs and bake as directed above.

Deviled Crab Meat

Since my mother always made this with cooked, fresh Baltimore lump crab meat already out of the shell, she did not have shells in which to bake it and so used ramekins or, when she could find them, large, scrubbed clam shells. It can also be done in an 8-inch round gratin pan, but it is nicer prepared in individual portions.

1 pound fresh lump crab meat, from Chesapeake Bay or Florida
Juice of ½ lemon
6 tablespoons sweet butter
½ cup finely minced green pepper
⅓ cup fine, white bread crumbs
1 tablespoon flour
½ cup half-and-half milk and cream, scalded and hot
2 hard-cooked eggs, yolks sieved and whites chopped

½ teaspoon cayenne pepper, or to taste
½ teaspoon prepared mustard, or to taste
1 teaspoon salt, or to taste
Freshly ground black pepper
2 tablespoons finely minced fresh parsley
¼ cup finely diced pimento

Preheat the oven to 375 degrees.

Butter the inside of 6 clam shells, 6 ramekins or individual gratin dishes, or an 8-inch round gratin dish, or 6 ceramic crab shell ramekins, if you have them.

Pick over the crab meat, eliminating all cartilage. Sprinkle with lemon juice and set aside.

Melt 2 tablespoons butter in a small skillet or saucepan and lightly sauté the minced green pepper until it just begins to wilt. Do not let it brown. Add to the crab meat. Melt 3 tablespoons butter in a large skillet, and in it sauté the bread crumbs, stirring frequently and toasting them until dry and light golden brown. Reserve. Follow the instructions for basic cream sauce on page 10, using 1 tablespoon each of butter and flour and the hot, scalded half-and-half. Simmer 3 or 4 minutes, or until the sauce is smooth and very thick. Add to the crab meat.

Stir in the sieved hard-cooked egg yolks, chopped whites, cayenne pepper, mustard, salt, black pepper, parsley, and 2 tablespoons of the buttered bread crumbs. Toss together lightly but thoroughly, so all will be mixed but not mashed. Finally toss in the pimento pieces, being careful not to mash them. Adjust the seasonings.

Divide the crab mixture into baking dishes and sprinkle with the remaining buttered bread crumbs. Bake in the preheated oven for 20 to 25 minutes for a large baking dish, 10 to 12 minutes for individual dishes. Serve immediately.

Yield: 6 appetizer servings; 3 to 4 main-course servings

Shrimp Creole

A stand-by at midnight suppers, this dish is best made with shrimp that come about 18 to 20 to a pound unshelled, for most convenient serving. Larger sizes will need to be cut in half to be manageable for buffet service.

1½ pounds shrimp, as purchased in the shell (about 18 to 20 per pound)	1 large clove garlic, peeled and chopped
4 tablespoons sweet butter	1 teaspoon salt
2 tablespoons corn or other light vegetable or olive oil	¼ teaspoon black pepper
	¼ teaspoon leaf thyme, crumbled
1 stalk celery, diced (about ½ cup)	1 bay leaf
1 medium onion, peeled and coarsely chopped (about ¾ cup)	1 one-pound can tomatoes, coarsely chopped with liquid reserved
½ large or 1 small green pepper, seeded and chopped (about ⅔ cup)	1½ cups long-grain converted rice, parboiled for 10 minutes
	1 to 2 cups boiling water, as needed

Peel and devein the shrimp and set aside. Heat the butter and oil in a large saucepan, and when bubbling stir in the celery, onion, green pepper, and garlic. Sauté slowly, stirring frequently until the vegetables are wilted but not brown. This will take about 7 minutes.

Add the salt, pepper, crumbled thyme, and bay leaf and sauté for a minute or two. Pour in the tomatoes with their liquid and 1 cup of water and bring to a boil.

Add the shrimp, reduce the sauce to a simmer, and cook, loosely covered, for about 5 minutes. Add the parboiled rice, continue cooking, and, slowly as needed, add boiling water until the rice is tender and the shrimp are cooked—about 15 minutes.

(continued)

Yield: 3 to 4 servings

Note: If you want to make this in advance for guests, prepare the shrimp in the sauce and cook the rice separately. Then combine to reheat just before serving, adding more liquid as needed and adjusting the seasoning.

Variation: A few drops of Tabasco sauce can be added during the last few minutes of cooking or reheating.

12

Sunday Dinners

On Sundays everyone awoke late, which at our house meant around eight-thirty or nine A.M. I was up earlier than that—usually by six or six-thirty, as I still am to this day. But back then I waited patiently, convinced that when I was an adult I too would sleep "late." I marked time by reading the comics in the newspapers that had been delivered to the door. And what a pile of newspapers it was, for on Sunday, to get all the comics, we had the *Brooklyn Eagle,* the *Herald Tribune,* the Sunday *News,* the *Journal-American,* and the *Sunday Mirror.* We also had *The New York Times,* but in those days that was a paper strictly for adults and no laughing matter, only the pictorial sepia-toned rotogravure section was of interest to children.

As soon as the breakfast table was cleared—usually by ten—we began to sniff and pick at dinner preparations, for the big meal of the day was usually served at one-thirty or two. Each week my mother complained, threatening to serve it at five in the evening ("like normal families who have only two meals on Sunday . . . why do I have to cook three?"), but each week there it was, set out on the big fumed-oak dining table that had been covered in a white or flower-printed cloth.

As she cooked the week's most elaborate meal, my mother loved to listen to a whole chain of Sunday morning radio programs, and their names bring to mind the mouth-watering smells of simmering split pea or mushroom and barley or cream of mushroom soup, sautéing onions, roasting meat or turkey, and the sweet smell of sugar caramelizing in pies or cakes. The "Horn & Hardart Children's Hour" ("Less work for Mother, just lend her a hand") with its young performers, Arthur Tracy, the Street Singer ("Marta, rambling rose of the wildwood . . ."); the A & P Gypsies ("Play Gypsy, dance Gypsy . . ."), and the Jewish language stations with programs such as "The Eternal Light" and the honey-rich, sweet-wine voice of Cantor Leibele Waldman or the bouncier, clattery popular songs sung in Yiddish by male or female vocalists who seemed to perform only on those stations and, as the announcement for them always reminded the listening audience, at Bar Mitzvahs, weddings, and other "simchas." Occasionally I tune in one of those stations, and the music invariably takes me back to all the Sunday mornings of childhood.

The midmorning errand performed by my father or my brother or myself—whomever my mother could catch and press into service—was to get fresh bread from the nearby bakery and, if the menu warranted it, cold, fresh sauerkraut, garlic dill pickles, green pickled tomatoes, and sweet red pickled peppers. The fruity, sour flavor of the pickled vegetables softened by the crackling-crusted, caraway-flavored sour rye bread was almost satisfying enough to make the rest of the meal unnecessary.

Smoked or pickled tongue was one of our favorite Sunday main courses, and though my mother often added plain boiled cabbage to it, what she most often served was stuffed cabbage, the beef- and rice-filled rolls in their golden sweet and sour raisin sauce being her idea of a proper vegetable. If roast beef was the main event, nut-brown, parchment-covered roasted potatoes came with it and usually peas, which I hated and would disperse all over my plate so my mother would not notice how many I had not eaten. She always noticed of course, regrouping them to show how many were left, as if I didn't know. Roast leg of lamb was another Sunday stand-by and the winner at that feast was the one who got the big lamb bone to gnaw on.

As my mother carried the food to the table, her standard weekly announcement was, "Now let's not rush . . . we have no place to go . . . let's take plenty of time," but by the time she served herself, those who had been served earliest were ready for seconds. My vision of my mother eating at those happy, noisy, groaning boards is of a woman jumping up and sitting down, cutting off bites that she chewed on the run to the kitchen to get more for the rest of us, of a woman whose plate always seemed to contain what looked like trimmings and odd pieces and quarter portions, who finished what others left, and who, by constantly pressing more portions on us and urging us to eat this and that, was the very one who set the rushed pace she had warned against.

Sunday afternoons meant naps for grownups or visits to grandparents, or more reading of comics, or, as we grew older, going off with our friends, always coming home, of course, in time for the third meal, the supper my mother swore she wouldn't bother with next week.

13

Poultry

SOUP CHICKEN AND THE THINGS
THAT HAPPENED TO IT

Since chicken soup was almost always a feature of Friday night dinners, that meant something had to be done with the fowl cooked in it. Now, of course, I would happily eat boiled (or poached) chicken with coarse salt and vegetables, or slivered into the soup, but as a child I regarded that as horrible. So did the rest of the family. If we were going to have sandwiches the next day the problem was solved, but generally my mother tried to serve the chicken at dinner. The result was one of the worst dishes I have ever eaten. She would sprinkle the whole boiled chicken with salt, pepper, and paprika, then rub it with garlic and chicken fat, and brown it in the oven. The result was like paprika-flavored balsa wood, chokingly dry.

Other times she saved the soup chicken for the following Saturday or Sunday and made chicken salad, chicken pie, or chicken à la king with it, according to the recipes that follow. If she was having a luncheon and wanted to make those dishes "on purpose," as she used to say, she would poach a capon because she felt that was more tender and moist than the fowl. It made a milder-flavored broth, though, so she eliminated the parsnip and parsley root when poaching it in order not to overpower the already faint flavor of chicken.

To make the next three recipes, cook a fowl or capon as directed for chicken soup (page 54). Skim the fat from the soup and reduce if necessary to produce a strong-flavored stock. It is also best to keep chicken in the soup if it is to be refrigerated overnight, so it does not dry out.

Chicken Pie with Biscuit Crust

White and dark meat can go into this dish, and it is far better with capon than with fowl. My mother made this in a large, deep baking dish without a bottom crust because she felt that it would get soggy and unpleasant. But it is more convenient and attractive to make individual-portion-sized pies in small ovenproof earthenware or glass or porcelain casseroles. A flaky biscuit crust was always the topping.

FILLING

Breast and thigh meat of a 6-pound cooked capon or fowl

3 large carrots, scraped and sliced in ½-inch rounds

8 to 10 small white onions

1 cup shelled fresh green peas, if available

8 small new potatoes or 4 medium-sized boiling potatoes, unpeeled

6 tablespoons sweet butter

5 tablespoons flour

3 cups hot, strained broth in which the chicken was cooked

Salt and white pepper to taste

3 to 4 tablespoons heavy sweet cream

2 tablespoons minced fresh parsley (optional)

Milk, for brushing the crust

CARAWAY BISCUIT CRUST

2¼ cups flour

4 teaspoons baking powder

1 teaspoon salt

Pinch of white pepper

2 teaspoons caraway seeds

1½ tablespoons cold sweet butter, cut

in small pieces

1½ tablespoons cold vegetable shortening, cut in small pieces

About ¾ cup ice water, or as needed

To make the filling, trim all skin and bones from the chicken pieces and break into large sections. Lay these in the bottom of the baking dish, which could be a 9-inch square pan that is about 2½ to 3 inches deep, or any dish of similar depth with an 8- to 9-cup capacity.

Parboil separately, in a little salted water, the sliced carrots, the peeled onions, and the unpeeled whole new potatoes until tender. Set the carrots and onions aside. Peel the potatoes and cut into ¼-inch-thick slices.

Blanch the peas in boiling salted water for 2 or 3 minutes. Drain.

Arrange the vegetables over the chicken pieces, with the potato slices first, then the onions, then the carrots, and finally the peas.

Melt 6 tablespoons butter in a heavy saucepan, and when hot and bubbling stir in the flour. Stir and sauté for 4 or 5 minutes, then pour in 2½ cups hot broth all at once. Beat with a whisk over low heat until thick and smooth—about 5 minutes. If the sauce is very thick, add a little more broth, remembering that you will add some cream later on. Add salt and pepper to taste.

Stir in enough cream to give the sauce a creamy color. It should be the consistency of melted ice cream. Stir in the parsley if you are using it. Pour the sauce over the pie filling.

Preheat oven to 450 degrees.

Sift together all dry ingredients; add caraway seeds and toss lightly. Using your fingertips, rub the butter and shortening into flour to form coarse flakes. Gradually add the water and stir in with a fork until all the flour is moistened and can be gathered in a ball. Turn onto a very lightly floured board and knead for half a minute. Pat or roll to fit inside the rim of the baking dish; the dough should be just a little less than ½ inch thick. Carefully lay over the tops of the vegetables, cut two or three gashes in the crust to let steam escape, and bake for about 15 minutes, or until the crust is light golden brown and the filling is hot and bubbling.

To serve, cut the crust in quarters and lay a piece on each dinner plate. Spoon chicken, vegetables, and sauce over or alongside crust.

Yield: 4 generous servings

Chicken à la King

This is a dish I have always adored, especially if I am tired and feel like something bland. It always seemed very special to me, primarily because my mother served it at luncheons or late suppers. She made it so well that often friends who were having parties would ask her to prepare the dish for them. It is very good on rice or toast, but prettiest in patty shells. Fresh peas were used when available; otherwise the green pepper was substituted.

Poached breast of a 5- to 6- pound fowl or capon
6 tablespoons butter
1 small green pepper, seeded and finely diced (if no fresh green peas are available)
1½ cups sliced mushrooms
¼ cup flour
4 cups hot broth in which the chicken was cooked
1 teaspoon salt, or to taste
¼ teaspoon white pepper, or to taste
Pinch of cayenne, or to taste
2 tablespoons sherry
1 tablespoon lemon juice, or to taste
1 cup shelled fresh green peas, when available
1 tablespoon finely minced, drained pimento
4 egg yolks
¼ to ½ cup heavy sweet cream
Crisp toast, steamed rice, or hot patty shells

Remove all the skin and bones from the chicken. Cut the chicken into fork-sized cubes or dice. You should have about 3 cups. Warm it in a little of the hot broth in which the chicken cooked.

Melt the butter and, if you are using green pepper, slowly sauté it until it begins to wilt. Add the mushrooms and sauté until they become golden brown around the edges. Sprinkle in the flour, blend until smooth, and sauté for 2 or 3 minutes. Pour in the hot broth and whisk or stir over low heat until smooth and moderately thick—about 5 minutes. Season with salt, pepper, and cayenne. Add the sherry, lemon juice to taste, and then the peas. Simmer for 5 minutes. Add the drained chicken and simmer 5 minutes longer.

Beat the egg yolks into ¼ cup sweet cream. Remove the chicken from the heat and slowly pour in the egg and cream mixture, stirring the sauce gently as you do so so as not to break up the peas and chicken. If more cream is needed, add it. Stir in the pimento and heat thoroughly but do not boil. Adjust the seasoning and serve.

Spoon over crisp toast, steamed rice, or into hot patty shells.

(continued)

Yield: 12 appetizer or 6 main-course servings

Note: If you want to make this in advance, cook up to point where the yolks are added. Reheat the chicken à la king thoroughly, then add the yolks, cream, and pimento just before serving.

Helzel

[Roasted Stuffed Poultry Neck]

Stuffed derma, made with a steer's intestines and also known as "kishka," was never served at our home, but this variation, in which the stuffing was put into the neck skin of any poultry bird—chicken, duck, goose or turkey— was often served. Parboiled, then roasted until crisp, the sliced helzel was served with baked egg barley, and was, in fact, often baked on a bed of the egg barley if not with the bird itself. The stuffing most often used was the one that follows. Sometimes, however, my mother stuffed it with her ham- burger mixture and let that bake in the skin.

This is easiest to make if you can get the long neck skin unslit, so that you have a tube. That way you merely sew the bottom closed, then fill and sew the top. If it is split, there is more sewing involved, as described below. Only a large poultry bird—at least 6 pounds and preferably larger—is really good for this purpose, because smaller birds do not provide a neck skin large enough to be worth stuffing.

1 neck skin of a large chicken, duck, goose, or turkey (at least 6 pounds in size), including the triangular skin of the crop
⅔ cup flour
2½ tablespoons diced, unrendered poultry fat
1½ tablespoons finely minced onion

1 clove garlic, peeled and finely minced
1½ teaspoons sweet paprika
½ teaspoon salt
Black pepper to taste
Chicken stock or water
Fat, for roasting

If possible, buy poultry with a neck skin that is not split. That is probably possible only if you shop at a live poultry market where the bird can be handled to your order. If only a slit neck skin is available, then work with it as directed, cutting down to include the crop skin.

In either case, singe the neck skin and pull out all feathers. Turn inside out, or open skin side down and clean off all tubes, bits of meat or sinews, and large lumps of fat from around the edge, but do not remove the fat lining the inside of the skin. If the skin is a tube, turn inside out and sew one end closed. Turn skin side out. If the skin is slit open, fold to form a tube, skin side out, and sew the bottom edge and three-quarters of one long side so you have a pocket that can be stuffed.

Place the flour in a mound on a wooden board or in a wide wooden chopping bowl. Chop the unrendered poultry fat into the flour in very fine bits, using a French chef's knife or a hand chopper. The result should be a coarse meal, such as you would have when making pastry. A pastry blender will not work for this, as it is not sharp enough to cut the fat. When you have a coarse meal, and when all the flour has been absorbed by the clumps of fat, blend in the onion, garlic, paprika, salt, and pepper.

Fill the skin, being sure not to pack it too tightly. The amount here will be just about right for the neck of a 6- to 7-pound bird. Sew the neck skin completely closed.

Poach in simmering stock, or water to which you have added a pinch of salt and a little fat of some kind. Poach for about 8 to 10 minutes, or until the filled skin stiffens and becomes firm. Place in a roasting pan with the bird, or lay over egg barley (page 86) ready for baking. Bake in a 350-degree oven for about 45 minutes, basting with fat several times and turning the helzel so it becomes crisp and golden brown on both sides. Serve a small slice or two as a garnish or appetizer.

If you roast the helzel with a poultry bird that will produce gravy, spoon some gravy over the slices before serving.

Yield: 3 to 4 servings.

Broiled Paprika and Garlic Chicken

1 broiling chicken (1½ to 2 pounds)	2 tablespoons kosher (coarse) salt
Juice of ½ lemon	½ teaspoon black pepper
1 large or 2 small cloves garlic, peeled	1½ teaspoons sweet paprika
	2 tablespoons sweet butter

Singe and clean the chicken if necessary, then split in half. Rub on both sides with lemon juice and let stand at room temperature for 15 to 30 minutes. Pat dry. Preheat the broiler.

Crush the garlic in a mortar with the coarse salt. Add the pepper and paprika, then mash in the butter with the pestle until you have a soft, creamy, well-blended paste. Spread half of this mixture over the skin side of the chicken. Place under the broiler, skin side up, and broil 2 inches from the heat for 10 to 15 minutes, or until the skin is golden brown but not blackened. Turn, spread the remaining butter mixture on the underside of the chicken, and continue broiling for about 10 minutes, or until the chicken is done. (Juices will run clear when the thigh is pierced with a fork).

Serve immediately. Home-fried potatoes (page 210) or mashed potatoes with onions (page 211) are especially good with this.

Yield: 1 to 2 servings

Roast Chicken

For a special touch of flavor, my mother filled the chicken cavity with parsley, as described below.

1 roasting chicken (3 to 4 pounds) or capon (5 to 6 pounds)
   Kosher (coarse) salt
   Salt and black pepper
2 to 3 cloves garlic, peeled
10 to 12 sprigs Italian parsley, washed and dried (optional)
1 medium onion (for a 3- to 4-pound chicken) or 1 large onion (for a capon), peeled and chopped
6 to 8 tablespoons sweet butter, margarine, or schmaltz (rendered chicken fat, page 7), in that order of preference
1 to 2 cups water or chicken stock, as needed

Clean and singe the chicken, if necessary. Sprinkle inside and outside with coarse salt and leave in the refrigerator overnight. Rinse and pat dry before roasting.

Preheat the oven to 350 degrees.

Rub the inside of chicken lightly with salt and pepper. Place the peeled cloves of garlic in the cavity and, if you like, the parsley, stems and all. It is not necessary to sew the opening closed, but it is a good idea to tie the drumsticks and wings in place with kitchen string.

Sprinkle the outside of the bird lightly with salt and pepper. Scatter the chopped onion on the bottom of an open roasting pan. Place a rack over the onion and lay the chicken on its side on the rack. Add the fat to the pan and place in the hot oven for 5 minutes, or until the fat melts. Baste the chicken thoroughly on its top side with melted fat. Allowing 25 minutes to the pound for roasting the chicken, for one third of the time roast with the first side up. Turn over and roast for another third of the time with the second side up. For the last third of the cooking time, roast breast side up, by which time all sides of the chicken should be golden brown. When the onion becomes a light golden brown add a little water or chicken stock to the pan to keep it from burning. Add more liquid as evaporation takes place.

The chicken is done when the drumsticks can be moved freely in their sockets and the juices run clear when a thigh is pierced with a fork or skewer.

Remove the chicken to a warm platter. Skim the fat from the gravy and pour the gravy through a strainer, rubbing through as much of the onion as possible. Pour into a saucepan. Check the seasoning and simmer until hot. Remove the parsley and garlic from the chicken and carve or cut into serving pieces.

Rice is especially good with this, as it is a pleasant foil for the buttery chicken gravy.

Yield: A 3- to 4-pound chicken will serve 2 to 4; a 5- to 6-pound capon will serve 4 to 6.

Variations: 1. Although it made for a less crisp skin, my mother sometimes rubbed paprika on the outside skin of the bird. This is a good idea if you use the rendered chicken fat.

2. This chicken can be stuffed with the kasha, bread, or matzoh-ball stuffing described on pages 152, 153, and 154. Allow 32 minutes per pound for roasting when stuffed.

Fried Chicken

Although we generally had this hot and crisp, on summer nights we ate it at room temperature. My mother would fry it at about four in the afternoon and then, after draining it on paper towels, would keep it on a platter on the kitchen counter. It was also a frequent feature at picnics, wonderful with potato salad (page 216), deviled eggs (page 42), plum tomatoes, slivers of cucumber, and thin slices of buttered pumpernickel.

(continued)

2 frying chickens (about 2 pounds each)

Juice of 1 large lemon

1½ cups flour, or as needed

1 scant teaspoon salt

¼ to ½ teaspoon black pepper

¼ teaspoon powdered ginger (optional)

2 eggs beaten with 2 tablespoons cold water

2 cups fine, dry bread crumbs, or as needed

Corn oil, for frying

Cut (or have the butcher cut) and disjoint the chickens into 8 sections each. Try to keep the skin intact during cutting. The backbones should be cut out and large breastbones removed so the pieces of chicken will lie flat. Clean and singe, if necessary. Place in a shallow bowl and rub all sides of all pieces with lemon juice. Let stand at room temperature for 30 minutes. Pat dry.

On a large piece of waxed paper or foil, combine flour with the salt, pepper, and ginger; blend well. Have the beaten eggs in a wide bowl that will permit dipping. Turn the bread crumbs onto a second sheet of waxed paper or foil. Dredge each piece of chicken very lightly with flour. Dip into the egg, letting excess drip off. Dredge well with bread crumbs. Place the breaded pieces of chicken on a rack suspended over a pan or platter. Let dry at room temperature for 20 to 30 minutes before frying.

Preheat the oven to 250 degrees.

Fill a deep, heavy skillet (preferably of black cast iron) with a 1-inch depth of oil. When the oil is hot (about 365 degrees), add a layer of chicken pieces; do not cram them in. It is best to do the same cuts together. Fry slowly for about 12 to 15 minutes, or until the first side is a crisp golden brown. Turn and fry the second side for 10 to 12 minutes, or until golden brown. Add oil if needed.

Drain the fried pieces on paper toweling. Place on a rack in an open roasting pan in the preheated oven to keep warm until all the pieces are fried. Do this even if you plan to serve at room temperature, as it degreases the breading.

When all the chicken is fried, and has had about 10 minutes in the low oven, remove and serve, or hold at room temperature until serving time. Leftover chicken should be stored in the refrigerator.

Yield: 4 servings

Chicken Fricassee with Meatballs

This was one of our favorite stand-bys and has become so in my household. It can be made ahead and freezes well, and it is delicious with either rice or cooked broad noodles.

1 broiling or frying chicken (3 to 3½ pounds) with all giblets except the liver
Double recipe for meatballs (page 38)
4 to 5 tablespoons butter, margarine, or schmaltz (rendered chicken fat, page 7), in that order of preference

2 medium onions, peeled and finely chopped
Salt and black pepper
1 tablespoon sweet paprika
1 small (individual size) can tomato juice
1 to 2 cups water, as needed
2 cloves garlic, peeled

The chicken should be cut and disjointed into 8 pieces. The breast and thighs can also be cut in half again, if you prefer small pieces. Clean and singe, if necessary. Prepare the meatballs using 1 pound of ground beef and doubling the other ingredients in the recipe.

In a 2½-quart Dutch oven, slowly sauté the chopped onion in 3 tablespoons of the fat until the onion is soft and yellow; do not let it brown. Remove and reserve. Add more fat to the pot if needed and brown the chicken pieces lightly until all sides are pale golden brown. Do this in several batches, as the chicken will not brown if crammed into the pan. Remove the chicken, sprinkle with salt and pepper, and reserve.

Return the onions to the pot and sprinkle with paprika. Sauté for a minute or two, until the paprika loses its raw smell. Add the tomato juice and 1 cup water.

Return the chicken to the pot and add the garlic cloves. The liquid should come about halfway up the chicken. Cover and simmer gently but steadily for 20 minutes. Gently and carefully add the meatballs to the pot, moving the chicken aside to make room and shaking the pot intermittently to separate the meatballs. These will be fragile while raw, but once cooked they will become firm and will not crumble or stick together.

Add more liquid to the pot if needed. Simmer, loosely covered, for another 20 to 30 minutes, or until the chicken and meatballs are done. Remove the chicken and meatballs and skim the fat from the gravy. Return the chicken and meatballs and reheat, checking the seasoning as you do so. Serve the chicken and meatballs with rice or noodles.

If you plan to make this in advance, add a little water before reheating.

Yield: 4 servings

Variations: 1. Tomato juice was sometimes eliminated and only water used. Chicken stock can be used instead of water, but the flavor is, strangely enough, more intense and interesting when water is used, with or without tomato juice.

2. Basically, this is a version of Hungarian chicken paprikash, but the Jewish version, because of kosher laws, eliminates sour cream. If you like, you can beat 2 tablespoons of sour cream into the gravy after the fat has been skimmed from it. Do not boil once the sour cream has been added; reheat by bringing to a slight simmer.

Kofatellen

[Chicken and Chicken Liver Croquettes]

These small fried meat cakes of chicken and chicken livers can be served as a hot appetizer with drinks, or in slightly larger form can be a main course. They are really first cousins to such delicacies as chicken croquettes, Pojarsky cutlets, and Middle Eastern kofta—the ground meat kebabs from which their name was probably derived. Although they are traditionally made with breast of chicken, kofatellen are almost as good with breast of turkey. But since that meat is a bit dryer, a little fat should be added to the mix. The special, easily identifiable aroma these little onion-flavored meat cakes send up when frying always tipped us off as to what was being cooked, and it was all my mother could do to save enough from anxious tasters to have adequate portions to serve.

1 pound raw, boneless chicken breast meat, well trimmed of sinews and membranes, cut up (about 2 cups)

About ¾ pound chicken livers, well trimmed of all connective tissue and fat

1 medium onion, peeled and cut up in chunks

2 eggs

1½ teaspoons salt

½ teaspoon white pepper

¼ to ½ cup matzoh or cracker meal

Schmaltz (rendered chicken fat, page 7), sweet butter, or margarine, for frying

Put the well-trimmed white meat of chicken through the fine blade of a grinder, along with the livers and onion. Do not use a food processor, as this will result in too fine a puree. Be sure the chicken is well trimmed, so the tissues do not jam the grinder mechanism.

Add the eggs, salt, and pepper to the ground mixture and beat well with a wooden spoon until all is smooth and thoroughly mixed. Add the matzoh or cracker meal, a little at a time, until the mixture is soft but not too liquid and can be lightly molded or dropped from a spoon in a single mass.

Add enough frying fat to a large skillet to come to a depth of ½ inch when melted. With two wet tablespoons, drop the meat mixture into the fat, using about 1 generous tablespoonful of the mixture to form a cake roughly 2 inches in diameter and about ½ inch thick. This size can be cut in half to make cocktail-size appetizers.

These cakes can also be molded with the palms of your hands, but wet your palms with cold water so the mixture will not stick.

Fry slowly until golden brown on one side; turn and fry the second side. Test one cake to see if it is thoroughly cooked and is no longer pink on the inside. Drain on paper towels and serve hot. Keep the finished cakes in a low oven until all are fried and ready to serve.

For extra crispness, the uncooked meat cakes can be dredged in additional meal before being fried.

Yield: About 6 servings as a main course; 10 as an appetizer

Variation: White meat of turkey with turkey or chicken livers (alone or combined) can be used instead of chicken. In that case, be doubly careful about removing tissues that might clog the grinder, and grind into the mixture about 2 teaspoons of raw fat trimmed from the turkey.

Braised Turkey

My mother firmly believed that turkey should be braised for most of its cooking time to avoid dryness and toughness. She also preferred to bake stuffing (page 152–54) separately so it did not become soggy. Basically she roasted turkey as she did chicken, eliminating only the parsley and adding more garlic, butter, salt, pepper, and sage-flavored poultry seasoning. (I include the parsley and sew the cavity closed as well as truss the bird.) She then placed the turkey on a rack in a roasting pan to which 2 or 3 large chopped onions were added, and basted it well with melted butter. She kept turning it as described for roasting chicken, but the roaster was kept covered until the last 45 minutes, when the bird was turned breast side up. That way the breast and wings and drumsticks became golden brown, if not completely crisp. A little stock, made by cooking the turkey neck, heart, and gizzard with a piece of onion and celery, was used for keeping the onions moist and was the basis of the gravy.

When the turkey was done, the grease was skimmed from the gravy and the pan juices were strained, with the onions pureed through the sieve. A natural gravy was generally served, but if you prefer yours thickened, reserve 3 tablespoons of the skimmed fat, heat it, and blend in 1½ tablespoons flour, then pour in the pan juices plus enough stock to make 2 cups. Simmer until smooth and thickened to the consistency of heavy cream. Season to taste.

Allow 18 minutes per pound for roasting turkey at 350 degrees.

Roast Squab Stuffed with Rice

In celebration of their twentieth anniversary, my parents had a caterer in to prepare a dinner for twenty-four friends. My mother obtained the recipe for the stuffed squabs the caterer made that day, and they became a family favorite. This works very well too with tiny chickens, such as the fresh Perdue Cornish chickens that weigh no more than 1¼ pounds. Frozen rock Cornish hens are not satisfactory simply because they are too dry and tasteless to be worth eating. My mother preferred thyme in this, while I favor nutmeg.

4 squabs or Cornish chickens (1 to
   1¼ pounds each)
Salt and black pepper
10 tablespoons sweet butter
¼ cup finely minced onion
   Livers of the squabs or chickens,
   raw and minced

1 cup long-grain converted rice
   Pinch each of black pepper and
   thyme or nutmeg, or to taste
2 to 3 cups hot chicken stock, as
   needed
2 tablespoons finely minced fresh
   parsley

Clean and singe the squabs or chickens, if necessary. Rub the insides lightly with salt and black pepper. Melt 4 tablespoons butter in a 1½-quart saucepan and in it sauté the onion until soft but not brown. Add the minced livers and sauté until they lose their red color—2 or 3 minutes. Add the rice and stir until well coated with butter. Add 1 teapoon salt, a little pepper, thyme or nutmeg, and 2 cups hot chicken stock. Cover the pan and simmer the rice for 12 minutes, or until still firm but tender enough to bite through. Add more stock if needed. Stir in 2 tablespoons butter and the parsley.

Preheat the oven to 400 degrees.

Lightly stuff the cavities of birds with the rice and sew or truss closed. If you like, you can also stuff the crop with just enough rice to round it out and sew or truss closed.

Sprinkle the outside of the birds with a little salt and pepper and rub with the remaining 4 tablespoons butter, which has softened at room temperature. Lay the birds on one side on a rack in an open roasting pan. Roast for 20 minutes, or until the first side is light golden brown. Turn and roast second side up, basting with pan juices for another 20 minutes. Turn breast side up for another 20 minutes, basting again with drippings.

The birds are done when their legs move easily in their sockets. This should take about 1 hour.

Untruss the birds and serve one to a portion. You may use butter drippings from the pan as gravy, or add a little chicken stock to the pan juices, bring to a simmer, season, and serve as gravy.

Yield: 4 servings

Variation: Instead of adding stock to the butter drippings in the pan, add about ⅔ cup heavy sweet cream, scrape in the coagulated pan juices, simmer for a few seconds, season, and serve that as gravy.

Broiled Squab

As elegant as we thought the rice-stuffed squabs were, this broiled variation was our favorite. Squabs must be watched carefully so they cook at the right temperature and do not dry out. Serve on slices of bread that have been toasted by being sautéed in butter.

For each serving:

1 squab
Lemon juice
Corn oil
3 tablespoons melted sweet butter
Salt and black pepper

1 slice good white bread, sautéed in butter until golden brown on both sides
Watercress, for garnish

The squab should be split in half from the back but not cut all the way through the breast skin. The backbone should be cut out completely. The squab should then be spread flat, butterfly style, and flattened with a tenderizer or the side of a cleaver. Singe and clean. Twist the wingtips, tucking them under the back of the squab. Sprinkle lightly on all sides with lemon juice and let stand at room temperature for 10 minutes. Pat thoroughly dry with a paper towel.

Preheat the broiler and brush the rack with corn oil. Coat both sides of the squab generously with melted butter. Sprinkle with salt and black pepper. Place on the rack, skin side up, about 5 to 6 inches from the flame or electric broiler coil. Broil for 15 to 18 minutes, or until the skin is golden brown. Turn, brush with a little more butter, and broil for 12 to 15 minutes longer, or until the juices run clear when a thigh is pierced with a fork or skewer.

Serve on freshly made toast with a clump of watercress.

Yield: 1 serving

Roast Duck

1 duckling, 4 to 5 pounds, fresh if
   obtainable, or thawed
Kosher (coarse) salt
3 cloves garlic, peeled
1 teaspoon black pepper

2 tablespoons sweet paprika
1 teaspoon powdered ginger
1 small onion, peeled
1 stalk celery with a few leaves

Wash the duck and singe; using a tweezer or your fingers, remove all pin feathers. Rub inside and out with coarse salt and place in the refrigerator for about 5 hours or overnight. Rinse and dry just before roasting.

Preheat the oven to 350 degrees.

Crush the peeled cloves of garlic with 1 tablespoon coarse salt in a mortar and pestle or just by rubbing the garlic in the salt. Mix in the pepper, paprika, and ginger. Rub a little of this mixture inside the duck. Place the onion and celery inside the duck cavity.

Rub the remaining garlic-salt mixture on the outside of the duck, sprinkling on a little more paprika if necessary. Place on a rack, breast side down, in an open roasting pan. Roast for about 50 minutes, or until the skin is golden brown and crisp. Turn and roast breast up for another 40 to 50 minutes, or until the duck is all crisp and the drumsticks move freely in their sockets. Remove the vegetables from the cavity, quarter the duck, cutting out the backbone. This is especially good with kasha (page 219) or baked egg barley (page 86).

Yield: 2 to 4 servings

Variation: I have found the duck becomes crisper if it is roasted already quartered. Rub with spices on both sides of each piece and roast on the rack, skin side up. Total cooking time may be a little less—about 1 hour and 15 minutes. If you like an extremely crisp skin, eliminate the paprika.

STUFFINGS

All of the following can be used for duck, goose, turkey or chicken, or for stuffed breast of veal. Always pack stuffing loosely, to allow room for expansion during cooking.

Kasha Stuffing

2 cups kasha (buckwheat groats), preferably fine but medium will do
4 large eggs, lightly beaten
4 cups boiling water
1 teaspoon salt
6 tablespoons schmaltz (rendered chicken fat, page 7), sweet butter, or margarine

1 medium onion, chopped
¼ pound fresh mushrooms, coarsely chopped, or 2 large dried Polish mushroom caps, soaked for 10 minutes in hot water, washed, and chopped
White pepper to taste

Put the kasha in a bowl and add half the beaten egg, stirring until the egg is absorbed. Turn into a cold skillet and slowly heat, stirring frequently, until the kasha grains are dry and separate and just beginning to brown. Pour in the boiling water and salt. Stir once, then simmer, covered, over moderately low heat until all the water is absorbed and the kasha is half cooked—about 10 minutes.

Melt the fat in a skillet, and in it slowly sauté the onion until it begins to soften; do not brown. Add the mushrooms, raise the heat, and sauté for a minute or two, or until their liquid evaporates. If you are using dried mushrooms, simply stir them into the sautéed onion and cook for a second or two.

Combine the sautéed onion and mushroom with the kasha and stir. Taste and adjust the seasoning with salt and pepper. Stir in the remaining beaten egg.

(continued)

Note: This stuffing can be prepared ahead and refrigerated, but should not be put into the bird or meat until just before roasting.

Yield: This amount will be ample for an 8- to 9-pound breast of veal or a 10- to 15-pound turkey. Use half the amount for half a breast of veal or for a 5- to 6-pound bird.

Bread Stuffing

About 4 cups cubed stale white bread, with crusts

4 tablespoons sweet butter, schmaltz (rendered chicken fat, page 7), or margarine

1 medium onion, chopped

2 stalks of celery, diced

3 chicken, 2 duck, or 1 turkey or goose liver, if available, cleaned and diced

1 cup water or poultry stock
   Salt, pepper, sage, and thyme to taste

2 tablespoons minced fresh parsley

2 extra-large eggs

Melt the fat, and in it slowly sauté the chopped onion and celery until soft but not brown. Stir in the diced liver and sauté until it loses its red color. Add the bread and stir. Stir in the stock or water until evenly distributed. Remove from the heat, season to taste, and stir in the parsley and eggs.

Yield: This amount will be stuffing enough for a 10-pound turkey; if stuffing an 8- to 9-pound breast of veal, reduce the recipe by about one quarter.

Note: This stuffing can be prepared ahead and refrigerated, but should not be put into bird or meat until just before roasting.

Potato Stuffing

This is best for breast of veal, duck, or goose. It is the same mixture used for potato pancakes (page 215), but bakes to a pudding or kugel as a stuffing. It should be prepared just before the meat or bird is to be roasted.

3 large baking potatoes, peeled

1 medium onion, peeled

1 extra-large egg

2 tablespoons matzoh meal or 1 tablespoon potato starch

1 scant teaspoon salt
¼ to ½ teaspoon white pepper
    1 tablespoon finely minced fresh
        parsley

3 tablespoons sweet butter,
    chicken fat or light
    vegetable oil

Grate the potatoes and onion alternately into a sieve set over a bowl, so the liquid will drain off. Pick up handfuls of the grated mixture and squeeze out as much liquid as possible into the bowl.

Pour the liquid from the bowl carefully, reserving the thick white starch that has settled at the bottom. Scrape this into the potato mixture. Add the egg, matzoh meal or potato starch, seasonings, and parsley. Mix well.

Heat the fat in a skillet and turn the potato mixture into it. Let simmer very slowly for a few minutes, until the fat is hot and the entire mixture is bubbling. Stir once or twice. Do not let potatoes fry or brown; they should remain at a simmer for 3 or 4 minutes. Stuff the bird and roast immediately.

Yield: Enough for a 5- to 6-pound duck, or half a breast of veal

Matzoh Ball Stuffing

Although not actually stuffed with matzoh balls, the same mix, loosened slightly so it will not become too dense and hard, makes a delicious stuffing for breast of veal, chicken, or a small turkey. It is not recommended for birds larger than 6 pounds, as it would take too long for the interior of the stuffing to cook, and by the time it did, the bird would be overcooked. This is one stuffing that must be prepared just before the bird or meat is to be roasted.

3 eggs plus 1 egg yolk
⅓ cup cold water
4 tablespoons schmaltz (rendered
        chicken fat, page 7), or as
        needed
½ teaspoon salt

Pinch of white pepper
¾ cup matzoh meal
½ medium onion, finely chopped
½ teaspoon thyme
1 tablespoon finely minced fresh
        parsley

Beat the eggs plus the egg yolk lightly with the water. Add 3 heaping table-spoons chicken fat and stir until the fat dissolves. Add the salt and pepper. Stir in the matzoh meal.

(continued)

Sauté the chopped onion in 1 tablespoon fat until it is very soft and bright yellow; do not let it brown. Add a little more fat if needed. Stir into the matzoh-meal mixture along with the thyme and parsley. Adjust the seasoning.

Stuff into your poultry or veal breast at once. Do not let this set, as when making matzoh balls.

Yield: This amount is correct for half a breast of veal weighing about 4½ to 5 pounds; make about one-third less for a 5-pound bird.

14

Passover

Of all the Jewish holidays of the year, none was more eagerly anticipated than Passover, for it meant two parties in a row, two new dresses, two wonderful meals at which to see great-aunts and uncles and cousins who lived in such exotically remote places as the Bronx, Forest Hills, or the City—Manhattan.

I knew very little about the reasons behind this holiday and so did not know why the Passover week began with Seder dinners on the first two nights. I supposed the system had been devised so children could go to both sets of grandparents, one on each night, because that is what we did.

Our routine was always the same—my mother's family the first night, my father's family the second. If one of my new dresses was a little prettier or more expensive than the other, it was saved for the second night, for that to us was a slightly more formal, and to me a more special, affair, primarily because my grandfather was a rabbi.

Grandpa Solomon, as we called our rabbi grandfather, wore formal white robes and a high-crowned satin hat, and since the ritual for the night required him to lean as he ate, he was ensconced at the head of the table on a sofa full of pillows covered by sheer, hand-embroidered white cotton and linen pillow slips. The table, which normally ran along the length of the dining room, had been turned around, and extended so that it went from the dining room through the archway into the living room that adjoined. Seders there were so crowded we sat on every kind of chair, piano bench, or stool, and children, because of size, were always given the seats within the archway frame, which made it hard to move one's chair back and leave the table.

My mother always made whispered remarks about the mediocre quality of the food prepared by Wilma, my grandfather's third wife, his first having been my grandmother. Wilma was Hungarian, and I would hear my mother say "they" did such terrible things as putting ground almonds in the gefüllte fish, which made it heavy, and grated carrots, which made it sweet. And because my mother felt Wilma's matzoh balls were always undercooked and indigestible, she ate cold beet borscht, a traditional alternate soup on the second night of Seder.

But, in spite of my mother's complaints about the food, it was still a gay event, for my grandfather invited all sorts of down-and-out acquaintances to come for the hearty meal, and my father, who invariably drank a lot of wine, was drunk and full of fun. Trince (I never knew his last name), an old, thin man with networks of red, broken blood vessels on his cheeks and nose, was always there wearing a magnificent yarmulka of blue velvet stitched with huge glass "jewels," and my grandfather gave my father his favorite yarmulka, a skull cap made of black silk intricately stitched with heavy, gleaming gold and silver thread. Trince played the violin, and my father, who had a wonderfully rich voice and who had sung in my grandfather's choir, would not only sing the traditional Passover songs, but would dance to them with Trince. It was at just such a Seder that I decided to summon the courage to tell my grandfather that I did not believe in God. Expecting an explosion of wrath, I was stunned into silence and chagrin when he said, "So? You'll go to heaven anyway."

But if I looked forward to the second night of Seder with a certain expectant awe, I looked forward to the first, at Grandpa and Grandma Breit's, with nothing but a sense of fun, for here would be the cousins I adored, eight boys, and I the only granddaughter for many years and therefore much appreciated and admired.

At the Breits', children were supposed to sit at a separate table, simply because there were too many people to fit around the big dinner table, but inevitably, we were all moved over to the big table by our parents as the evening wore on.

As a rule, my mother and an aunt or two went over the day before or the morning of the Seder, to help my grandmother with the preparations, and usually I and one or two of my cousins went along as well.

There was fish to be chopped in the huge wooden bowl because my grandmother believed it had to be chopped, not ground, to make a proper gefüllte fish. There was the mix of eggs, chicken fat, and matzoh meal for the matzoh balls, to be made early in the day, then chilled several hours before the dumplings were cooked. There were pots of chicken soup to be cooked and therefore several chickens to be singed, and the faintly fleshy smell of burning feathers when I singe a chicken now still takes me back to those pre-Seder preparations. Wine had to be funneled into cut-crystal decanters and horseradish had to be grated.

Since hard-boiled eggs in salt water were the first course at the Seder meal (eggs signifying rebirth and hope and salt water a reminder of tears), someone had to peel the eggs, and that was often my job. And they had to be perfectly, evenly, gleamingly peeled. That meant letting them chill in ice-cold water, then gently tapping them on all sides on the edge of the sink or table, then rolling them between the palms of my hand to crack the shell, all over, and only then peeling it off. Any broken egg was a reject, to be saved for the following night's chopped liver.

I also opened walnuts and pounded them fine with my grandmother's huge, heavy brass mortar and pestle that now glistens on my own kitchen shelf, and I was the official taster for the charoses, the salad of chopped apples and walnuts sweetened with Concord grape wine and spiced with ginger. I loved this wonderfully sweet and exotic mix, and each year I asked my mother why we could not have it at other times. (I have made it since and find it delicious on hot, toasted English muffins). My mother said, "Certain things are eaten at certain times and that's why not", an answer that also had to hold me for the hard-boiled eggs in salt water as well. (I have tried those at other times and they taste awful—a dish that does not travel well in time.)

There was the table to be set with the best freshly pressed white linen cloth that would soon bear Rorschach blots of red wine. The heavy, embossed silver candlesticks had to be polished, and the big silver or heavy glass wine goblets reserved for this night had to be set out—silver for the men, glass for women and children, since there was not enough silver for all.

The afternoon of Seder preparations that stands out above all took place when I was about eight, and my Aunt Estelle came over bringing her son Wally, aged nine, and my favorite cousin. It was early in the morning when we all got there, and the gefüllte fish had not yet been started. My grandmother liked to add carp to the holiday fish, along with pike and whitefish, but she felt carp had to be kept alive until just before it was cooked. And so there was a huge golden fish swimming in the bathtub when we all assembled. The water in the tub was icy cold, a fact that Wally noted and thought was cruel to the carp. He turned the hot water on and let it run into the tub to warm the fish. By the time the busy adults in the kitchen were aware of the sound of running water, the bathroom was full of steam and the fish had turned over on its back. My grandmother was horrified at the thought of starting with a carp that was dead and not absolutely raw, and she sent my mother to the fish market for a replacement.

Distant (to me) relatives such as my grandmother's sister, Tante Regina, who was poor and lived on the Lower East Side, were always at the Seder. She brought with her a big shopping bagful of Passover candy—hard candy with soft, jamlike fruit centers that we children loathed but had to eat to please her. Then she would chase us into corners to hug us so hard it hurt and to implant a big wet kiss we hated on our cheeks. When she left at evening's end, the shopping bag was as full as when she had arrived; in it was food enough for a week and old clothing everyone had brought to give her.

As a bonus, there was always at least one unexpected guest at this Seder—an aunt or uncle who lived in some really far-off city such as Tulsa or New Orleans, Omaha or Norfolk, who would come as a surprise to my grandparents. Other members of the family knew who it would be each year, but no one ever told me, knowing I would certainly tell and spoil the surprise. There was always a chill of excitement as my grandparents, trembling with combined laughter and tears, embraced one of the children whom fate had moved so far away.

15

Meat

As it did to most American families, dinner at our house meant meat, potatoes, and a vegetable or two, and much of the meat was simply broiled. Although well prepared, the roast leg of lamb, broiled lamb chops, lamb or beef stews did not differ from their standard versions, so recipes for them are not included here.

Ham was a meat my mother came to cook rather late in life. We always had bacon at home and she would eat ham in restaurants, but I was close to sixteen before I remember her actually buying a ham and baking it. Once she did, it became a fairly regular feature of Sunday dinners, always done the classic American way, with a glaze of brown sugar, cloves, mustard, and pepper. She also made ham steaks, broiled or baked, but again from standard recipes, many of which she cut from magazines and newspapers.

But pork was something else again, and I always felt it was the word that scared her. She did eat pork knowingly, willingly, and enthusiastically in Chinese restaurants, but if we ever teased her by calling ham "smoked pork" she was furious; she said that she would never have "real" pork in her house. So much for the irrationality of habit.

Roast Beef

My mother's preparation of roast beef was so simple it is hard to make a bona-fide recipe of it. Although she sometimes used prime rib, either with bone in or boned and rolled, she disliked the wastefulness of this cut and generally used top sirloin. She also, on occasion, did an eye round of beef exactly the same way. Both of these cuts produce delicious roast beef only if they are served very rare to medium rare. Any more cooking than that toughens them and turns the meat gray and hard. They should also be sliced paper thin, as they are not as tender as prime rib and so do not lend themselves to thick slices.

Top sirloin is a very wide cut, and if you want a relatively small amount, say 3 to 5 pounds, the cut would be so narrow it could not stand up. The whole wide cut is not practical unless you want a roast of 7 pounds or more. For that reason, butchers split the meat horizontally, then tie each half snugly with a good layer of beef fat on all sides. The half that has the muscle sinew running through it is the tenderest but if you have a family of picky eaters who blanch at such tissue, get the smaller half that does not have the sinew.

Take the tied roast from the refrigerator 30 minutes to 1 hour before roasting. Preheat the oven to 350 degrees. Insert small slivers of garlic in six or eight spots in the roast. Rub the meat on all sides and ends with pepper (no salt) and dredge lightly with flour on all sides, including the ends. Place on a rack in an open roasting pan and place in the middle of the preheated oven. Allow 18 minutes per pound for very rare beef, 20 minutes for medium rare, 22 or 23 minutes for medium, and 30 minutes for well done. Or use a meat thermometer that registers the degree of doneness you want.

It is not necessary to turn or baste this roast. When done, remove the meat to a platter and keep warm.

Pour off the fat from the pan (it is excellent for roasting potatoes or making French fries). The amount of hot water you add to the pan will depend on how much coagulated meat dripping remains on the bottom of the pan. Pour hot water in slowly, bringing it to a boil in the pan on top of the range and scraping the coagulated juices into the water with a wooden spatula. You can add water as long as the color remains fairly dark; if it becomes too pale you have added too much and will have to boil it down to reduce it. The correct amount of water for a 5- to 6-pound roast will be about 1½ cups. Pour into a saucepan. Season with salt and heat thoroughly. Slice the meat, sprinkle with salt, and serve the clear pan gravy in a heated gravy boat.

If you use eye round of beef, prepare it as above but roast it in a 425-degree oven, allowing half the amount of cooking time per pound.

For richer gravy, my mother put coarsely chopped onion on the bottom of the pan and placed the roast on a rack over it. When the onion was medium golden brown, she added just enough water to the bottom of the pan to keep it from burning. The resultant juices, skimmed and strained, were the gravy.

Boiled Beef

Following the recipe for chicken soup (page 54), substituting beef for chicken as indicated. If your primary interest is in the beef, place the beef (preferably first-cut flanken) in boiling water. If you care more about the broth, place the meat in cold water. Boiled beef can also be made according to the recipe for mushroom and barley soup (page 58). Serve with beet horseradish (page 15).

Beef with Sauerkraut

This was a favorite family winter dish, and the nose-twitching aroma of simmering sauerkraut was enough to lift our spirits as soon as we came home and sniffed it on cold, bleak winter afternoons. Flanken is the tenderest, juiciest cut for this dish, but lean chuck works fairly well. First-cut brisket is a possible, if slightly less tender, alternative.

3 pounds first-cut flanken or other boiling beef, in 1 piece
6 to 8 cups water, more as needed
2 pounds fresh sauerkraut, if available, otherwise use canned (but not packaged)
2 small onions, peeled and one sliced, the other diced

2 or 3 dried Polish mushroom caps, soaked in warm water for 20 minutes
2 tablespoons schmaltz (rendered chicken fat, page 7), margarine, or sweet butter
1½ tablespoons flour
Salt and black pepper to taste

Place the meat in a straight-sided stainless steel or enameled pot and cover with water—about 6 to 8 cups should do it. Bring to a boil, reduce to a simmer, and skim foam off the surface as it rises. When the broth is clear, cover the pot and simmer the meat gently but steadily for about 1 hour, or until half tender. Add water as needed to keep the level up. Do not add salt.

Remove the meat from the pot and reserve the stock.

Taste the sauerkraut, and if it is very sour, rinse in a strainer under running water until the flavor is still piquant but not stingingly so. Canned sauerkraut will need more rinsing than the fresh. Using a 3-quart enameled Dutch oven, place half of the sauerkraut in it. Lay the half-cooked piece of unsliced meat on the bed of kraut. Strew the sliced onion and dried mushrooms over the beef. Top with the remaining kraut. The meat should be completely covered by the kraut, so you may need to push it down into the bottom layer. Pour in the reserved meat stock until it comes just slightly below the top level of the kraut. If there is not enough stock to do this, add water to reach that point.

Cover the pot and bring to a simmer. Simmer slowly but steadily for another 1 or 1½ hours, or until the meat is meltingly tender when pierced with a fork. The kraut will be cooked by that time. Add water or stock if the kraut becomes too dry during cooking.

Remove the meat from the pot and set aside. Keep the sauerkraut over low heat. In a small saucepan or skillet, melt the fat. In it sauté the diced onion until it turns deep golden brown, but not black. Stir in the flour and let that brown slowly until it becomes a deep cocoa-brown color. Turn the roux (einbrenne) into the sauerkraut, raising the heat so the kraut liquid is at a low boil. Stir and cook until the flour-fat mixture is absorbed.

Taste the kraut for seasoning, adding salt, if necessary, and black pepper. Return the meat to the kraut, burying it again as much as possible, and reheat for 10 minutes over low heat.

The meat may be sliced or served in chunks, along with the kraut. It is best served with dry, floury boiled potatoes.

This dish improves with age, and it is best prepared the day before it is to be eaten. Add a little water before reheating to prevent scorching.

Yield: 4 servings

Pot-roasted Brisket of Beef

First-cut brisket is really the only good cut for this method of cooking, as it is thin enough and fat enough to cook thoroughly without becoming dry and tough. Obviously any braising cut can be used, but the results will be less successful. Brisket is also an easy cut to slice. Potato pancakes (page 215) and applesauce (page 227) were the classic accompaniments to this dish. Sweet and sour string beans or cabbage (pages 187 and 188), or a cucumber salad (page 200), are also good with it. Sandwiches of cold sliced leftovers were a bonus treat.

4 pounds first-cut beef brisket, in 1 piece	1 tablespoon sweet paprika
Salt and black pepper	2 cloves garlic, peeled and cut in half lengthwise
1 to 2 tablespoons rendered beef fat or margarine, if needed	Pinch of thyme (optional)
2 large onions, peeled and coarsely chopped	2 to 3 cups hot water, as needed

Sprinkle the meat lightly on all sides with salt and pepper. Place in a heavy Dutch oven large enough to hold the meat flat and brown the meat on all sides. There should be enough fat on the meat itself for the browning. Turn the meat with tongs or a pair of wooden spoons; do not pierce it with a fork. It should take about 10 minutes for all sides to become golden brown; do not let them blacken. Remove and set aside.

If needed, add whichever fat you are using to the pot and sauté the chopped onion. Sauté slowly until it just begins to turn pale golden brown. Stir in the paprika and sauté for a minute more. Add the garlic, thyme, and 2 cups of hot water.

Return the meat to the pan and baste the top with the pan liquid. Add a little more hot water to come to a depth of about 1½ inches in the pan. Cover loosely, bring to a boil, reduce the heat, and simmer gently but steadily for 2½ to 3 hours, turning the meat several times during the cooking and adding a little hot water as needed to keep the onion from scorching. When the meat is completely tender when tested with a fork or skewer, remove from the pan. Skim off the fat from the pan juices and strain the skimmed juices, rubbing the onion through the sieve into the gravy. Heat the gravy and adjust the seasoning. Slice the pot roast, place on a warm serving platter, and serve with the gravy in a heated sauceboat.

Yield: 6 to 8 servings, depending on shrinkage

Beef Tongue

Smoked tongue was always purchased ready to cook, and often pickled tongue was also. But when they had time, both my grandmother and mother preferred to pickle beef tongue at home, just as they did corned beef. The beef and smoked tongue were cooked the same way—in huge kettles filled with enough water to cover the meat. For smoked tongue a large onion, peeled and quartered, was added to the pot, along with a bay leaf or two. With pickled tongue, a few fresh spices such as those used in the pickling were added.

The tongues cooked, loosely covered, in water that was maintained at a gentle but steady boil, for anywhere from 2½ to 4 hours, depending on size and toughness. Tongue is done when the tip yields readily if pressed between thumb and forefinger, and when the two protruding bones in the thick (schlung) end slip out of place.

Run a hot cooked tongue under cold water so it can be handled, then trim off the schlung and peel. Peel only the amount of tongue you expect to use at a given meal, as it keeps better unsliced and with the skin on. There are often deliciously tender morsels of tongue and an occasional sweetbread to be dug out of the schlung, and we all used to crowd around for those prizes during the carving. My mother sliced tongue on the diagonal starting at the wide end, to get large slices.

Serve hot, with creamed spinach (page 196) or boiled cabbage and boiled new potatoes with parsley or dill. Hot mustard is an excellent accompaniment to tongue. The meat is, of course, wonderful cold and sliced for sandwiches.

Pickled Tongue

When my mother cooked smoked tongue and prepared cabbage to go with it, she cooked the cabbage in a half-and-half combination of fresh water and the cooking liquid from the tongue.

If you make your own pickled tongue and corned beef, you need not use the nitrites that are generally found in commercial products. Saltpeter (potassium nitrate) is not considered a harmful chemical, as is sodium nitrate, but it can be eliminated if you prefer.

1 fresh beef tongue (5 pounds)

1½ cups kosher (coarse) salt, or as
needed

2 teaspoons saltpeter (this is solely
to retain a bright red color
and its use is optional)

10 cloves garlic, unpeeled but lightly
crushed

3 large bay leaves, crumbled

3 whole, small, long hot dried red
peppers or 2 teaspoons crushed
hot red pepper flakes

1 scant tablespoon black
peppercorns

1 tablespoon coriander seeds

1 tablespoon mustard seeds

Water as needed

Fresh tongue is extremely perishable, so set about pickling it as soon as you get it; do not keep it unpickled in the refrigerator for more than 2 days, and then only if you are sure it was very fresh when purchased. Buying it from a kosher butcher is the best way to ensure freshness.

Wash the tongue under cold running water. Pierce all over with a thin skewer or long needle. Place in a wide-mouthed, 5- to 7-quart stoneware or earthenware crock. Add all the remaining ingredients to 2 quarts of water in a saucepan and bring to a boil. Simmer until all the salt is dissolved. Cool thoroughly, then pour over the tongue. Pour in enough additional cold water to completely cover the tongue or to come within 3 inches of the top of the crock.

Unless the tongue is wedged snugly in place in the crock, it will float above the brine and so will spoil where uncovered. To avoid that, weight the tongue down. To do that, you will need a large plate or a wooden lid that will fit inside the crock and be beneath brine level. Place the plate or lid on top of the tongue. For a weight, you can use a thoroughly scrubbed stone or, what I have found to work very well, a large glass filled with water and placed dead center on the plate.

Cover the crock with two or three thicknesses of cheesecloth or a dish-towel and tie a string around the sides to keep it in place. A piece of foil can be placed loosely over the towel. The crock should not be tightly covered, as the brine will ferment and spoil the tongue if it is airtight. The cloth and foil covers are simply to prevent dust from getting in.

Ideally, the tongue should be kept in a cool room for one week before being refrigerated. If you do not have such a place, put it in the refrigerator at once, knowing it will take almost 10 days longer to become pickled.

Turn the tongue over in the brine every 2 days. Taste the brine to see if it is becoming less salty, and if so, add a little salt each time. Retie the cloth and lay the foil over. After 1 week in a cool room, refrigerate for 3 weeks, still turning every 2 or 3 days. Rinse and cook as described above.

Pickled or "Corned" Beef

The pickling is done exactly as it is for tongue (see preceding recipe) except that corned beef made with first- or second-cut brisket of beef (the only cuts to consider) will be thoroughly corned in 2 to 2½ weeks—1 week in a cold room and 1 week in the refrigerator, or 3 weeks in the refrigerator. This beef should not be pierced. Prepare, weight, and turn exactly as for tongue. Do not trim off the fat, as it will keep the meat from drying during the pickling.

Although steaming is sometimes used as a method of cooking corned beef, that is a very lengthy process at home, and it is better to poach the meat gently in water to cover as described for pickled tongue, adding a few extra, fresh pickling spices. Again, this is good served with cabbage and boiled potatoes, or sliced cold in sandwiches, or made into hash.

Pan-Broiled Steak

Even though my mother did not observe kosher laws, she had developed a taste for certain cuts of kosher meats that she was in the habit of using often, most especially forequarter cuts of meat for steak. She did make sirloin and porterhouse steaks as well, but we also had rib steak, skirt steak, and shoulder steak, if they looked well marbled and were tender when pressed between thumb and forefinger. Whichever she used, she liked a good edge of fat on the meat and always did what she called "pan broiling," or pan frying. It is still my favorite way to cook steak or hamburgers, although I prefer lamb chops done under the broiler.

To pan-broil steak, you need a heavy, black cast-iron skillet. Nothing else will do. The steak should be at room temperature, not cold. Sprinkle a light, even coating of kosher (coarse) salt on the pan and heat thoroughly. Slap the steak on; the pan should be hot enough for the steak to sizzle. Reduce the heat very slightly and fry until the steak can be lifted easily for turning. If it sticks, it is insufficiently seared. If you are doing two steaks, they should not be crammed into the pan; there should be an inch between them and at least half an inch of clearance around the sides. When the first side is brown, turn and brown the second side. Lower the heat slightly after the searing if you like well-done or medium meat; otherwise leave high.

The steak is done rare when red juices begin to flow on top of the first side. It is not necessary to resalt the pan when turning the steak over. Turn with a spatula or tongs so as not to pierce the steak, and do not re-turn or it will develop a peculiar flavor. Once you get the knack and discover just how you like the steak done, you will be able to time this accurately. I find that a 1-inch-thick room-temperature steak needs about 7 to 8 minutes on the first side, 5 to 7 minutes on the second.

This is an extremely smoky process, and I would think twice about attempting it without the proper venting over the stove, the only really proper venting being a vent fan that opens to the outdoors. Otherwise the whole house will be filled with smoke.

A little butter spread on top of the finished steak, along with a few grindings of fresh black pepper, adds a satisfying touch.

Pan-Broiled Hamburgers

When in a rush, my mother made plain chopped beef seasoned primarily with pepper and cooked on a salted pan as described above. She always ground the meat herself and always did the mixing with a fork so the meat would not be too compressed and result in hard, dense hamburgers. Generally she used the hamburger mixture below:

¾ pound beef chuck plus ¾ pound
    beef round, ground together
    through the medium blade of the
    grinder
1 medium egg, lightly beaten

1 generous tablespoon grated onion,
    with juice
Pinch of salt
½ teaspoon black pepper
Kosher (coarse) salt, for frying

Using a fork, combine the beef with the egg, grated onion, salt, and pepper. Remember, the salt on the pan will also flavor the meat, so do not add more than a tiny pinch to the mixture. Shape into 6 hamburgers. These can be prepared in advance and kept in the refrigerator until frying time. Again, bring to room temperature before frying. Cook on an iron pan sprinkled with coarse salt as described for steak (see preceding recipe). Use a wide, flat spatula for turning.

Serve on a plate, or in buns or toasted English muffins, with the usual trimmings.

Yield: 3 to 6 hamburgers

Variation: Once in a while my mother prepared the meat as described above, then broiled one side of the hamburgers under the gas broiler. When seared, she turned them over, let the uncooked side broil for 2 to 3 minutes to seal, then spread a thin coating of brown mustard over them and continued the broiling. These were always served on buns or toasted English muffins.

Meat Loaf with Tomato Sauce

The idea of finding slices of egg in the middle of a meat loaf always was exciting when we were kids. The egg may, of course, be eliminated, especially if you want meat loaf slices for sandwiches on the following day.

3 pounds fairly lean (but not too lean) ground chuck

2 extra-large or jumbo eggs, lightly beaten

2 tablespoons grated onion

½ scant teaspoon black pepper

2 teaspoons salt

2 hard-cooked eggs, peeled (optional)

1 medium green pepper, seeded and diced

1 medium onion, peeled and diced

2 tablespoons sweet butter, margarine, or corn oil

1 cup coarsely cut-up canned tomatoes, liquid reserved

1 can (8 ounces) tomato sauce

1 clove garlic, peeled and split in half vertically

1 small bay leaf

Take the meat from the refrigerator and mix it with the beaten eggs, grated onion, pepper, and salt 30 minutes before you intend to start baking it. Shape half the meat into a layer and place the hard-cooked eggs lengthwise on it. Top the remaining meat and shape into a loaf. The loaf should be roughly an oval or oblong about 2½ inches high in the center if you do not use eggs, or a little higher if you do. Place in the center of a 9 x 15-inch baking pan. There should be about 1½ to 2 inches of space between the loaf and the sides of the pan.

Preheat the oven to 350 degrees.

Sauté the green pepper and onion in the butter until soft but not brown. Stir in the canned tomatoes, tomato sauce, garlic, and bay leaf. Keep the reserved liquid from the canned tomatoes on hand to be added to the sauce if it thickens too rapidly.

Simmer the sauce for a minute or two, then pour around the meat loaf in the pan. Place in the middle of the oven. After 15 n.inutes, or when the top of the meat loaf is sealed, start basting with the sauce. Bake for 45 minutes to 1 hour if the eggs are inside; if there are no eggs, bake for 1½ hours to be moderately well done, or a little less if you like it rare, as I do. Add the tomato canning liquid to the pan juices if they thicken before the meat loaf is done.

Serve the meat loaf sliced. Skim the fat off the sauce, adjust the seasoning, and serve on the side or spooned over the slices. Rice is a good accompaniment for this.

Yield: 6 to 8 servings

Stuffed Peppers in Sweet and Sour Tomato Sauce

Medium-sized peppers work best for this recipe. If the peppers are too large, the meat filling will take so long to cook that the peppers will fall apart. It is also more difficult to have the rice cook thoroughly if the filling is too large a mass. Small peppers can be used to make appetizer portions. Most important of all, however, is that the peppers be uniform in size so they will cook evenly. Use a very heavy-bottomed Dutch oven-type pot for this and shake frequently so the peppers do not scorch. Enameled cast iron is the perfect material, but cast iron will also do, for although a bit of lemon juice is added, it is done close to the end of the cooking time, and the sauce is dark anyway; there is not the problem of discoloration as with white sauces.

8 medium firm, bright-green peppers, free of blemishes and soft spots and preferably even on the bottom so they can stand upright.	½ teaspoon black pepper
	1 can (35 ounces) whole tomatoes
	1½ to 2 cans (each 16 ounces) tomato sauce, as needed
½ cup long-grain converted rice	1 large onion, studded with 6 or 8 cloves
2 cups water, lightly salted	
3 pounds lean ground beef chuck	1 large bay leaf
1 large onion, peeled	4 or 5 black peppercorns
2 extra-large eggs, lightly beaten	¼ cup lemon juice, or to taste
Salt	3 tablespoons sugar, or to taste

Wash and dry the peppers. Cut around inside fold of the top and remove the inner piece around the stem. That will give you an open top but one with a sort of ledge or lip around it, which holds the meat better than if the top were sliced off straight across. Reach inside the pepper and remove the seeds and as much of the white membrane material as possible. Rinse thoroughly, to get rid of all seeds, and drain.

Parboil the rice in 2 cups lightly salted water for about 6 or 7 minutes, or until it looks as though it is just beginning to soften. Drain the rice thoroughly and reserve.

Place the ground chuck in a roomy mixing bowl. Grate the onion into the meat, then add the eggs, 2 teaspoons salt, black pepper, and rice. Mix thoroughly but lightly with a fork so the meat does not become too densely packed but is well blended. Fill each pepper with the meat, gently pushing the meat into the crevices. Do not pack it too densely, however, or the pepper will crack. The meat should come slightly above the top of the pepper in a small mound. (See note 2 below.) Stand the peppers in a 3- to 4-quart casserole that will hold them upright, leaning against each other, but one in which they will not be tightly crammed together.

Drain the tomatoes, reserving the liquid, and cut up coarsely. Add to the pot with half of the liquid (reserving the remainder) and enough tomato sauce to come halfway up the sides of the peppers. Add the clove-studded onion, bay leaf, peppercorns, and a pinch of salt. Bring to a boil, reduce the heat, cover loosely, and simmer gently but steadily for 1 hour, checking to see if more tomato liquid is needed as the sauce thickens and basting the tops of the peppers with sauce. Shake the pot back and forth several times to prevent the peppers from sticking to the bottom. If the peppers flop over, try to prop them upright against each other.

After 1 hour, add the lemon juice and sugar alternately to achieve a balance of flavors that is perhaps just ever so faintly more sour than sweet. The exact amount of lemon juice and sugar needed to achieve that balance will depend on the acidity of the tomatoes and lemons. Add salt as needed. Simmer for 20 minutes more. Remove the bay leaf and onion and spoon the sauce over the peppers when serving.

Yield: 4 to 8 servings

Notes: 1. If there are leftover stuffed peppers, they must be reheated very carefully or the peppers will burn by the time the filling is hot. Remove the leftover peppers from the refrigerator several hours before you start to reheat them. Place them over low heat and bring the sauce to a simmer, thinning it with a little water if it is thick enough to scorch. Turn off the heat, keep the pot covered, and let the peppers warm gradually in the heated sauce for an hour or so before you actually start to recook them. It is best to do the final thorough reheating in the oven, as they are less likely to burn. If, however, you do it on the top of the range, be sure the heat is very low and that you add liquid as needed. Although they will not look quite as nice, left-over peppers are more easily reheated if they are cut in half vertically.

2. If you have meat left over after filling the peppers, shape into balls, roughly the size of the pepper fillings, and cook in the sauce along with the stuffed peppers. These meatballs often appeal to children who may not like the flavor of the peppers.

Glazed Sweet and Sour Stuffed Cabbage

This was a great specialty of my mother's, one which she prepared as a main course or an appetizer, but which she mainly categorized as a vegetable, serving it with tongue or pot roast.

¼ cup long-grain converted rice	2 to 3 tablespoons brown sugar, or to taste
1 cup water, lightly salted	
1½ pounds lean ground beef chuck	2 to 3 tablespoons strained lemon juice, or to taste
1 small onion, peeled and grated	
1 scant teaspoon salt, or to taste	1 onion, peeled and studded with 4 or 5 cloves
½ teaspoon black pepper, or to taste	
1 large head (about 3 pounds) green cabbage	½ cup raisins
	6 to 8 small gingersnaps, as needed, crushed
½ cup tomato puree	

Parboil the rice in 1 cup lightly salted water for about 7 minutes. Drain thoroughly. Combine with the beef, grated onion, salt, and pepper and mix thoroughly but lightly with a fork. The meat should be well mixed but not compacted.

Prepare the cabbage. Remove withered or faded outer leaves. You will use only the big outer leaves for this recipe, so buy cabbage that is in good condition so you do not waste too many of those large leaves in trimming. With a sharp-pointed knife, cut the core out of the cabbage. Let a strong stream of water run into the cavity left by the core, so the leaves will be loosened.

Gently remove the outer leaves one by one, trying not to crack them in doing so. Rinse each leaf under running water and stack them. You should have between 12 and 14 leaves. The inside of the cabbage can be saved for cole slaw or soup.

Place the leaves in boiling water that is lightly salted and parboil for about 8 minutes, or until limp and rollable but not thoroughly softened. Drain and cool slightly. Place each leaf on a board, rib side up, and trim off the thick portion of the rib, but do not cut through the leaf.

Turn each leaf over so the rib side is down and the base of the leaf is toward you. Place 1 generous tablespoon meat filling at the base and roll toward the tip, tucking in the sides as you do so. Place the stuffed rolls, seam side down, in a deep, heavy pot, such as a Dutch oven, and arrange so they fit snugly and hold each other in place. Place a second layer over the first. Cover with an inch of water. Blend the tomato puree with 2 tablespoons brown sugar and 2 tablespoons lemon juice. Add with the clove-studded onion. Bring to a boil, reduce the heat, cover, and simmer gently but steadily for about 30 minutes, shaking the pot several times to prevent sticking.

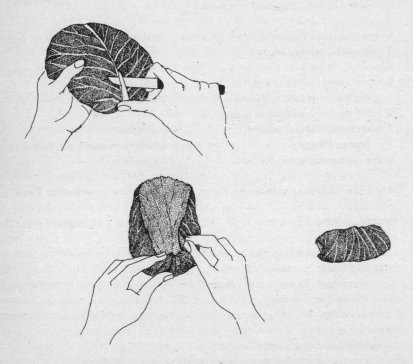

Add the raisins, a little water if necessary, and continue cooking another 15 minutes. Add 6 crushed gingersnaps and let simmer about 15 minutes longer, until the sauce is smooth and thick. If it is still very liquid, add more gingersnaps. Adjust the seasoning with salt, sugar, and lemon juice as needed to achieve the correct sweet and sour balance. Discard the onion. Total cooking time for the rolls will be about 1 to 1¾ hours.

Preheat the oven to 375 degrees.

Arrange the cabbage rolls in a single layer in an open baking pan that is at least 3 or 4 inches deep. Pour the sauce over the rolls, covering them completely. Bake in the preheated oven for 30 to 40 minutes, or until the sauce is thick and the tops of the rolls are browned.

Yield: 12 to 14 rolls; 1 per serving as an appetizer, 3 as a main course

Note: If you want to prepare this dish partially in advance, you can stop after the rolls have been cooked in the pot, or go one step further and arrange them in the baking pan with the sauce, ready to be baked just before serving. Once baked, they can be reheated in the oven. Remove from the refrigerator 1 hour before, cover with foil, and place in a 375-degree oven for about 45 minutes, adding a little water if the sauce becomes too thick. Remove the foil for the last 10 minutes of reheating.

Fried Veal Rib Chops with Potatoes

6 **veal rib chops, ½ inch thick**
  Salt and black pepper
2 **cups dry bread crumbs, or as**
  needed
1½ **cups flour, or as needed**

2 **extra-large eggs, beaten with 2**
  tablespoons water
  Corn oil, for frying
4 **large, cold boiled potatoes, peeled**
  and cut into ½-inch-thick slices

Pat the chops dry on both sides and sprinkle lightly on both sides with salt and pepper. Set out two sheets of waxed paper, or two dinner plates, and place the dry bread crumbs on one, the flour on the other. Have the beaten egg and water in a wide bowl.

Coat both sides of each chop with flour, tapping off excess, then dip into the egg so that both sides are covered and let excess drip off. Dredge on both sides with bread crumbs. As the chops are breaded, place them on a rack that has been set over a pan or platter and let them dry at room temperature for about 20 minutes before frying.

Heat a little less than a ½-inch depth of oil in a large, heavy frying pan, preferably cast iron. When the fat is hot but not quite smoking, add as many chops as can go into the pan without touching. Fry at a slow but steady sizzle until the first side is golden brown.

(continued)

Turn and fry for 3 or 4 minutes, then cover the pan loosely, reduce the heat, and let fry slowly for about 10 minutes. When golden brown on both sides, the chops should be removed to drain on paper towels. Fry the remaining chops, if any.

Add the sliced potatoes to the hot fat, sprinkle with salt and pepper, and fry over moderate heat for about 10 minutes, or until the potatoes are golden brown on both sides and bits of the breading from the chops cling to them. Turn the potatoes gently with a wooden spatula several times during cooking. It should not be necessary to add more oil to the pan with the potatoes, as they should fry in shallow fat.

Arrange the chops and potatoes on a heated platter and serve with string beans Lyonnaise (page 186) or cucumber salad (page 200).

Yield: 3 to 6 servings

Stuffed Breast of Veal

This is an economical dish that takes on elegant proportions, especially if a whole veal breast is prepared. Stuffed and then braised to a rich golden brown, it suggests a whole animal as it is presented at the table. This can be roasted, but the veal will retain its juices and be far more tender in less time if it is braised—browned lightly, then cooked covered in the oven with a little liquid and some chopped vegetables that make a velvety, spicy gravy. Since the stuffing provides the starch for this meal, the only necessary addition is a vegetable, best in the form of a cold green salad or cucumbers in vinegar. Because the breast of veal must be carved between the ribs, which are generally wide, portions look enormous, but the amount of meat is actually far less than it seems. Any of the stuffings in Chapter 13, pages 152–54, may be used, but my preference is divided equally between the matzoh ball (page 154) and the kasha (page 152). It is not a good idea to stuff less than a half-breast of veal. A smaller cut will be in a strip that is cut at both ends, so there is no natural pocket and two openings will have to be sewed—a tiresome and arduous task. Leftovers of this dish keep well and can be reheated, or the veal meat can be served cold even if the stuffing cannot.

Whole breasts of veal vary in size. The general range is from 6½ pounds if the calf was small to 9 or 10 if it was large. If you use a whole breast you can prepare two different stuffings, placing them in different halves of the breast, and serve guests a slice of each.

1 breast of veal (8 to 9 pounds)
4 cups of any stuffing on pages
     152–54
4 cloves garlic, peeled and 2
     of them crushed
   Salt, black pepper, and sweet
     paprika
1 teaspoon powdered ginger
1 teaspoon thyme
2 to 3 tablespoons schmaltz
     (rendered chicken fat, page
     7), sweet butter, or
     margarine

2 medium onions, peeled and
     coarsely chopped
2 carrots, scraped and coarsely
     diced
3 or 4 small pieces cracked ginger
2 or 3 sprigs parsley
1 can (12 ounces) tomato juice,
     as needed
1 to 2 cups water, or as needed

Have the butcher cut a pocket as large as possible in the veal breast, but be sure he does not cut through to the edges or the top. The fat should not be trimmed from the top of the veal, as it will keep the meat moist during cooking. Have the butcher saw notches between the ribs on the underside of the breast so it will be easy to carve between them, but be sure he does not cut into the pocket area, either on top or bottom, or the stuffing will ooze out.

Rinse the veal and pat dry. Preheat the oven to 375 degrees.

Prepare 4 cups of stuffing, knowing that you will probably not use all of it. The amount will depend on the width and depth of the pocket, but it is better to have a little more than less.

Rub the crushed garlic around the inside of the pocket; reserve the garlic. Rub also with a little salt, pepper, and paprika. Stuff the pocket. Do not cram it too full, as the stuffing will expand. Also, do not place the stuffing past the 1- to 1½-inch margin at the opening of the pocket or it will be messy to sew.

When the breast is stuffed, sew the opening with small stitches, using a large needle and unwaxed cotton kitchen thread.

Rub the outside of the breast, top and bottom, with the remaining crushed garlic, salt, pepper, paprika, and powdered ginger. Sprinkle with the thyme.

Place the fat, chopped onion and carrots, the 2 peeled cloves of garlic, and the cracked ginger in the bottom of a roasting pan with a cover. Place the veal breast on top of the vegetables and slide into the preheated oven. Do not cover.

Check after a few minutes, and when the fat has melted, baste the top of the roast. Let the roast remain uncovered for between 20 and 30 minutes, or until the top of the breast and the vegetables are beginning to turn golden brown. When brown, pour half the tomato juice over the roast and add 1 cup of water to the bottom of the pan. Add the parsley, cover the roasting pan, slide back into the oven, and after roasting for 10 minutes, reduce the heat to 350 degrees.

Roast, covered, for about 3½ hours, including the time taken for the roast to brown. Check every 30 minutes to see if more tomato juice and water are needed to keep the vegetables from burning, and to baste the roast. It will probably take the entire can of tomato juice and between 1 and 2 cups of water.

When the meat near the back of the ribs can be pierced easily with a long-pronged fork, the roast is done. Remove it to a heated platter and keep warm. Skim as much fat as possible from the pan juices. Pour them through a strainer into a large saucepan, discarding the parsley but rubbing through the cooked carrots, onion, and garlic. Skim again. Adjust the seasoning, and if the gravy is too thick (which it should not be), thin with a little water. Simmer to reheat. Remove the thread and carve the breast of veal, cutting slices between the ribs to include the stuffing.

Arrange on a heated platter. Serve the gravy on the side in a heated sauceboat.

Yield: 8 to 10 generous servings

Note: If you use only half a breast of veal, obviously you will divide all other ingredients in half, including stuffing.

Variations: 1. If you would like to use two stuffings, make 2 cups of each, stuffing half the pocket with one, then the other half with the second. Begin to carve by cutting the breast in half where the stuffings meet so each guest can have a slice of each half.

2. Although sour cream in the gravy is not traditional, it does add a mellowing touch. To add it, prepare the gravy as described, and when it is very hot beat in the sour cream, which has been brought to room temperature, allowing about 2 teaspoonfuls per cup of gravy. Heat but do not boil.

Veal Goulash

3 pounds boneless shoulder of veal, well trimmed and cut in 1½-inch cubes

2 tablespoons butter, schmaltz (rendered chicken fat, page 7), or margarine

2 medium onions, peeled and coarsely chopped

1½ teaspoons salt, or to taste

½ teaspoon black pepper, or to taste

1½ tablespoons sweet paprika

1 large green pepper, seeded and diced

1 teaspoon caraway seeds, lightly crushed

Pinch of thyme

1 large clove garlic, peeled and sliced in half lengthwise

1 to 2 tablespoons distilled white vinegar, as needed

1 cup tomato juice or liquid from canned tomatoes, or 1 teaspoon tomato paste dissolved in 1 cup water

1 to 2 cups water, as needed

Remove the meat from refrigerator 30 minutes before you begin to cook it. Heat the fat in a heavy 2½- to 3-quart Dutch oven and in it slowly sauté the onion until soft and bright yellow. Do not let it brown. Stir in the salt, pepper, and paprika and sauté for a second or two, or until the paprika loses its raw smell. Add the meat and turn through the spice mixture. Cover and braise over low heat for about 10 minutes, stirring once or twice. Add the green pepper, caraway seeds, thyme, garlic, 1 tablespoon vinegar, and whichever tomato liquid you are using. Add enough water to make a depth of 1½ inches. Cover, bring to a boil, reduce the heat, and simmer gently but steadily for about 2 hours, or until the meat is very tender but not falling apart. Add more vinegar if the sauce needs sharpening, and add water during the cooking if needed to prevent scorching and to maintain the original level. If the sauce is too thin, reduce by boiling, uncovered, for 3 or 4 minutes.

Skim the grease from the surface, adjust the seasoning, and reheat. This dish improves in flavor if made a day before it is to be served, in which case remove the fat from the top after it has coagulated in the refrigerator.

Serve with noodles (page 82), pinched dumplings (page 84), or boiled potatoes.

Yield: 6 to 8 servings

Variations: 1. Although veal was much preferred at home, my mother sometimes used beef for this. The recipe is as above.

2. My own addition to this recipe is ⅔ cup of sour cream, beaten with a fork until thin and allowed to stand until it reaches room temperature; it is then stirred into the goulash sauce. If you want to do this in advance and then be able to reheat without having the cream coagulate, blend ½ teaspoon of flour into the cream before stirring it into the goulash sauce.

Braised Shoulder of Veal

1 boneless rolled shoulder of veal
      (4 pounds), well tied
2 cloves garlic, peeled
      Salt and black pepper
2 tablespoons sweet butter,
      margarine, or corn oil

1 small carrot, scraped and coarsely
      chopped
1 medium onion, peeled and coarsely
      chopped
2 teaspoons sweet paprika
2 sprigs parsley
1 cup water, or as needed

Take the veal out of the refrigerator 30 minutes before cooking. Cut 1 clove of garlic into thin slivers and push the slivers into the center of the veal through the openings at the ends. Sprinkle lightly on all sides with salt and pepper.

Heat the fat in a 2½- to 3-quart Dutch oven, preferably oval, and slowly brown the veal on all sides. This should take about 15 minutes. Remove and set aside. Add the carrots and onion to the hot fat and sauté slowly until the onion turns light golden brown. Stir in the paprika and sauté for a minute or two until it loses its raw smell.

Return the meat to the pot, setting it over the sautéed vegetables. Add the parsley sprigs and the remaining garlic clove and 1 cup of water, or as needed to make a depth of 1 inch. Cover and simmer slowly but steadily for about 2½ hours, adding more water as needed and turning the veal several times.

When thoroughly tender, remove the veal and keep warm. Skim the fat from the pan juices. Discard the parsley. Strain the juices, rubbing the carrots, onion, and garlic through the sieve into the sauce. Reheat and adjust the seasoning. Cut the string off the meat, slice, and serve, with the pan juices in the heated sauceboat.

Yield: 6 to 8 servings

Sweetbreads

We considered these mild, tender morsels to be the ultimate special-occasion food, either sautéed or, even better, combined with mushrooms and green peas in a savory sauce and heaped in crisp, buttery puff-pastry patty shells.

Sweetbreads are bought in pairs that may range in weight from ¾ pound to 1½ pounds, depending on their size. Calves' sweetbreads are the smaller, more tender and more delicate, but are very hard to come by. Beef sweetbreads are heavier and must be cooked slowly to avoid toughness; and they require greater weight to be flattened. It is necessary to flatten sweetbreads when frying, broiling, or sautéing; but this need not be done if they are to be cut in small chunks to be served in sauce. They are flattened so they will cook evenly. Before they are fried, sautéed, sauced, or whatever, sweetbreads require the following basic treatment:

Wash them under running cold water, then soak in a large bowl of ice water for 1 hour, or until they look very white and all traces of blood have disappeared. Place in a potful of fresh water to cover, along with a stalk of celery that has a few of its leaves, 2 or 3 slices of onion, 5 or 6 peppercorns, a sprig or two of parsley, and 1 tablespoon of lemon juice. These quantities are for preparing two pairs of sweetbreads. Bring to a boil, reduce the heat, and simmer very gently for about 20 minutes, or until the sweetbreads look solid and completely cooked. Drain, reserving the cooking liquid if needed, as for the recipe on page 181. Rinse the sweetbreads under cold water to cool, then gently pull off all membranes and trim out tubes, clumps of white fat, and tissue. Lay the sweetbreads in a single layer in a glass or ceramic pie plate or dish.

Cover with a layer of waxed paper, then fit another dish or pan inside the first so it can be pressed down on the sweetbreads. Place weights evenly over the top plate. Heavy cans or an old flatiron make efficient weights. Place in the refrigerator for at least 7 hours, and preferably 24, before cooking. Turn the sweetbreads over once halfway through the flattening process. Be sure the weights are distributed to the edge of the plate or the sweetbreads around the rim will remain lumpy.

Sautéed Sweetbreads

It is customary in Jewish homes and restaurants to broil sweetbreads, but my mother always felt, correctly I think, that this method tended to make them too dry and tough. She preferred the sautéed version below.

2 pairs of calves' sweetbreads,
    parboiled and flattened as
    described above
Salt and black pepper
Flour, for dredging

Sweet butter or corn oil, or a
    combination of both, for
    frying
2 to 4 slices buttered toast

Garnishes: lemon wedges and crisp
    bacon slices

Remove the parboiled, flattened sweetbreads from the refrigerator 30 minutes to 1 hour before you intend to sauté them. Pat gently on both sides with a paper towel to remove some, but not all, of the moisture on them. Sprinkle the sweetbreads on both sides with a little salt and black pepper. Dredge lightly on all sides in flour.

Heat enough butter to form a ¼-inch film on the bottom of a large, heavy skillet. A little corn oil can be added to prevent the butter from burning, but if you are careful this should not be necessary. When the fat is hot, add the sweetbreads. Sauté over moderate heat until the first sides are medium golden brown. Turn and brown the second sides. If the heat is adjusted properly, the insides of the sweetbreads will be piping hot by the time both sides are golden brown. The total sautéing time should be about 15 minutes.

Serve the sweetbreads on hot buttered toast, allowing half a pair as a first course or a whole pair as a main course. Lemon wedges and slices of bacon are perfect garnishes.

Yield: 2 to 4 servings

Note: If you can get only beef sweetbreads, they will need a little longer time to sauté, as they are heavier; and because they are larger you will probably get 3 appetizer portions to a pair.

Sweetbreads and Mushrooms in Patty Shells

1 pair sweetbreads (about 1 to 1½
   pounds)
  Stock in which the sweetbreads
   were poached
3 tablespoons sweet butter
1 tablespoon finely minced onion
10 medium mushrooms, cleaned and
   sliced

2 tablespoons flour
½ cup fresh green peas
  Salt, white pepper, and nutmeg
   to taste
2 to 3 tablespoons heavy sweet
   cream
4 puff-pastry patty shells,
   homemade or purchased

Soak, cook, and trim the sweetbreads as described in the recipe for basic preparation on page 179, but do not press. Instead, cut into fork-sized dice; you should have about 2 cups. Remove the vegetables from the liquid in which the sweetbreads were poached and boil rapidly to reduce to about 2 cups.

Heat 2 tablespoons butter in a saucepan, and when hot add the onion. When it just begins to soften, stir in the mushroom slices and sauté until they begin to turn golden around the edges. Add the sweetbreads and sauté quickly for a minute or two. Add the remaining tablespoon butter, and when melted stir in the flour gently, using a wooden spatula. Sauté until the flour is absorbed and takes on a pale golden-brown color, about 3 minutes.

Pour in 1½ cups hot stock, stir gently, and simmer to make a smooth sauce. Add the peas. If the sauce is too thick to simmer without scorching, add a little more reduced stock. Simmer until the peas are tender, about 7 minutes. Adjust the seasoning, stir in the cream, and heat thoroughly but do not boil. Check the seasoning again.

While the sweetbreads are cooking, heat the patty shells in the oven. Divide the sweetbread mixture between the shells, letting some sauce and filling overflow. Cap with the tops of the patty shells and serve at once.

Yield: 4 appetizer or 2 main-course servings

Variation: A tablespoonful of sherry can be added with the stock, before the peas cook.

Carnatzlach

[Rumanian Ground Beef Sausages]

These peppery, garlic-scented broiled beef "sausages," were much like the ground lamb kebabs one comes across in the Middle East. My grandmother would broil and serve these on a bed of rice with cucumber and onion salad or cold sauerkraut on the side. I like to sprinkle them with chopped onion or scallion. "Carnatzlach" is the Yiddish name for what Rumanians call *mititei*.

2 pounds ground lean beef chuck	1 teaspoon black pepper
3 cloves garlic, crushed in a press	½ teaspoon allspice
1 teaspoon salt	½ cup cold club soda, or as needed

Combine all the ingredients except the soda and mix well, kneading the mixture with your hands so it becomes dense and compact. Add soda gradually, kneading between additions until the dough is smooth, fine, and almost elastic. Wet the palms of your hands and roll portions of the mixture into sausagelike cylinders, each about ¾ to 1 inch thick and 3½ to 4 inches long.

Arrange in a single layer on a platter and cover with waxed paper or foil. Chill for at least 5 hours, but preferably 24, to develop the flavor fully.

Let stand at room temperature for 1 hour before cooking. Broil for about 10 minutes, turning frequently so all sides brown. Turn with tongs or a wooden spatula so the sausages do not break. These are also good when charcoal broiled.

Yield: 6 servings

16

Sour Pickles

The kosher garlic dill pickles I remember with the greatest longing, and whose equals I have searched for in vain, were those made by my grandmother, kept in big wooden barrels (when the family was large and close to home) or in smaller crocks or jars (as the family dispersed).

Anytime I sniff that pungent perfume of kosher pickles with its fresh-air scents of dill and cucumber spiced with the aroma of the briny pickling fluid, I remember the front porch of the upper part of the two-family house in which she lived. One barrel held the much adored pickles, another was filled with small, hard, deep-green pickled tomatoes, and the third held translucent, straw-colored fresh sauerkraut. The barrels were concealed from view, if not from our noses, by an old-fashioned porch glider.

Usually when I visited my grandmother, so did several of my cousins, and four or five of us would cram onto that glider and begin rocking back and forth, ever more vigorously, bumping into the barrels until the boards that covered them would jump up, sending forth fragrant whiffs of the pickling wonders within.

Admonished by parents and grandparents not to spoil our appetites with pickles (how could grownups not know that pickles did not jade appetites but, rather, piqued them?), we at first resisted the odoriferous blandishments. Then carefully, stealthily, we knelt against the back of the glider and dipped in. Oh the ecstasy, as teeth snapped through firm but tender skin to the cool, spicy interior that slowly, juicily released its counterpointed flavors of hot peppers, garlic, dill, the piny bay leaves and exotic mustard seeds and the faintly winy-cidery tang of the pickling liquid made yeasty with a crust of sour rye bread.

Then we dipped in again—after all, who would miss six or eight pickles, with such a large supply? (My mother once said with her usual flair for hyperbole that each barrel held an acre of pickles.) In that case, we asked, who would miss twelve or sixteen or even twenty, if five of us gave in to temptation with a vengeance?

Summer pickles made with dill gone to seed were the best, but winter pickles, standing out in the cold, were snappier.

The dark green pickles, lighter celadon-green tomatoes, sweet red peppers or round, pickled hot red cherry peppers, and the pale fresh, raw sauerkraut, all heaped in big cut-crystal bowls, replaced salad at certain Sunday dinners in winter. They lent a particularly sharp and clarifying accent to main courses such as potted beef brisket with its onion, paprika, garlic, and ginger-touched gravy and the crisp, oniony potato pancakes and homemade applesauce served with it. Or to pickled tongue served with boiled potatoes, or to the dish we called "chicken fricassee," paprikash minus sour cream, garnished with tiny dumplings of ground beef and chicken giblets, all to be piled over grainy kasha or baked egg barley.

Pickles were our favorite summer snacks after broiling days at the Brooklyn beaches. Parched by sun and salt-sea swimming, a group of us bought pickles, as sour as could be had, and chipped in for a loaf of caraway-flecked sour rye bread, and ate bread and pickles alternately as we walked home.

As with so many other things, they don't make pickles or pickled tomatoes the way they used to. First of all, the ancient wooden barrels that imparted their own mellow, flavorful patina to the vegetables pickled therein have given way to plastic, which with luck imparts no flavor at all.

It has also become all too common to add alum to pickles to give them a false, too-brittle crispness. As for tomatoes, it is more difficult each year to find perfect hard green specimens picked before they have had a chance to ripen at all, for even the slightest tinge of pink results in what most devotees consider a "rotten" pickled tomato.

For the record, my preference was, and still is, for the sourest of sour pickles. New pickles, still closer to cucumbers, may be taken from the brine after two or three days, and half-sours also have their fans. But to me, unless a cucumber has turned a glassy, olive-green color, and unless its pungency brings tears to the eye at first bite, it is not fit to be called a pickle.

17

Vegetables, Salads, and Pickles

Oddly enough, given his occupation, my father hated most vegetables, and when they were being served he would say in Yiddish to my mother, "Nicht keine gruner"—as though we children would not realize after so many repetitions that he was saying, "No greens."

In spite of the family knowledge of an unusually wide variety of vegetables, my mother did a typically poor job of cooking them. Typically, in this case, means typical of Jewish cooks of that generation, who generally overcooked vegetables to extinction. There were, however, a number of more complicated and traditional vegetable dishes she did very well, and which we all looked forward to.

For other vegetable recipes besides the ones in this chapter see the following: mushrooms and onions on toast (page 37), creamed mushrooms on toast (page 36), black radish and onion salad (page 35), roasted peppers with garlic (page 41), grilled red peppers (page 42), eggplant caviar (page 33), vegetable sandwich (page 45), stuffed peppers in sweet and sour tomato sauce (page 169), and glazed sweet and sour stuffed cabbage (page 171).

Potato salad and all potato recipes are in the following chapter.

Baked Acorn Squash

Acorn squash are at their best in fall and winter. Prepared this way, they are especially good with lamb and pork dishes and with baked ham steak.

2 medium acorn squash   3 tablespoons sweet butter
   Salt, black pepper, and nutmeg

Preheat the oven to 350 degrees.

Cut each squash in half vertically. Scrape out the seeds from the center cavities. Being careful not to cut too deeply into the squash, trim off any slight bulge from the bottom of each half so the squash will sit level in a baking pan.

Set the squash halves in the baking pan without having them touch one another. Sprinkle the cavities and cut edges with a little salt, pepper, and nutmeg. Divide the butter among the four halves, placing it in the cavities.

Pour a 1-inch depth of boiling water into the pan around the squash. Bake in the preheated oven for 30 to 40 minutes, basting the cut edges of the squash with melted butter from the cavity several times. Add more boiling water to the pan if necessary. The squash is done when the flesh is tender all the way to the shell.

Remove from the hot water carefully so as not to spill the melted butter. Serve at once.

Yield: 2 to 4 servings

String Beans Lyonnaise

1 pound young, tender string beans   1 large onion, peeled, sliced, and
4 tablespoons sweet butter, or as   separated into rings
   needed   Salt and black pepper to taste

Wash the string beans. They may be cut into 1½- to 2-inch lengths or left whole, depending on their size and your preference. Boil in salted water until tender but slightly firm; this will take about 10 minutes. Drain thoroughly and keep warm.

Melt the butter in a medium-sized skillet, and when it is hot stir in the onion rings. Sauté *very* slowly, stirring frequently, until they melt to softness and are bright yellow; this will take about 20 minutes. Do not let them brown. Add more butter if needed during the sautéing.

Stir the onions and their butter into the string beans. Adjust the seasoning, reheat together for a few minutes, and serve immediately.

Yield: 4 to 6 servings

Sweet and Sour String Beans

This was usually served with the Friday night roast chicken, or with pot roast and potato pancakes, or with tongue. It is also a good accompaniment to baked ham.

1 **pound young, tender string beans**	1 to 2 **tablespoons brown sugar, or to taste**
3 **cups water**	2 **tablespoons sweet butter**
1 to 2 **tablespoons lemon juice, or to taste**	1½ **tablespoons flour**
	2 **cloves (optional)**
	Black pepper to taste

Wash the string beans and cut into 1½-inch lengths. Boil in the water along with 1 scant teaspoon salt and 1 tablespoon each lemon juice and brown sugar. Cook for about 12 minutes, or until the beans are tender but not too soft. Drain off the cooking liquid; reserve and keep hot.

Heat the butter in a small saucepan, and when it is hot and bubbling, stir in the flour. Cook over low heat, stirring frequently, until the flour has turned a mellow cocoa brown. Pour in, all at once, 1½ cups of the hot, reserved cooking liquid from the beans. Add the cloves and stir and simmer until smooth. If the mixture becomes too thick, add a little more of the cooking liquid.

Turn the sauce into the beans. Adjust the seasoning with additional lemon juice and sugar until there is a good flavor balance, slightly more sour then sweet. Add salt and pepper. Simmer together for 10 minutes, then serve immediately.

Yield: 4 to 6 servings

Sweet and Sour Cabbage

This was a particular favorite with boiled smoked beef tongue (page 164) or with pot-roasted brisket of beef and potato pancakes (pages 163 and 215). The grated sour apple is my own addition, one of the few innovations my mother approved.

2 pounds green cabbage
3 cups boiling water
   Salt
1 tablespoon brown sugar, or to taste
2 tablespoons lemon juice, or to taste
2 tablespoons sweet butter

1½ tablespoons flour
1 sour apple, peeled and grated
   (optional)
½ cup seedless black raisins, soaked
   in warm water for 15 minutes
White pepper to taste

Shred the cabbage fine, discarding the tough outer leaves and thick ribs. Add to the boiling water, along with 1 teaspoon salt and 1 tablespoon each brown sugar and lemon juice. Cook until the cabbage is tender but not too soft, about 15 minutes. Drain, reserving the cooking liquid and keeping it hot.

Melt the butter in a saucepan, and when it is hot and bubbling, stir in the flour. Cook over low heat, stirring frequently, until the flour is a mellow cocoa-brown color. Pour in, all at once 2 cups of the reserved cooking liquid and stir and simmer until smooth.

Turn the sauce into the cooked cabbage. Stir in the grated apple, add the raisins, and bring to a simmer. Add more lemon juice and brown sugar as needed to achieve a good flavor balance, slightly more sour than sweet. Add salt and pepper to taste and simmer for 15 minutes. This is one vegetable dish that is very good when reheated on the following day.

Yield: 4 to 6 servings

Krautfleckerel

[Sautéed Cabbage with Noodles]

If ever I wanted to get a rise out of my mother, all I had to do was suggest that this dish should be made with onions, an idea she regarded as a heresy. I sometimes include them, for variety's sake. This dish also changes character with the fat used for the sautéing. It is much lighter and blander made with butter, a little greasier but richly flavorful with schmaltz, the rendered chicken fat. It is really meant as a light main course, rather than a side dish. An appetizer of cold jellied pickled fish (page 113) or pickled herring (page 25) would be suitable before it, and some coffee cake or a fruit pie would be a good finish.

Some prefer this dish with long, wide noodles, others with noodle squares, still others made with macaroni bowties (*farfalle*). Again, I vary it with my mood.

2 pounds green cabbage
Kosher (coarse) salt
6 to 8 tablespoons sweet butter or
schmaltz (rendered chicken
fat, page 7), as needed

1 large onion, peeled and
coarsely chopped (optional)
8 ounces noodles, noodle
squares, or bowties
Salt and white pepper to taste
Pinch of sugar, if needed

Shred the cabbage fine, trimming off and discarding the toughest ribs and wilted outer leaves. Place in a colander, sprinkle with coarse salt, and let stand at room temperature for 30 minutes, until the cabbage has wilted and its liquid has drained off. Squeeze out as much liquid as possible from the cabbage.

Heat 6 tablespoons fat in a large skillet, and when it is hot and bubbling, add the onion. Sauté until it begins to soften but is not brown. Stir in the cabbage and sauté over low heat, stirring frequently until lightly browned. This should take about 25 minutes. Add fat if needed.

While the cabbage is sautéing, cook the noodles or bowties in rapidly boiling salted water until tender, but do not let them get too soft, as they will cook longer when added to the cabbage. Drain well and keep warm.

When the cabbage has begun to brown, stir in the cooked noodles. Add salt and pepper to taste, and a tiny pinch of sugar only if the cabbage is acidic. Cover loosely and let the mixture braise over very low heat for about 10 minutes. Add fat if needed. Adjust the seasoning and serve at once. This dish cannot wait to be served, as the noodles will become too soft and the cabbage will develop an unpleasantly strong flavor.

Yield: 4 main-course servings

Corn, On and Off the Cob

As it is in most American families, summer sweet corn was a great favorite. We began eating it in June, when the pale-yellow local varieties came into the markets, then went on to the golden bantam of midsummer and then to the country gentleman, which we all preferred. This last type, rarely seen in markets these days, came in August and was distinguished by irregular rows of ivory-white teeth, and when we went to the Catskills for the summer, we all treasured a local purple bantam corn that looked as though it had been smeared with indelible ink. It was wonderfully sweet and juicy.

Corn was perhaps the only vegetable my mother did not overcook. She cooked it in boiling salted water, always with some of the inner, tender green leaves of the husks, which she said made it sweeter. My father insisted that she cut his kernels off the cob, and occasionally she provided that luxurious touch for all of us. The milky, freshly cut kernels would be served in a small, warmed bowl—really a fruit saucer—with lots of butter, salt, and white pepper. Leftover ears would be saved for corn fritters for the following morning's breakfast or to accompany a dinner of fried fish or fried chicken.

Corn and Lima Bean Succotash

This is something we had only when both corn and lima beans were fresh.

2 cups shelled raw lima beans (about
     1½ pounds in pods)
2 cups cooked corn kernels (about 4
     ears of corn)
3 tablespoons sweet butter

Salt and black pepper to taste
1 tablespoon finely minced, well-
     drained pimento (optional but
     festive)

Cook the lima beans in boiling salted water until tender but firm (about 7 minutes). Drain well. Combine the lima beans and cooked corn kernels with the butter, salt, and pepper. Heat over a low flame, loosely covered, until the vegetables are hot and permeated with butter. Add a few drops of water if the mixture seems too dry, and a little more butter if needed. Toss in the pimento and heat thoroughly.

Yield: 4 to 6 servings

Fried Eggplant

Eggplant was considered a very unusual vegetable in our neighborhood, one rarely found in the vegetable markets. Usually we had it only when my father brought some home, and my mother prepared it either the following way or as eggplant caviar (page 33). The version below makes an interesting first course, or a side dish with broiled lamb chops or broiled chicken. It is a perfect addition to an assorted vegetable plate.

1 medium dark, unblemished
   eggplant
   Kosher (coarse) salt
1 cup flour, mixed with ½ teaspoon
   white pepper, or as needed
1 jumbo egg, beaten with 1½
   tablespoons lemon juice, or as
   needed

1 cup fine bread crumbs, mixed with
   ½ teaspoon crumbled leaf thyme,
   or as needed
6 tablespoons sweet butter, or as
   needed
¼ cup corn or olive oil
   Salt to taste
   Lemon wedges, for garnish

Using a stainless-steel knife, peel the eggplant and cut into round, ½-inch-thick slices. You will have between 6 and 8 slices. Place in a colander and sprinkle liberally with coarse salt. Let stand for 45 minutes so the bitter juices can drain off. Using a paper towel, wipe each eggplant slice dry on both sides.

Place the flour blended with the pepper on a sheet of waxed paper. Have the beaten egg and lemon juice in a wide bowl. Have the crumbs mixed with crumbled thyme on another sheet of waxed paper.

Lightly dredge each eggplant slice on both sides with the flour mixture, tapping off excess. Dip both sides into the beaten egg, letting excess drip off. Dredge each slice generously on both sides with bread crumbs. Mix additional flour, eggs, or crumbs if needed.

Place the breaded eggplant slices on a rack over a platter or pan and let dry for 10 minutes.

Heat the butter with the oil in a large skillet. The butter will enhance the flavor of the eggplant, and the oil will keep the butter from burning. Add the eggplant and fry slowly until golden brown on the first side. Turn and slowly brown the second side. The total frying time should be about 15 minutes, after which the inside should be thoroughly cooked but not mushy and the outside should be crisp and a medium golden brown. Drain the slices on paper towels. Sprinkle with salt and serve garnished with lemon wedges.

Yield: 6 to 8 slices; 3 to 4 servings

Mushroom Schnitzels

Delicious with broiled steak and roast beef or lamb, these savory cutlets are also good as appetizers. Vegetarians will find them especially satisfying. Small mushrooms are fine for this dish; it is unnecessary to pay premium prices for the larger sizes. Just be sure they are fresh, firm, and relatively clean.

1½ pounds firm, clean white
    mushrooms
1 medium onion, peeled and finely
    chopped
4 tablespoons sweet butter plus
    enough for frying

1 tablespoon finely minced fresh
    parsley
2 extra-large eggs, lightly beaten
5 to 6 tablespoons matzoh meal
    Salt, white pepper, and nutmeg
    Lemon wedges, for garnish
    (optional)

If the mushrooms are sandy, wash them quickly under cold running water and carefully wipe each one dry. If they are clean, merely wipe them with a damp towel. Trim off the bottom of the stem end and discard. Chop the mushrooms until fine.

Sauté the onion in 4 tablespoons butter until it just begins to soften. Stir in the chopped mushrooms and sauté over a moderate flame, stirring frequently until the mixture is thoroughly dry and just beginning to turn the faintest golden brown in color. Turn into a mixing bowl. Add the parsley and stir in the beaten eggs. Add the matzoh meal gradually until the mixture is thick enough to drop from a spoon in a soft mass. There should be some liquid still visible. Season with salt, pepper, and nutmeg.

Heat enough butter in a large skillet to make a ¼-inch depth of melted butter in the pan. When the butter is hot and bubbling, drop in the mushroom mixture, 1 heaping tablespoonful at a time. Fry slowly until the first side is golden brown. Turn with a wide spatula and slowly brown the second side. Total frying time should be about 10 minutes per batch. Do not overcrowd the pan with cutlets; they can be close together but not touching. Drain fried cutlets on paper towels and keep warm until all are fried. Serve with lemon wedges.

Yield: About 16 schnitzels; 6 to 8 servings as appetizer or side dish

Sauerkraut

Sometimes cooked with beef as described on page 161, sauerkraut was also prepared by itself to be served with steamed knackwursts, or with boiled smoked tongue (page 164). Its flavor improves with age, so prepare it a day or two before you want to serve it. Fresh sauerkraut from a barrel is the best to use, as it is the firmest, freshest, and least acidic. Canned is the next best substitute, but the type sold in sealed plastic packets is almost invariably too soft and sour.

2 pounds fresh sauerkraut	2 tablespoons schmaltz (rendered
1 teaspoon salt	chicken fat, page 7), sweet
Black pepper to taste	butter or margarine
1 tablespoon caraway seeds	1 small onion, peeled and finely
(optional)	minced
Water to barely cover	2 tablespoons all-purpose flour

Place the sauerkraut in a strainer and let cold water run through it until it is no longer too acidic, but do not wash out all of its pungency. How much washing it will need will depend upon the original state of the sauerkraut. Pick up handfuls of the sauerkraut and squeeze out as much water as possible, then pull apart to fluff out and separate the strands. Place in a 2-quart enameled pot. Add the salt, pepper, caraway seeds, and enough water to come just below the top of the sauerkraut. Cover, bring to a boil, reduce the heat, and simmer gently for about 1 hour, stirring occasionally to prevent scorching at the bottom and adding a little water if the top becomes dry.

Heat the fat in a small saucepan and in it sauté the minced onion until it is a deep golden brown, but do not let it blacken. Sprinkle in the flour and sauté slowly, stirring several times, until the flour is a mellow cocoa color.

Turn the roux (einbrenne) into the simmering sauerkraut and stir gently with a wooden spoon while the liquid simmers, so the roux blends into the sauce. Simmer for 30 minutes to 1 hour, or until the sauerkraut is tender but not overly soft and most of the liquid has been absorbed. If it becomes dry before it is tender, add a little more water.

Yield: 4 to 6 servings

Variation: To serve with frankfurters or knackwursts, parboil the wursts for 5 minutes, then bury in the sauerkraut and continue cooking for 15 minutes. Serve with boiled potatoes.

Creamed Onions

Because this appeared on Thanksgiving, it stands out as a special reminder of that day and is a dish I still love. The smaller the onions the better, but most important of all is that they be uniform.

1 pound small onions, preferably pearl onions	Salt, if needed
3 cups rapidly boiling salted water	Pinch each of mace and cayenne pepper
2 tablespoons sweet butter	1 tablespoon finely minced fresh parsley
2 tablespoons flour	
½ cup heavy sweet cream, scalded and hot	

Peel the onions carefully so as not to remove too much of their insides, but be sure to remove all the papery white layers that will toughen in cooking.

Cook until tender in rapidly boiling salted water. Pearl onions will be done in about 8 minutes; larger sizes will take a little longer. They should be tender but firm. Drain, reserving the cooking liquid.

Melt the butter in a saucepan, and when it is hot and bubbling, stir in the flour. Sauté, stirring, for 3 or 4 minutes without letting the flour take on color. Add, all at once, ½ cup of hot onion liquid and the hot, scalded cream. Whisk until smooth, adding salt if needed and a tiny pinch each of mace and cayenne pepper. Pour over the onions and simmer for 10 minutes. Adjust the seasoning and stir in the parsley. Serve at once.

Yield: 4 servings

Spinach

I always had trouble understanding why spinach was considered a punishment and why only Popeye's inducement of strength could convince kids to eat it. Probably I liked it because my mother always cooked it with either a piece of onion or a clove of garlic, either of which would counteract that characteristic, unpleasant acid flavor. One of my favorite lunches when I came home from school was something we called a "spinach Mary Ann." It was chopped buttered spinach shaped in some sort of small, individual-size double ring mold that made it possible to have a ring of spinach set into a ring of rice, just how I can no longer remember. But I do know that a poached egg went into the center of the whole thing. Spinach, chopped or creamed and topped with poached eggs, was another popular lunch or light supper, and sometimes my mother would turn the creamed spinach into a small baking dish and baked the egg in it. All variations of eggs in spinach were known around our house as "eggs in nest."

Chopped Spinach

2 pounds fresh leaf spinach
½ teaspoon salt
1 large clove garlic, peeled, or 1
    small onion, peeled and thinly
    sliced

3 to 4 tablespoons sweet butter
Salt and white pepper
Pinch of nutmeg (optional)

If the spinach is in bunches, separate into leaves. Discard wilted or large, tough leaves, and the larger, tougher stems. Wash the leaves in several changes of very cold water until absolutely free of all sand. Drain the spinach but do *not* shake off water. In any pot not made of iron or aluminum, which can change the flavor of spinach, put the garlic or onion slices, ½ teaspoon salt, and then the spinach, along with any water clinging to its leaves. Cover the pot, bring to a boil, reduce the heat, and simmer for 3 or 4 minutes. Turn the spinach over and simmer for another 3 minutes, or until tender. Drain thoroughly, pressing out as much moisture as possible. Chop fine. The garlic or onion slices may be picked out, but the final result tastes much better if they are chopped in right along with the spinach. Return to the pot, add the butter, and simmer over low heat until the butter has melted into the spinach and all liquid has evaporated. Season with salt, and pinch each of pepper and nutmeg, to taste. Serve as is, atop rice, or garnished with hard-cooked egg slices.

Yield: 3 to 4 servings

Variation: For a main course, top each portion with one or two poached eggs.

Creamed Spinach

Prepare chopped spinach as described in the preceding recipe, but after it is chopped do not add butter or reheat it. Prepare a cream sauce as directed on page 10 with 1½ tablespoons sweet butter, 1½ tablespoons flour, and ⅔ to ¾ cup hot, scalded half-and-half milk and cream. Simmer the sauce for 5 minutes, then turn into the spinach, which has been chopped with cooked onion or garlic. Season with salt, white pepper, and nutmeg. Simmer together very gently for about 5 minutes.

Spinach and Mashed Potatoes

This was a combination much beloved by my mother's father, who liked it so much he ate it as a main course, shunning whatever else my grandmother may have planned to serve with it. The best combination is chopped spinach and mashed baked potatoes mixed together with a big lump of sweet butter and plenty of salt and pepper. It could of course be prepared with mashed boiled potatoes, but the baked potatoes have a more interesting flavor. Creamed spinach is too liquid and starchy to be used this way.

Mashed Yellow Turnips (Rutabagas)

This very simple dish was one I disliked as a child and I love now. To prepare it, simply peel one large, round yellow turnip, being careful to keep flakes of wax off the peeled surface. Rinse and cut into ¼-inch cubes. Cook in rapidly boiling, well-salted water until the cubes are tender. This will take about 20 minutes. Drain thoroughly and mash with a potato masher.

Return to the pot and stir over low heat for 2 to 3 minutes so all water evaporates. Beat in a large lump of sweet butter and a little scalded cream or milk, as for mashed potatoes. Season with salt and pepper.

Yield: 4 to 6 servings

Variation: Those who find the flavor of the turnip unpleasantly strong will prefer this prepared with a half-and-half mixture of mashed potatoes.

Stewed Tomatoes with Rice

This can be prepared with canned tomatoes, but fresh are preferable, as it is almost impossible to get rid of the overpowering "canned" flavor. The best tomatoes to use for it are the ripe Italian plum tomatoes that are in season from mid- to late summer, but any rich, dark red tomatoes will do. Do not attempt to make this of the impostors known as "hard-ripe tomatoes" or of any grown in a greenhouse.

My mother felt that peeling the tomatoes meant a loss of flavor, but I find the skins so unpleasant that I remove them before cooking. Although many recipes for stewed tomatoes call for a breadcrumb thickening, my mother preferred rice. She also felt onions added enough sweetening to make sugar unnecessary. This dish is especially good with fried fish (page 121) or codfish cakes (page 123).

3 pounds red, ripe tomatoes
1 large onion, peeled and coarsely
   chopped
5 tablespoons sweet butter
   Salt and black pepper to taste

½ cup long-grain converted rice,
   parboiled for 10 minutes and
   drained
   Pinch of sugar, if needed
   Minced fresh parsley, for garnish

Tomatoes have the best flavor if they are peeled after being held over an open flame with a long handled fork until the skins char off. However, that becomes tedious when so large a number are being prepared. It is easier therefore to skin them after blanching them for 1 minute in boiling water. Drain off the water and peel the tomatoes. Cut out the stem end and cut the tomatoes in large chunks—in halves or quarters, if you are using plum tomatoes. Catch juices and reserve with the tomatoes.

Sauté the onion in the butter very slowly until it is soft and yellow; do not let it brown. Add the tomato pieces and turn through the onion and butter. Sprinkle with a little salt and pepper, then cover and simmer for 5 minutes. Check to see if there is enough liquid in the pot to simmer; if not, add a little hot water. Cook slowly for about 10 minutes longer, at which time the liquid should come between one-third and one-half of the way up the tomatoes.

Add the parboiled rice and continue cooking until the rice is tender, about 10 minutes longer, adding a little water if the mixture becomes dry.

(*continued*)

Adjust the seasoning, adding a pinch of sugar if needed, and serve in small, deep plates, topping each portion with minced parsley.

Yield: 6 servings

Variation: Dill can be substituted for parsley. A dash of celery salt or some basil (1 leaf if fresh, a tiny pinch if dried) can be added during cooking. If basil is used, garnish with parsley, not dill.

Tzimmes of Kohlrabi, Carrots, and Peas

Figuratively, a tzimmes is a big, complicated fuss; literally, it is a dish that combines many different ingredients. The classic Jewish tzimmes is sweet, based on prunes and other dried fruit, sweet potatoes, carrots, and sometimes brisket. My mother never made this type of tzimmes, but used the term to describe a combination of kohlrabi, carrots, and peas. The first two vegetables were always present, but string beans might replace peas when the latter were unavailable. My family's version is very close to the mixed vegetable combination the Germans called *Leipziger Allerlei.*

The vegetables may be cooked together, but they retain a little more of their individual flavor if cooked separately and then combined.

5 to 6 medium kohlrabi	Salted water to cover
4 medium carrots	3 tablespoons sweet butter
1½ cups shelled green peas (about 1½ pounds in pods) or ¼ pound string beans	2 tablespoons flour
	Salt and white pepper to taste
	Minced fresh parsley, for garnish

Trim the leaves and stems off the kohlrabi bulbs. The leaves may be washed and sliced and cooked with this mixture, but that is not typical. They may be reserved and cooked as a separate vegetable, much as spinach or cabbage is prepared. Peel the green outer covering off the bulbs, making sure you remove all of the stringy, woody outer coating until you reach the soft, white, smooth-textured inside. Cut the peeled bulbs into matchstick strips.

Scrape the carrots. If they are small, slice in ¼-inch rounds; if they are wide, cut in vertical halves or quarters and then slice. If using string beans, trim and cut into 1-inch lengths. Cook the kohlrabi, carrots, and shelled peas or beans separately, each in salted water, until tender but slightly firm. Drain off all liquids into a clean saucepan and keep hot. Combine the vegetables in a pot.

Melt the butter in a saucepan, and when hot and bubbling, stir in the flour. Cook slowly, stirring frequently, until the flour is a pale golden brown, just a little lighter than cocoa. Add, all at once, a cup of the combined hot vegetable cooking liquid and whisk over low heat until smooth. Season with salt and pepper and pour over the vegetables, turning them through the sauce gently. Simmer another 10 minutes, then remove from the heat and adjust the seasoning. If the sauce is too thick, thin with a little additional vegetable liquid. Serve sprinkled with parsley.

Yield: 4 servings

SALADS

Green salads were always a bone of contention at our house. My mother complained that each night she cut up salad and each night no one ate it. That was true, probably because most of the time, her concept of salad meant big wedges of iceberg lettuce and sliced or quartered tomatoes. If there was any dressing, it was Russian. We all hated the lettuce, which only occasionally was varied with romaine or Boston. But other vegetable salads and pickles, such as those that follow, were favorite side dishes.

Cole Slaw

As a rule I avoid cole slaw because I dislike the combination of raw cabbage and mayonnaise. But my mother's slaw is something else again, crunchy with carrots and green peppers, fragrant with onion, and dressed with oil and vinegar. It remains the best cole slaw I have ever had.

1 pound green cabbage, shredded	2 teaspoons salt
1 small onion, peeled and chopped	½ cup distilled white vinegar
2 young carrots, scraped and chopped	2 teaspoons sugar, or as needed
	¼ cup corn oil
1 small green pepper, seeded and chopped	2 teaspoons dill seeds
	White pepper to taste

Combine all the vegetables and chop together until fine and well mixed. Toss in the salt and let stand for 30 minutes. Pour off any liquid that accumulates in the bowl. Add the vinegar and toss well but lightly. Let stand for another 20 minutes, tossing once or twice. Drain off excess vinegar. Add the sugar, oil, dill seeds, and pepper and toss lightly but thoroughly. Chill for several hours or overnight. Adjust the seasoning and serve.

Yield: 4 to 6 servings

Cucumber Salad

The best cucumbers to use for this, or any other cucumber dish, as a matter of fact, are the small unwaxed Kirby cucumbers (also known as "Chicago dills") generally used for pickling, but also delicious raw. They are more compact than regular cucumbers and do not have such a large, watery seeded core. The long European greenhouse cucumbers are the best alternates.

4 or 5 Kirby cucumbers, 2 medium
        regular cucumbers, or 1 long
        greenhouse cucumber,
        peeled
        Kosher (coarse) salt
 1 medium onion
 ½ cup water, or as needed
	½ cup white distilled vinegar, or as
	        needed
	    White pepper
	    Pinch of sugar, if needed
	    Minced fresh parsley or dill, for
	        garnish (optional)

Peel the cucumbers, and if they have a large seed area, cut them in half vertically and with a teaspoon scoop out the seeds. If the seed area is small, leave whole. In either case, slice thin, place in a bowl, and sprinkle with about a tablespoonful of coarse salt, tossing lightly to mix cucumbers and salt. Nest another plate inside the first and weight the cucumbers down. Let stand in the refrigerator for 1 hour.

Pour off the accumulated liquid and taste the cucumbers. If very salty, rinse and drain. If not, leave them as they are.

Peel the onion, cut in half vertically, and then slice downward and separate into splinters of onion. Add to the cucumbers. Cover with a half-and-half mixture of cold water and vinegar. Add a dash of white pepper and a little sugar if the liquid is too sour. Let chill an hour or two. Stir in the parsley or dill before serving.

Yield: 4 to 6 servings

Greek Salad

Also known as "spring salad," this was served as a side dish, or mixed with pot cheese and sour cream as a summer main course. When served as a salad, tomatoes can be added, but they should be eliminated if sour cream is to be added. I also like the peppery addition of crisp watercress leaves. The basic ingredients, however, are red radishes, cucumbers, and scallions; even green peppers are optional. Kirby cucumbers are more solid than the usual variety, so use them if available. This salad requires no dressing.

1 bunch firm, young red radishes (about 10 to 12 radishes)	½ bunch watercress (optional)
2 small Kirby cucumbers or 1 medium regular cucumber	4 or 5 ripe Italian plum tomatoes or 1 medium regular tomato
6 to 8 scallions	1 large clove garlic
1 small green pepper (optional)	Pinch of kosher (coarse) salt
	Black pepper

Wash the radishes well and trim off leaves and roots. Slice in rounds. Leave slices whole if the radishes are small but cut the rounds in halves or quarters if radishes are large. Peel the cucumbers. Cut in half vertically and with a teaspoon scoop out the seeds and discard. Dice the flesh. Trim and wash the scallions and slice thin both white and tender green portions. Seed and chop the green pepper, if you use it. Wash and dry the watercress and pull the leaves off the stems; discard the stems. Cut the tomatoes in small chunks.

Cut the peeled garlic clove in half. Place a pinch of coarse salt in the salad bowl and rub the cut sides of the garlic in it, rubbing all over the bottom and sides of the bowl. Add the vegetables and black pepper to taste and toss together lightly but thoroughly. Serve at once, discarding the garlic halves as you come upon them.

Yield: About 4 servings

Charoses

[Passover Apple-Walnut Salad]

Representing the mortar that the ancient Hebrews used to build their temple, this aromatic salad of apples, walnuts, and wine is traditional at Passover, spread on pieces of matzohs and eaten along with sweet and bitter herbs. I occasionally get a longing for it midyear. It is good on toasted English muffins or with toasted stale pound cake, in both cases served at breakfast or with tea. I have tried to improve upon this by using something other than the sweet kosher-style Concord grape wine, but that is the authentic ingredient and nothing else makes this taste quite right.

3 medium apples (1 pound), preferably McIntosh or Northern Spy	¼ to ½ teaspoon powdered cinnamon
½ cup chopped walnuts	1½ tablespoons sugar, or to taste
¼ to ½ teaspoon powdered ginger	3 tablespoons red Concord grape wine

Peel, core, and chop the apples moderately coarse. Toss with the chopped walnuts and add the ginger, cinnamon, and sugar to taste. Stir in 2 tablespoons red wine and adjust the seasoning. This should ripen in the refrigerator for at least 6 hours before it is served and is even better if it stands for 24 hours. Before serving, stir in 1 additional tablespoon wine.

Yield: About 1½ cups

Pickled Beets

3 cups sliced, cooked beets, preferably home cooked but canned will do, cooking or canning liquid reserved	1 large onion Salt and sugar, as needed
	1 cup distilled white vinegar
	4 or 5 cloves

Home-cooked beets will have a better flavor and texture, but perfectly acceptable pickled beets can be made of the canned variety. If you cook your own, peel first and reserve the cooking liquid. Reserve the liquid also from canned beets.

Peel the onion and slice into thin rounds, which should then be separated into rings.

Using a wide-mouth, straight-sided crock or jar, or a narrow bowl, arrange in it alternate layers of beets and onion rings. Sprinkle a little salt and sugar over each onion layer.

Measure 1 cup of beet liquid; if you do not have that much, add water to make up that amount. Combine with the vinegar in a saucepan and bring to a boil with the cloves. Pour over the beets, with the cloves, tapping the jar several times so the liquid seeps into all layers and corners. Taste the liquid and adjust the seasoning, with salt and sugar as needed. When cool, cover the container and let stand in the refrigerator at least 24 hours before serving. Check the seasoning during pickling. The beets will develop more satisfying flavor after 48 hours.

Variation: Substitute 1 tablespoon caraway seeds for the cloves.

Kosher Garlic Dill Pickles

The following is a basic recipe that may be altered to suit varying tastes, and which should be adjusted slightly to the number of pickles being done in a particular size and shape of crock or jar. (I use a crock with a 5-quart capacity, which takes from 2½ to 3½ pounds of cucumbers, depending on size.) It is essential that the pickles be covered by the brine.

To accomplish this, the cucumbers to be pickled should be stood on end close together on the bottom of the crock, so they hold each other firmly in place. Even so, they may loosen and float to the top. To avoid that, place a plate or disk of wood directly in the brine, over the pickles, and weight them down, either with a clean stone or a 10-ounce glass two-thirds full of water. If it is necessary to skim the gray film off the brine's surface, replace the weight each time it is removed. The pickling receptacle should have a wide mouth so a salad or bread-and-butter plate, or similar sized disk of wood, can fit inside it. It should be made of ceramic, glass, or wood, not plastic or metal. Unwaxed Kirby cucumbers are the only type that will work for pickling.

Because of the yeast it contains the crust of rye bread will result in a mildly fermented brine, similar to the Russian and Polish kvass, and will give a subtle, mildly fermented flavor to the pickles.

In making these pickles it is important that you do not use mixed pickling spices, because the cinnamon, cloves, and other sweetly aromatic spices in them will detract from the pickles' flavor. Also, it is important that you do not used iodized salt in the process, as that will leave a bitter aftertaste; if you cannot get kosher (coarse) salt, use uniodized table salt, substituting about two-thirds of the amount called for. These are fresh brine pickles, and no vinegar should be used.

24 to 30 small, very firm Kirby cucumbers, free of bruises or brown spots	**3 bay leaves**
7 or 8 cloves garlic, unpeeled but lightly crushed	**12 to 14 springs dill, preferably with seed heads, well washed**
1 teaspoon coriander seeds	**1 teaspoon dried dill seeds, if the dill has no seed heads**
1 teaspoon mustard seeds	**Heel of sour rye bread with caraway seeds**
1 teaspoon black peppercorns	**3 quarts of water, or as needed**
4 or 5 small, dried hot red peppers, or ½ teaspoon crushed, dried hot red Italian peppers	**¾ cup kosher (coarse) salt, or as needed**

Thoroughly wash a wide-mouthed bean pot, crock, or glass jar. Carefully wash the cucumbers, rubbing gently with a sponge, a soft brush, or your hands to remove all traces of sand. Discard any with bruises. Stand the cucumbers on end around the sides and across the bottom of the crock or jar, so that they hold each other in place but not so tightly that they will crush each other. A second upright layer can be added if the jar is tall enough. To the crock add the garlic, all herbs and spices, and bread.

Mix 3 quarts of water with ¾ cup coarse salt and stir until the salt dissolves. Pour the salt water into the crock to completely cover the pickles. The brine should overflow so you can be sure no air pockets remain. If it does not, place the crock under the faucet and let water run in slowly until it does overflow. You may wash out a few spices in the process, but that will not be critical.

Place the jar on a stain-proof surface in a cool place, but not in the refrigerator. A temperature between 65 and 70 degrees is just right. Place a dish or wooden disk directly over the pickles, in the brine, and top with a weight as described on page 203. Cover the crock loosely with a dish towel or a double thickness of cheesecloth.

Check the pickles every 24 hours and remove any white or gray foam that has risen to the surface; this will prevent rotting. Shake the crock slightly to distribute spices and be sure to re-weight. Add salt or other seasonings if the brine seems bland. The pickles will be half sour in about 4 to 5 days, and very sour in about 10 days. When they have reached the degree of sourness you like, they can be stored in the refrigerator in tightly closed jars. Pour some strained brine into the jars to cover the pickles. They will keep for about 5 weeks, assuming they have not been eaten long before.

Yield: 24 to 30 pickles

Pickled Green Tomatoes

Small, hard, unripe green tomatoes can be prepared exactly as the cucumbers above. Place them in the crock, bottoms down. If the tomatoes are thick-skinned, it may be necessary to prick their surface in several places with a fine needle, so the solution will penetrate. It is very important that the tomatoes be small (about the size of Italian plum tomatoes), very hard, and dark bright green.

18

The Joys of Being
Sick in Bed

Even illness had its own special menu at our house.

It would all begin when my mother declared me officially sick—sick enough to stay home from school and, therefore, sick enough to stay in bed. Immediately the day took on a holiday air and I resigned myself to bedded-down luxury, helpless in the face of nature.

The illnesses I remember most were the head colds and grippes of winter, and my progress in recovering could be measured by the food my mother served, for she always had strong ideas on exactly what one should eat when. Miraculously, her instinct seemed infallible, and when I did not know what I wanted, she did.

Meals always appeared on pretty trays, set with colorful mats, the best china and silver, and, when possible, a flower. In the earliest stages of an illness, the menus were based on what seemed to be an infinite variety of teas: plain, with lemon and sugar or honey, or with crystals of amber rock candy that slowly melted below the surface of the tea in tiny golden streams. Sometimes it was a flowery, rosy brew of dried raspberries, other times a clear, sunny, gently perfumed camomile, or bosky sassafras.

My favorite came in late afternoons or evenings, especially when I had the flu. It was steaming dark and strong tea spiked with Rock 'n' Rye and flavored with a clove-studded lemon slice. That, two aspirins, the sweet, exotic fumes of the camphorated oil on my chest, and the candy-sweet scents of the tincture of benzoin being sent into the air from a nearby vaporizer sent me off in a drowsy torpor of half-dreams, three of which were recurrent and unforgettable.

In one dream, I was Princess of Everything, a title I devised as being sufficiently all-inclusive. In another, I owned a bridge across the Atlantic Ocean, and had hotels and restaurants along the way, so travelers could drive to Europe in comfort as I became rich. A similar goal inspired my third dream, in which I had built a roof over the entire world so everyone, everywhere, had to pay me rent.

Such ambitious dreaming amid the snug warmth of flannel nightgowns, a floppy and scalding hot-water bottle, bed socks, and drifts of blankets left me pretty thirsty, and there was always an assortment of fruit juices on hand when I awakened. Sometimes it was freshly squeezed orange juice, or orangeade chilled with cracked ice. Lemonade was served in a tall, icy glass, its rim frosted with sugar.

There might be fresh grapefruit juice, of which I was especially fond when the grapefruit was pink, or pineapple juice, with or without grape juice added to it. The tall fruit juice glasses always held a bent glass straw—the hospital kind—that allowed me to lean back on my mountain of pillows and sip at ease.

As I began to feel better and therefore more restless, I called for hair ribbons and my mother's best silk bed jacket, and waited impatiently for alcohol rubdowns and dustings of perfumed bath powder. Cutouts and coloring books cluttered the bed, as did horse-rein spools and the shaded wool worked through them to produce endless ropes of no use whatever.

As the bed trays became more interesting, so did the daily radio menu of soap operas. The day began with "John's Other Wife" (his secretary) at about nine, went through the midday bathos of "Our Gal Sunday" (can a girl from a simple mining town out West find happiness as the wife of England's richest and handsomest nobleman, Lord Henry Brinthrop?), and "Vic and Sade" who were forever on the lookout for someone known as "the brickmush man." It ended at dusk with "Stella Dallas" (the story of mother love and sacrifice) in which my favorite character was always introduced as "insane but wealthy Ada Dexter."

Toast was a big item in my mother's culinary pharmacopeia. At first it was served plain and dry, but that was soon followed by crisp, sweet cinnamon toast, then baby-bland milk toast that tasted soothingly of fresh air. Thick slices of French toast, crisp and golden outside but moist and eggy within, would probably come next, always topped with a melting knob of sweet butter and a dusting of confectioner's sugar. I knew I was close to recovery when I got the toast I liked best—almost-burned rye bread toast covered with salt butter.

Shortly after that, chicken soup would appear, first as a clear golden broth perfumed with knob celery, leeks, dill, and the sweet root of parsley, petrouchka. Later it would be served adrift with bits of chicken, carrots and celery, sprinklings of parsley, and rice or broad, buttery noodles.

Beef tea was an alternate soup, and to make it my mother put chunks of tough but juicy beef into a narrow necked glass milk bottle, which was then set in boiling water where it stayed for hours, until all of the beefy broth had been extracted. This was then salted and served in warm mugs, or poured over riced potatoes.

Eggs had a prominent place on these convalescent menus. Lightly poached, they would be served on toast or in the center of what my mother called a "bird's nest" of creamed spinach. They might be stirred into those tiny macaroni starlets, pastina, to which butter and grated cheese would be added, or scrambled with spicy caraway seeds. Finally, they arrived in my favorite guise—fried with crisp brown edges and a sprinkling of coarse salt and black pepper.

It was only when my mother considered me more than half well that she began to serve milk. She and my grandmother were both of a mind that milk was bad for a fever or a cough, because, they said, it caused congestion. Once milk was permitted it came in thick, whipped eggnogs fragrant with vanilla and nutmeg. Or it was baked into custard in chocolate-brown earthenware cups. Cinnamon-topped rice pudding studded with currants and warm baked apples with cream, cloudlike floating island pudding and pink junket were other stand-bys my mother used as "build-up" foods. So was red Jell-O, whipped when half set to become a snowy, mousselike froth.

All of my childhood illnesses seemed to have a prescribed number of days in bed, and each had its own treatments and menus with the food geared to my rate of improvement. By the time I was able to have a full-scale meat and potatoes dinner, I was also able to be out of bed and dressed, and I knew the period of glorious luxury had ended, and I felt cured, and very well cared for and loved.

19

Potatoes and Grains

Boiled Potatoes and . . .

Boiled potatoes figured in many of my mother's menus, not only as vegetable accompaniments to meat and fish, but as garnishes in cold borscht and schav. When available we ate new potatoes, valued for their delicate flavor and waxiness. Usually we had old potatoes, preferably from Long Island. If the potatoes were very old and sandy, they would be peeled before being boiled to tenderness in lots of well-salted water. When drained, the potatoes were returned to the dry pot, placed over low heat and shaken back and forth for a few seconds until they became dry and floury. If they were cooked with their skins, they were peeled after they were done and then dried over low heat. New potatoes were sometimes served in their jackets, with just a slim strip peeled off around the middle.

Hot boiled potatoes were also delicious in cold sour cream, as part of a light dinner or summer lunch; or if served with meat or soups, they might be topped with coarsely chopped or sliced onion that had been sautéed very slowly in butter until tender, bright yellow but not brown. The onion and its butter would go over the potatoes, which were served alongside the soup on a separate plate. My father also loved boiled potatoes mixed with schmaltz, the rendered chicken fat (page 7), and crumbled griebenes, or cracklings (page 7).

Home-Fried Potatoes

At our house, this meant fried raw potatoes, and the fat my mother used was generally the commercial Rokeach Nyafat, a product I now find taste-less and greasy. A combination of suet and butter would produce a similar result, but margarine can be used by those who are kosher. New potatoes are best for this dish, as they hold their form. If none are available, use old Californias or Long Islands. Maine potatoes will usually become too sticky and mushy.

2 pounds new red or brown potatoes, or old California or Long Island whites	and rendered beef suet, or all clarified butter
⅓ to ½ cup half-and-half combination of sweet butter	1 teaspoon salt, or to taste Black pepper to taste

Peel the potatoes and cut into ⅛-inch-thick slices. Heat ⅓ cup fat in a large, deep, heavy skillet, preferably of black cast iron, and add the potatoes with the salt and pepper. Turn the potato slices through the fat gently with a wooden spatula until all are coated. Cover tightly and fry very slowly for about 20 minutes, or until the potatoes are beginning to be tender and the underside is brown. Turn, cover, and slowly brown the second side. In about 15 minutes all of the potatoes should be tender. Serve at once.

Yield: 4 servings

German Fried Potatoes

Made with leftover boiled potatoes and an approximation of the potatoes generally served in luncheonettes and diners with breakfast eggs, these were a great favorite of my father's. They can be made either with boiled new po-tatoes, in which case the final result will be firm and nearly crisp, or with old potatoes, in which case they will be softer, more crumbly, and lustier. Onions are optional—nice with meat, less nice for breakfast. If potatoes are being cooked for this purpose, boil them in their skins and peel when cold. Under no circumstances should the potatoes be sliced when hot.

2 pounds boiled new or old potatoes	**1** teaspoon salt
3 tablespoons sweet butter	Black pepper to taste
1 tablespoon corn oil or rendered bacon fat or suet	**1** teaspoon sweet paprika

Potatoes should be peeled and sliced when cold; the slices should be about ¼ inch thick. Heat the butter and oil in a large, deep, heavy skillet, preferably of black cast iron. Add the potatoes, salt, pepper, and paprika and turn through the hot fat. Fry slowly, uncovered, stirring gently with a wooden spatula several times so all the potato slices heat and take on a golden-brown, crusty finish. Serve at once.

Yield: 4 servings

Variation: 1 small onion, finely minced, can be sautéed until it starts to soften in the fat before the potatoes are added. Proceed with the rest of the recipe as above.

Mashed and Riced Potatoes

Always incorporating very white old potatoes that were properly dry and mealy, this dish was made with an old fashioned wire potato masher, never with a whip or beater. I still prefer the more solid result to the soupier alternative. Potatoes were boiled after being peeled and were dried in a pot as described for boiled potatoes (page 209). They were then mashed in the hot, dry pot in which they were cooked, along with a generous lump of sweet butter (about 2 tablespoons per pound of potatoes) and just a trickle of hot milk or cream, so they would stand in peaks much like a heavy porridge. Salt, pepper, and mace or nutmeg were added, and sometimes chives as well.

We also liked these topped with rings of onions that had been melted in butter and a sprinkling of toasted bread crumbs; or, still another alternative, with crumbled griebenes, or cracklings (page 7).

The potatoes were boiled in the same way for riced potatoes and were then pressed through a ricer (see illustration page 69). Sometimes melted butter was drizzled over them, but usually these were topped with the beef tea described on page 68.

Lyonnaise Potatoes

The dish that went by this name at our house was simply the preceding recipe minus paprika. For it, use 1 medium onion, thinly sliced and separated into rings. Saute the rings in fat until tender and yellow, but not brown. Remove and reserve, add potatoes and salt and pepper, and fry as above. Return the onions to the pan for the last 5 minutes of frying time. Serve at once, sprinkled with minced parsley.

Potatoes au Gratin

Although we pronounced "gratin" to rhyme with "rotten," this dish was considered the height of fancy cooking. The only reason my mother didn't make it more often was that we all tended to leave the meat, fish, or whatever main course was served with them. White Cheddar was the cheese my mother used, but Parmesan is less overpowering and more elegant.

2 pounds new potatoes	½ cup grated white Cheddar or
Boiling, well-salted water	Parmesan cheese
1½ cups basic cream sauce (page 10)	2 to 3 tablespoons fine, dry bread crumbs
Salt and white pepper to taste	2 to 3 tablespoons sweet butter
Pinch of mace	

Wash the potatoes and boil, unpeeled, in lots of well-salted water until tender but firm. Drain and let cool, uncovered. When thoroughly cold, peel and cut into ¼-inch-thick slices. Butter a 9-inch round pie plate or square baking pan. Preheat the oven to 375 degrees. Prepare the cream sauce, seasoning it with salt, white pepper, and a pinch of mace.

Arrange the potato slices in the baking pan, sprinkling a little cheese between each layer and reserving 3 or 4 tablespoons for the topping. Cover with cream sauce, sprinkle with the remaining cheese and bread crumbs, and dot generously with butter. Bake for about 20 minutes, or until sauce is bubbling and the top is crusty brown.

Yield: 4 to 6 servings

Roasted Potatoes

The small red potatoes result in the thinnest, crispest skins. Idaho potatoes have a crustier finish but are wonderfully light and dry inside.

1 pound small new red or brown potatoes, small old red potatoes, or Idaho baking potatoes	1 cup solid vegetable shortening or corn oil 1 tablespoon diced suet, if available Salt to taste

Preheat the oven to 400 degrees.

Peel the potatoes. If you are using Idahos, cut them in quarters. Place in an 8 to 9-inch baking pan with the shortening or oil and suet. There should be enough fat for a depth of about ½ inch in the pan. Roast the potatoes for about 45 minutes, turning several times so they brown easily and do not stick to the pan. Drain on paper towels and serve at once. Salt at the table after they have been cut open.

These are especially good with meat roasts; pan drippings from the roasting meat can be added to the potatoes as they are cooking.

Yield: 3 to 4 servings

Stuffed Baked Potatoes

8 large baking potatoes, preferably Idaho	Salt and black or cayenne pepper to taste
3 tablespoons sweet butter	Minced chives (optional)
4 to 5 tablespoons hot half-and-half milk and cream, or as needed	Sweet paprika 3 tablespoons grated Cheddar or Parmesan cheese, approximately (optional)

Preheat the oven to 450 degree.

Wash and dry the potatoes and wrap in foil. Bake in the preheated oven until done, about 45 minutes. Pierce with a skewer, or a thin knife blade to see if the potatoes are done all the way through.

Remove from the oven but do not turn the oven off. Cut the potatoes in half lengthwise to form boats. Scoop the insides out into a mixing bowl.

(continued)

Discard (or eat) 8 half shells. Mash the potatoes with a fork or potato masher, working in the butter and enough hot half-and-half to make a light and fluffy mixture, but one that is not too thinly whipped or liquid. Season to taste, adding chives if available. Heap the potato mixture into the 8 remaining half shells. Sprinkle with paprika and, if you like, with a little grated cheese—about 1 teaspoonful per potato half. Return to the oven and bake for a few minutes, until the potatoes are thoroughly hot and the tops are golden brown. Serve at once.

Yield: 8 servings

French Fries

My mother did not use the true deep-frying method for these potatoes, but fried them instead in a 1-inch depth of vegetable shortening or corn oil, usually with some rendered beef suet added for flavor. "Silver dollars," which we preferred, were simply round french fries. Idaho or other baking potatoes are the best to use for this.

2 pounds large baking potatoes	¼ pound rendered or diced beef suet
Solid vegetable shortening or corn oil, for frying	Salt to taste

Peel the potatoes and cut into strips; ours were always fairly thick. Soak in ice water for 30 minutes. Remove the potatoes from the water and dry thoroughly on a towel. Heat a 1-inch depth of fat in a large, heavy skillet, preferably of black cast iron. If the suet has been rendered, add it to the fat to come up to the 1-inch level. Otherwise add it diced to the liquid fat so it fries along with the potatoes. Add just enough potatoes to form a single layer in the pan. They should not be too crammed in, but it is all right if they barely touch. Fry slowly, turning several times until rich golden brown on both sides and tender within. Remove with a slotted spatula, drain on paper towels, and keep hot until all are fried. Sprinkle with salt just before serving.

Yield: 4 to 6 servings

Variation: Peel the potatoes and cut into ½-inch-thick round "silver dollars." Soak and fry as above.

Potato Pancakes

These should be prepared and fried as close to serving time as possible. They were the standard accompaniment to pot-roasted brisket of beef (page 163) or glazed sweet and sour stuffed cabbage (page 171).

7 or 8 medium old potatoes (about
     2½ pounds)
1 large onion, peeled
2 eggs, separated
2 tablespoons potato flour or
    matzoh meal

1 scant tablespoon salt
1 teaspoon white pepper
   Corn oil, for frying
Applesauce (page 227), as
    accompaniment

Peel the potatoes and cover with cold water until you are ready to make the pancakes. Grate the potatoes and onion into a strainer that is suspended over a bowl to catch the juices. If this is hard for you to manage, grate the potatoes into a bowl, then turn into a strainer suspended over another bowl. Grate the potatoes and onion alternately, as the onion juice will help prevent the potatoes from darkening. Using a wooden spoon, or picking up handfuls of the grated potato mixture, squeeze or press out as much liquid as possible. Reserve all liquid and let it settle in the bowl for 2 or 3 minutes.

Put the pressed potato and onion mixture in a clean bowl. Carefully pour off the watery part of the reserved liquid but do not discard the thick, starchy paste at the bottom of the bowl. Scrape that into the potato mixture.

Add the egg yolks, potato flour or matzoh meal, salt, and pepper and mix thoroughly. Beat the egg whites to stiff and shiny peaks and fold them into the potato mixture.

Heat a ½-inch-depth of oil in a heavy skillet, preferably of black cast iron. Drop the potato mixture into the hot oil, about 2 tablespoons per pancake, and fry, turning once so the pancakes are a deep golden brown on both sides. Drain on paper towels. Total frying time for each batch of pancakes should be about 10 minutes. Keep fried pancakes warm while the rest are being fried. To do that, put the fried, drained pancakes on a rack in an open baking pan and place in a low oven (about 250 degrees). Do not hold for more than 15 minutes before serving or they will become soggy. Serve with applesauce.

Yield: 6 servings

Potato Kugel

Although this is not a true kugel in the typical sense of a thick, baked pudding, it was as close to it as my mother ever came. She did not like the thicker variety because she said, quite correctly, that it always stayed soggy and heavy in the middle. This dish is simply one giant potato pancake, which she fried on top of the stove if she did not mind tending to it closely, or baked in the oven when she wanted more leeway if guests were coming.

Follow the above recipe exactly. Heat a ½-inch depth of corn oil in a heavy, ovenproof 12- to 13-inch skillet, preferably black cast iron. Turn the potato mixture into the hot oil and spread evenly to the edges of the pan. Drizzle a little hot oil over the top. Place in an oven preheated to 400 degrees and let bake about 45 minutes. If the top does not start browning after 30 minutes, remove the pan from the oven, and using a large spatula or a large plate to flip the pancake onto, turn the pancake. Do not worry if it breaks in turning, because it will cook back together somewhat and in any case it will be cut for serving. Continue baking until the top is crusty brown and the center is cooked.

Serve cut in wedges. This recipe can, of course, be made in a comparable-size square or rectangular pan. What is important is that the potato mixture be no more than ¾ inch thick.

Yield: 6 servings

Variation: The kugel can also be done in the skillet on top of the stove, in which case it must be turned. It will take about 30 minutes to cook and needs careful attention because there is more danger of burning.

Potato Salad, Neat and Messy

We had two different styles of potato salad, depending on whether my mother used firm new potatoes, or old mealy varieties. The new potatoes retained their neat sliced shapes, while the mealier potatoes became almost mashed as they were mixed. My mother preferred the first, I the second, and no one else in the family seemed to care. My mother always waited for the potatoes to cool before mixing them with dressing so they would not become too mashed.

Neat Potato Salad

2 pounds new potatoes
   Rapidly boiling salted water
1 tablespoon distilled white vinegar,
      or as needed
1 teaspoon salt
   Black pepper, to taste
2 extra-large or jumbo eggs, hard
      cooked, peeled, and mashed with
      a fork

¼ cup finely minced celery
1 teaspoon grated Spanish or
      Bermuda onion (optional)
¾ cup mayonnaise, or as needed
1 teaspoon prepared mustard

Wash the potatoes and cook them, in their jackets, in plenty of rapidly boiling salted water. Drain when tender and let cool until you can handle them. Peel off the jackets and cut the potatoes into round slices a little less than ¼ inch thick. Spread the slices out and sprinkle lightly with vinegar.

When at room temperature, place the slices in a large mixing bowl. Add the salt, pepper, eggs, celery, and onion. Toss lightly. Blend the mayonnaise and mustard together and turn through the salad as gently as possible. Add more mayonnaise or seasonings if needed. Cover the bowl and let stand in the refrigerator overnight or at least 5 hours before serving.

Yield: 6 to 8 servings

Messy Potato Salad

6 medium old boiling potatoes (about
      2 pounds)
   Rapidly boiling salted water
2 tablespoons distilled white vinegar
1 teaspoon salt
   Black pepper to taste
2 extra-large or jumbo eggs, hard

cooked, peeled, and coarsely
   chopped
1 tablespoon very finely minced
      onion
¾ cup mayonnaise
1 teaspoon prepared mustard

Scrub the potatoes and cook them, in their jackets, in plenty of rapidly boiling salted water. When tender, drain and let stand until they can be handled, but the hotter the better. Peel and cut into quarters lengthwise, then into ¼- to ½-inch-thick slices. Spread out and sprinkle with the vinegar. While the potatoes are still very warm, place them in a mixing bowl with all the other ingredients and stir with a wooden spoon. The potatoes should break down slightly and form both solid and partially mashed parts that combine with the hard-cooked egg yolks and mayonnaise. Let stand overnight in the refrigerator or at least 5 hours before serving.

Yield: 6 to 8 servings

Baked Sweet Potatoes

I have always felt that the best sweet potatoes (or yams) were those most simply prepared, and I have never been able to understand why sugar should be added to something that is naturally so sweet. Sweet potatoes, scrubbed and baked until tender, then broken open and mashed with a big lump of sweet butter and salt and pepper were always an exciting event, and the very smell of them baking in the oven was comforting on a winter afternoon. When I was a child, they used to be sold on street corners in New York from stands such as those that now sell chestnuts, giving off a tantalizing scent of hot baking potatoes and charcoal.

I much prefer small, firm, pale-yellow sweet potatoes to the softer, mushier orange yams, but both can be cooked the same way. Bake as you would white potatoes (page 213), but pierce a hole in the sweet potato after it has baked for 20 minutes so it does not burst.

Mashed Sweet Potatoes

This was another favorite, and simple to prepare. Sweet potatoes were boiled in their skins, then peeled and mashed (with a potato masher) with sweet butter, salt, and pepper or nutmeg. Just the smallest trickle of warmed heavy sweet cream might be added to give them a satin finish, but never sugar or aromatic spices such as cinnamon or cloves.

Candied Sweet Potatoes

Having said my piece about sweetened sweet potatoes, I must add that the one exception was at Thanksgiving, when, for reasons I cannot explain, candied sweet potatoes seemed essential.

6 sweet potatoes (about 2½ pounds)	Pinch of powdered ginger
Boiling salted water	4 tablespoons sweet butter
⅔ cup brown sugar	2 tablespoons lemon juice

Boil the scrubbed, unpeeled sweet potatoes in salted water until tender but firm. Let cool and then peel. Cut in half lengthwise.

Preheat the oven to 350 degrees. Butter a baking pan that will hold the potato halves comfortably without having them touch.

Place the potatoes in the pan, cut side down. Combine the brown sugar and powdered ginger and sprinkle over the tops of the potatoes. Add the butter and lemon juice to the pan and bake for 25 to 30 minutes, basting the potatoes frequently with the melted butter and lemon juice and sugar, which will form a syrup. The potatoes should be thoroughly hot and have a rich, dark, caramelized glaze.

Yield: 6 servings

Kasha

[Buckwheat groats]

This basic recipe for nutty buckwheat groats is the standard one printed on the box in which kasha comes. My mother preferred fine kasha, but I generally use the medium or coarse grain, preferring the smaller size only for stuffing. Kasha was the standard accompaniment to duck, but it is good with all roast poultry. We never served kasha in chicken soup, but I know that is standard practice.

1 cup kasha	1 tablespoon sweet butter
1 egg, lightly beaten	Salt to taste
2 cups boiling water	

Put the kasha in a wide bowl and, with a fork, mix the beaten egg in until the egg is absorbed and all grains seem moistened. Turn into a heavy, 10- to 12-inch skillet and place over moderately high heat. Stir frequently and cook until each grain is dry and separate. Pour in the boiling water and shake the pan so the water settles evenly. Cover and steam over low heat for 20 to 30 minutes, or until the kasha is puffed up and tender. Halfway through the cooking, stir in the butter and season with salt.

Yield: 4 servings

Variations: Sautéed onion or mushrooms, with the butter in which they were sautéed, can be stirred into the kasha instead of plain butter. Minced chives are also good tossed into this. For kasha stuffing, see page 152.

Kasha Varnishkes

Prepare kasha as described above. When done, toss with 4 ounces macaroni bowties (*farfalle,* in Italian) that have been cooked in well-salted water and stir in ½ cup coarsely chopped onion that was sautéed in butter. Add seasonings. This should be fairly peppery to be interesting.

Spanish Rice

Although this was often served as an accompaniment to broiled or fried fish (page 121) or codfish cakes (page 123), it also was the basis for shrimp Creole (page 131). It was one of my mother's stand-bys for parties because it could be made in advance.

1 medium onion, chopped (about ½ cup chopped)	1 teaspoon sweet paprika
	¼ teaspoon hot paprika or a pinch of cayenne pepper
½ green pepper, seeded and chopped fine (between ⅓ and ½ cup chopped)	1 one-pound can tomatoes, coarsely chopped, with liquid reserved
2 tablespoons sweet butter	1½ cups water, or as needed
1 cup long-grain converted rice	1¼ teaspoons salt

Sauté the chopped onion and green pepper in the butter in a heavy-bottomed 2½- to 3-quart saucepan. Cook slowly, so vegetables wilt slightly but do not brown. This will take about 7 minutes. Stir several times.

Stir in the rice and both paprikas or cayenne pepper. Sauté for 2 or 3 minutes, until the spices lose their raw smell and all the rice grains are coated with butter and become translucent. Add the chopped tomatoes. Combine the tomato canning liquid (usually about ½ cup) with enough water to make 2 cups. Bring to a boil and pour over the rice and vegetables, adding the salt.

Bring to a boil, cover tightly, reduce the heat, and simmer very slowly for about 20 minutes, or until the rice is tender but not mushy. Check several times during the cooking to see if the rice is too dry. If so, add a little boiling water.

When done, taste and adjust the seasonings.

Yield: 4 to 6 servings

Note: If you want to make this several hours or a day ahead of time, use 1 extra tablespoon of butter in the cooking. Then place the cold rice in the top of a double boiler, or in its original pot set in a larger pan of water, and heat.

Mamaliga

[Rumanian Cornmeal]

This is really a very thick cornmeal mush, much like Italian polenta, served instead of potatoes or rice with gravy and meat—usually with pot-roasted brisket of beef (page 163), beef stew or veal goulash (page 177), or with sautéed chicken livers with mushrooms and onions (page 38). It is also very good simply with a lump of sweet butter and some salt and pepper. I have also had it in Bulgaria, in a dish called *kachamak,* for which crumbled brindza sheep's milk cheese and butter are stirred into the hot, cooked porridge, which is then lightly baked for a few minutes until the cheese melts.

For breakfast, my mother often made fried mamaliga. She would prepare the porridge as described below the night before, then put it in a buttered baking pan or plate so that it would set into a 1- to 1½-inch-thick cake. This she cut into squares, which were fried slowly in hot butter until light golden brown on both sides.

Italian food buffs will recognize all of the above as pertaining to polenta.

4 cups water	2¾ cups finely ground yellow
4 teaspoons salt	cornmeal

Pour 2 cups of water into a heavy, 2½- to 3-quart saucepan. Stir the remaining 2 cups cold water with cornmeal and salt. Bring the water in the pot to a boil, and when bubbling rapidly, slowly pour in the cornmeal mixed with water. The boiling should never stop or the cornmeal will form lumps. Keep stirring as you pour the cornmeal into the water. Reduce the heat, cover, and simmer gently for about 10 minutes, until the porridge is thick and all liquid is absorbed. Stir several times with a wooden spoon to be sure the mixture is not scorching on the bottom.

Serve at once, with butter, meat, or gravy or in any of the ways described above.

Yield: 6 to 8 servings

20

Funerals

My mother's reflex reaction to any special event, joyous or sad, was to call the butcher. A death in the family was no exception. "At least let there be a plate of soup in the house," she said, explaining why she ordered a chicken, and, "At least let there be some meat to slice when visitors get hungry," she added, thus accounting for the pickled tongue or pot roast or roast beef or turkey. Sorrow was bad enough without compounding it with hunger. Sometimes the food was to be left at home if she expected condolence callers, but usually at least some of it went to the house where shiva was being observed.

It was the shiva house—the house of mourning, usually where the deceased had lived—that frightened me as a child. Mirrors were shrouded with sheets, living room furniture was pushed back to accommodate bridge chairs for visitors and the plain wooden crates or the small bare benches sent by the funeral parlor for the immediate mourners to sit on. Those mourners wore stockings or, at most, slippers (since they were not permitted to wear shoes) and black clothes usually with a cut near the lapel, although in later years the cut was made more practically in a strip of black grosgrain ribbon that was then pinned to the clothes. Men did not shave for the seven days of mourning nor did women wear lipstick, no radio or music was played (unusual for a family in which everyone, it seemed, played the piano), and the house was full of visitors from times and places far removed.

Mothers introduced children to long-lost relatives with pride as the children squirmed, and when I was older my mother always admonished me to dress nicely at funerals (but not too nicely) so she could show me off to a distant cousin or aunt. Tears alternated with laughter as funny stories were recalled and photographs of the deceased were passed around, along with others of new and unseen babies and brides.

Most visitors brought food if they had not already sent some. Not only the sorts of things my mother prepared, but lofty soufflélike sponge cakes fragrant with vanilla, nut- and cinnamon-filled coffee cakes, pounds of delicatessen meats such as whole, garlic-flecked salamis, bologna, liverwurst, peppery sides of pastrami, and whole corned beefs, their glistening fat waiting to be steamed to melting, succulent tenderness. There were jars of soup, boxes of candy, and big, flat baskets that held a kaleidoscopic array of dried tropical fruits wrapped in orangy cellophane, each packed with a little bone or ivory two-pronged fork. There were tins of salted nuts and high steamer baskets of hothouse fruits with big satin bows ("Dopes," my father loved to say. "Don't they know that hothouse fruit has no taste? Who cares if it looks beautiful? What good is it if you can't eat it?" he would ask, as my mother upbraided him for being an ingrate.)

But the most memorable spread was the one laid out immediately after the funeral and burial, again usually at the home of the deceased and at its best when that was my grandmother's house and the family was still large and close together. One such funeral was for her husband (my grandfather), the other for a son (my uncle) who died at thirty-seven. Though his young family lived in Brooklyn, his wife was unable to cope with crowds, food, and the attendant fuss, so the shiva was observed at my grandmother's.

Somehow, magically, one or two of the less immediate family members, or perhaps the neighbors, set out the spread while relatives went to the cemetery, and since all the funerals I remember took place in the morning and in cold or rainy weather, the meal they came back to was more or less a breakfast, with dairy foods and plenty of hot coffee as a welcome restorative.

But before coffee or food, even on empty stomachs, there would be shots of schnapps—rye whiskey thrown down neat with nothing more than a shudder as a chaser, for both men and women, although the latter sometimes sipped theirs down in thirds. The toast "lachaim"—to life—had special meaning at such an event, and that meaning never passed unremarked.

But they also ate to life, starting with the symbolic hard-cooked egg and piece of bread. The table, whether set in kitchen, dinette, or dining room, was covered with the best damask cloth and groaned under the weight of bowls of gleaming silver-blue pickled herring with sour cream and onion rings, ruby fillets of maatjes herring with minced scallions, dishes of coral canned salmon to be served with finely minced Bermuda onion in white vinegar, trays of smoked fish such as whitefish, alabaster sturgeon, satiny sable, all looking as though they had been gold leafed, and paprika-edged smoked carp. Sliced tomatoes and onions dotted with wrinkled, salty black musselines olives, baskets of pumpernickel rye bread, matzohs, bagels, onion rolls, and bialys, dishes with slabs of cream cheese and butter, slices of imported Swiss and buttery Muenster cheese, were all there to be nibbled on while someone at the stove dished up to order eggs, any style, fried or scrambled plain or with lox and onions, or blintzes puffy with cinnamon-sugar cottage cheese fillings that appeared magically from some beneficent relative to be fried crisply brown and topped with sour cream as needed.

Then for the coffee cakes, the crunchy rugelach and schnecken of crisp yeast dough enveloping chewy fillings of walnuts, cinnamon, raisins, and sugar, gold and chocolate marble cake sometimes with streaks of fudge running through it, high sunny cheesecakes, pecan rings and almond braids, streuselkuchen crumbcakes, an endless array of cookies from neighbors and friends, perhaps apple strudels and poppyseed rolls, and more that I have probably forgotten.

With the family grown small, even funerals come infrequently now, and there is no one left to observe shiva. But one cousin and I who share the memory of that funeral food, and feel it a palliative for sadness, usually go to Ratner's after a funeral (now that Rappaport's, our favorite, is closed) and duplicate as best we can some of the standards of the postfuneral breakfast.

The foods eaten at one funeral always recall another—and all recall to me the most memorable circumstances surrounding the funeral of my Uncle Al. He was the big, bald, rotund, jolly favorite of everyone in the family, a happy-go-lucky man who had a hard time making a living and who traveled and lived all over the country to do so, and so was most often away. His visits to Brooklyn always seemed like holidays, with much card playing, eating, and, way into the night, laughter, always laughter.

His death, which came suddenly and early of a heart attack, really did cause my mother agony. He died in Virginia, but he was to be buried in the family plot on Long Island, so my cousins, his sons, came North with the body, and my mother, in spite of her anguish, helped them with funeral preparations. The first task was to go to a funeral home and order the coffin and arrange for the service, and, inevitably, to bargain for the whole affair. My cousins could afford only $600, but the coffin they liked cost $900, and so my mother took over with the funeral director, who had handled all the family deaths until that time. "Look, Sherman," she said to him, "be smart. Give the kids the coffin they want for six hundred dollars. You know, Sherman, you buried my mother, my father, one brother, now another brother. Be smart, Sherman, and you'll bury me." Sherman eventually thought this made sense and dropped the price $300.

But this was not the end of Uncle Al's funeral, for when the cemetery workers opened the grave he was to occupy in the family plot, they discovered in it a stray leg—my grandfather's leg, which had been amputated many years before he died. In the orthodox Jewish tradition, it was buried in the grave he was eventually to occupy, so that he could go to his Maker intact. But when my grandfather died, he had obviously been buried in the wrong grave, without his leg. My mother was incensed. "Imagine Morris Breit in his grave all these years without his foot," she said. "I'll sue!"

She never did, though, but saw to it that the gravediggers opened my grandfather's grave and buried his foot before they readied the new grave for my uncle. When all was done, and when she was sure there would be no charge for correcting the error, she let herself go and cried for Uncle Al.

21

Desserts

Although my mother did have packaged pudding and fruit gelatin desserts, and sometimes canned fruit, on hand, those were emergency measures not often resorted to. Most often dessert was some form of cake or pie, or one of the recipes in this chapter. My brother and I complained bitterly if stewed fruit or applesauce appeared, since we felt fruit didn't count as dessert, but now delicious spiced compotes, based on fresh or dried fruits, are among my favorites. The thought of cake or anything baked, except perhaps the lightest fruit tart, seems excessive after a full meal. Heavier desserts, such as rice, bread, or noodle puddings, were relegated to dinners when the main courses did not contain meat and were fairly light. Dessert then became a substantial part of the meal.

Applesauce

It may be hard to imagine anyone getting excited about so simple a preparation as this, but homemade applesauce is hard to come by these days, and a treat when it is available. McIntosh apples are best for applesauce, though Northern Spies and Cortlands will also work well. In all cases, and especially with McIntosh, cooking the peel with the apple results in a pleasant blush tone to the final result. *(continued)*

2 pounds apples, preferably
    McIntosh
½ to 1 cup water, as needed
    1 two-inch strip lemon peel

¼ cup sugar, or to taste
½ teaspoon powdered cinnamon,
    or to taste
Optional seasonings: Heavy sweet
    cream, lemon juice, white wine, or
    cloves

Core and quarter the apples, but do not peel them. Place in a large, heavy saucepan and add just enough water to cover the bottom of the pan. Add the lemon peel. Cover the pot and bring to a simmer. Let cook gently for about 15 minutes, or until completely soft but not totally fallen apart. If more water is needed to prevent scorching during the cooking, add a little, but the less the better. It is best for the apples to cook in their own juices.

Place a strainer or food mill over a clean pot or bowl and puree the apples through it, discarding the skins and lemon peel. Return the puree to the pot and set over very low heat. Gradually stir in sugar to taste. For my taste, applesauce is best when it is still slightly sour and apple-y, not candy sweet. Add cinnamon to taste and simmer slowly until the sauce is very thick. Serve hot, warm, or cold.

If served cold, a trickle of heavy sweet cream is delicious added after the sauce is spooned into individual fruit dishes. Lemon juice, white wine, and cloves are other possible seasonings.

Yield: About 4 cups (this will vary with the amount of moisture in the apples you use)

Variation: A slightly more interesting if less conventional method is to make applesauce without pureeing it. Cook the apples until done, pull out the skins, and beat the sauce lightly with a wooden spoon, so you still have some pieces in it. Add sugar and cinnamon and cook down further to eliminate moisture.

Baked Apples

4 baking apples, preferably
    Rome Beauties
    Juice of ½ lemon
3 to 4 tablespoons sweet butter

4 teaspoons sugar, or to taste
    Powdered cinnamon to taste
    Heavy sweet cream, for
        garnish (optional)

Preheat the oven to 375 degrees. Wash, dry, and core the apples. Do not cut all the way through the bottom when coring. Pare off a 1- to 1½-inch strip of peel from the top of each apple. Sprinkle the inside and top with a little lemon juice.

Set the apples in a baking dish 3 to 5 inches deep. Divide the butter among the apples, placing some in each center hollow and reserving a little for the top.

Sprinkle the sugar inside each hollowed-out core and over the top where pared. Sprinkle the top and core with cinnamon and dot the peeled edges with flecks of butter.

Pour a 1-inch depth of boiling water into the baking pan, around the apples. Place in the oven and bake, uncovered, for about 30 minutes, or until the apples are tender enough to be pierced with a fork and are light golden brown on top. Baste once or twice with the pan juices.

Remove to a serving dish. Serve warm or chilled, with or without cold, heavy sweet cream.

Yield: 4 servings

Stewed Rhubarb

This, and baked apples with cream, were the only fruits I considered special enough to be served for dessert when I was a child. Rhubarb was especially exciting because it was a sign of spring, indicating that summer and vacation could not be too far off.

This is also very good over vanilla ice cream, the way my father preferred it.

3 pounds rhubarb	**3 or 4 pieces cracked ginger**
1½ to 1¾ cups sugar, to taste	**Whipped cream, for**
1 cup water	**garnish (optional)**

Wash the rhubarb. If young and tender, do not peel. If the stalks are tough and heavy, strip off the outer red covering. Cut into 1-inch pieces. Place in a heavy enameled saucepan and sprinkle with 1½ cups sugar. Add 1 cup water and the ginger. Cover and simmer gently for about 10 minutes, or until the rhubarb is tender but not falling apart. Adjust the seasoning, adding more sugar if necessary and letting it dissolve in the hot syrup. Chill before serving. A small dab of whipped cream on each portion is delicious.

Yield: 6 to 8 servings

Spiced Peach Compote

Although this same preparation was sometimes made with fresh apricots or small blue plums or nectarines, peaches were the most suitable—especially the big, sunny ripe Georgia peaches. The peaches may be peeled for a more refined presentation, but they seem to taste better when cooked with their skins on.

6 medium peaches	6 to 8 cloves
1½ cups water	2-inch stick cinnamon
1½ cups sugar	Grand Marnier

If you want to peel the peaches, plunge them into boiling water for 2 or 3 minutes, then slip the skins off. If you are not going to peel them, rub off any fuzz that might be on them with a rough cloth and wash them well.

Bring the water to a boil with the sugar, cloves and cinammon stick. Boil, uncovered, for a minute or two, or until a light syrup forms. Add the peaches and simmer until the peaches are tender, about 7 to 10 minutes, depending on their size. Place the peaches in a tall, narrow bowl or jar. Flavor the syrup to taste with Grand Marnier and pour over the fruit, which should be covered with the syrup; the spices should be left in the syrup. Chill for at least 24 hours before serving.

Yield: 6 servings

Dried Fruit Compote

2 pounds mixed dried fruit	2 slices lemon, studded with 3 cloves
1 cup water	each
1 cup white wine, or to taste	2-inch stick cinnamon
½ to ¾ cup sugar, to taste	Lemon juice to taste

Follow the instructions on the package as to whether or not the fruit needs soaking. The best dried fruit is that which does not have sulphates added; these need overnight soaking. Place the fruit, soaked or unsoaked, in a heavy saucepan with the water, wine, ½ cup sugar, the clove-studded lemon slices, and cinnamon and simmer until tender, about 20 minutes. If more sugar is needed, add as necessary. After the fruit is cooked, flavor with lemon juice and more white wine. Chill thoroughly before serving. Although the lemon slices are not served with the fruit, they are usually stored with it. This compote tastes best when made a day or two in advance.

Yield: 6 to 8 servings

Variation: Prunes alone can be stewed as above; if you prefer, eliminate the wine and substitute water.

Cup Custard

Individual brown earthenware custard cups lined in white were the traditional holders for this lovely, nutmeg-scented custard. I hardly considered it edible in anything else although, of course, it could be baked in one large baking dish.

6 **extra-large egg yolks**	½ to 1 **teaspoon vanilla extract, to**
4 to 5 **tablespoons sugar, to taste**	**taste**
Pinch of salt	**Nutmeg to taste**
3 **cups milk**	

Preheat the oven to 350 degrees.

Beat the egg yolks with 4 tablespoons sugar and a pinch of salt until they just begin to foam. Add the milk and stir until the sugar is dissolved. Taste and add more sugar if the custard does not seem sweet enough. Add vanilla to taste. Strain the custard into a pitcher.

Pour into 6 individual custard cups or a 1-quart soufflé dish or similar baking dish. Sprinkle with nutmeg.

Place the cups or baking dish in a baking pan and pour in boiling water to come three-quarters of the way up the sides of the cups or dish. Place in the oven and bake for 45 minutes to 1 hour, or until a knife inserted in the center of the custard comes out clean. Custard in the one large baking dish will take about 10 minutes longer to set than that in smaller cups. Remove from the hot water at once; let cool and chill in the refrigerator.

Yield: 6 servings

Biscuit Tortoni

This was my mother's idea of a super-elegant dessert to be served at luncheons or dinner parties, or for one of our birthdays. She always made it in the traditional pleated paper cups and froze it in the emptied ice-cube tray in days before refrigerators had freezers. Although the macaroons are easily and quickly crushed in a blender or a food processor, both of those methods result in very fine even crumbs. The texture is far more interesting if the crumbs are a bit coarser and uneven. My mother crushed hers by putting them in a brown paper bag and going over them with a rolling pin, or if she was not preparing too large a quanity, she used a heavy brass mortar and pestle. If you cannot find the proper paper cups at fancy kitchen equipment shops, small, individual ramekins or even demitasse cups can be used. Portion size should vary between two and three heaping tablespoonsfuls of the mixture; because of its richness, it is doubtful that anyone could eat more than that. The tortoni can also be frozen in a 6-cup soufflé dish or a comparable square dish, and served in wedges or squares, but it is not quite as authentic.

1 extra-large egg white	6 tablespoons confectioners' sugar
14 crisp Italian macaroons (Amaretti)	1 tablespoon light rum
(about ⅓ cup crushed)	1 teaspoon vanilla extract
1 cup heavy sweet cream	Pinch of salt

Let the egg white stand in a bowl so it will warm to room temperature. Chill a bowl and beater for whipping the cream.

Crush the macaroons, using a blender or food processor if you want to save time and like them very fine, or as described above, with a rolling pin or mortar and pestle, for a coarser, more interesting texture. You should have ⅓ cup. Set aside.

Pour the cream into a chilled bowl and begin whipping. As it thickens, gradually beat in the sugar, 1 tablespoon at a time. The cream should be as thick as possible without turning to butter, so watch it carefully. Beat in the rum and vanilla.

Beat the egg white with a pinch of salt until it stands in stiff and shiny peaks. Fold into the whipped-cream mixture.

Divide the mixture among 6 to 8 pleated paper tortoni cups or individual ramekins, allowing 2 to 3 heaping tablespoons of mix per portion. If using a single 6-cup soufflé dish, be sure the mixture is not more than 1½ inches deep. Sprinkle generously with crushed macaroons. Cover each cup, ramekin, or the soufflé dish with aluminum foil and freeze until firm, at least 5 hours. This can easily be done several days ahead and kept frozen until served. Take out of the freezer 5 or 10 minutes before serving, so the mixture will soften and be creamy.

Yield: 6 to 8 servings

Variation: ⅓ cup chopped, toasted, blanched almonds can be folded into the cream mixture before the egg white is added.

Rice with Milk

In its simplest form, this was served to us when we were recuperating from an illness. It is delicious either warm or slightly chilled, sprinkled with cinnamon sugar. In either case, cold, heavy sweet cream can be poured over it. Folded with whipped cream it became an elegant dessert, sometimes topped with a spoonful of cherry or blueberry sauce.

2 cups water	3 tablespoons sugar, or to taste
½ cup long-grain converted rice	1½ teaspoons vanilla extract
4 cups milk	Cinnamon sugar, for topping
Pinch of salt	

Bring the water to a boil in a very heavy, 1½-quart saucepan. Add the rice and cook for 5 minutes. Drain thoroughly.

Heat the milk to the boiling point in the saucepan and add a pinch of salt. Stir in the drained rice. Lower the heat and simmer, stirring constantly, for about 5 minutes. Cover the pot and cook very gently for 45 to 55 minutes, stirring occasionally. The rice should be completely tender and creamy and the milk almost completely absorbed.

Stir in the sugar and vanilla. This can be served warm or chilled, with cinnamon sugar.

Yield: 6 to 8 servings

Variations: 1. If you wish, fold in ½ cup heavy sweet cream, whipped, after the rice is thoroughly chilled. Top, if desired with a fruit sauce (follow a standard recipe for stewed cherries or blueberries, then puree the fruit into a syrup either by rubbing it through a sieve or by using a food processor)

2. If you like raisins, a tablespoonful can be stirred into the rice during the last 20 minutes of cooking time.

Custard Rice Pudding

3 extra-large eggs
4 cups milk
⅔ cup sugar
Pinch of salt
1¼ teaspoons vanilla extract
1 generous teaspoon grated lemon rind
1 generous teaspoon grated orange rind

¼ cup black raisins or dried currants
1 cup cooked rice, at room temperature
Powdered cinnamon or nutmeg to taste
Heavy sweet cream (optional)

Preheat the oven to 350 degrees.

Beat the eggs into the milk and strain into a mixing bowl. Add all the remaining ingredients except the cinnamon or nutmeg and the optional sweet cream. Butter an 8-inch square glass or ceramic baking dish and turn the pudding mixture into it, smoothing the top so the depth is even.

Place the baking dish in a larger pan. Pour in enough hot water to come halfway up the sides of the rice pudding dish. Bake for 30 minutes, then stir gently so the rice is distributed evenly through the custard. Continue baking for 30 minutes, then stir again. Carefully smooth the top to level it, then sprinkle with cinnamon or nutmeg. Continue baking for another 20 minutes, or until the custard is set. Lift the pudding dish from the water bath and cool.

The pudding may be served slightly warm or after being chilled in the refrigerator. Heavy cream can be poured over individual servings.

Lokshen Kugel
[Noodle Pudding]

1 pound noodles between ½ and 1 inch wide, preferably the latter
7 eggs
½ cup sugar
1½ teaspoons vanilla extract
1 teaspoon powdered cinnamon
3 tablespoons raisins

2 cups creamed large-curd cottage cheese
3 to 4 tablespoons sweet butter, for topping
Sour cream and cinnamon sugar (optional)

Cook the noodles in 3 quarts of rapidly boiling, lightly salted water until tender but still al dente, about 10 minutes.

While the noodles are cooking, preheat the oven to 350 degrees. Butter a 9 x 13 baking dish, preferably of heavy ceramic or heatproof glass.

Beat the eggs with the sugar, then beat in the vanilla and cinnamon. Drain the noodles, but do not dry too thoroughly; if noodles are too dry, the pudding will be heavy. Turn the hot noodles into the egg mixture, adding the raisins and the cottage cheese. Combine thoroughly but gently so you do not break up the noodles. Turn into the buttered baking dish. Dot the top generously with butter and bake for about 50 minutes, or until the pudding is set and the top is golden brown. Serve hot, plain or sprinkled with cinnamon sugar and with sour cream on the side.

Yield: 8 to 10 servings

Tapioca Pudding

Because of the glassy, round grains of tapioca set into this dish, we called it "fish-eye pudding," but we loved its vanilla flavor and eggy richness. It can be made with quick-cooking tapioca, but the version below has more body.

3 tablespoons seed pearl tapioca	3 tablespoons sugar
2 cups milk	3 egg yolks
Pinch of salt	1 teaspoon vanilla extract

Place the tapioca, milk, and salt in the top of a double boiler. Set over boiling water and cook, covered, for 15 to 20 minutes, stirring frequently, until the grains of tapioca are large and glassy clear and the mixture is creamy. Stir in the sugar. Remove from the lower potful of water.

Beat the egg yolks until light and foamy, then slowly add to the hot tapioca, stirring constantly. Set back over gently bubbling water and cook, stirring constantly, for 5 to 7 minutes, or until the custard is thick enough to coat a spoon.

Remove from the heat and stir in the vanilla.

Pour into 4 individual sherbet glasses or other dessert dishes. Chill until completely set.

Yield: 4 servings

Noant

[Passover Honey Nut Candy]

The contrasting scents and flavors of sweet honey, spicy ginger, tangy orange peel, and the crunch of walnuts made this one of the more memorable Passover treats. My grandmother used to pour the mix out on a lightly oiled platter to harden to a stiff taffy consistency, but much of it was stolen in tiny pinches while still gently warm and soft. Do not attempt to make it on a rainy or very humid day, because it will not harden.

1 cup honey, preferably dark and unfiltered	½ teaspoon powdered ginger
	Grated rind of ½ medium orange
2 cups sugar	1½ cups coarsely chopped walnuts
1 tablespoon lemon juice	

Have on hand a platter or cutting board that is about 12 to 14 inches long and 6 inches wide. Candy poured onto the board is easier to cut, but candy poured onto a platter with a small rim becomes just a little thicker and more interesting.

In a heavy, 2-quart saucepan, combine the honey, sugar, lemon juice, and ginger and stir very gently until blended. Place over low heat and cook slowly, stirring constantly until the sugar is completely melted. Raise the heat slightly and continue cooking, stirring frequently, until the mixture turns a deep golden brown and forms a soft ball when a few drops are added to a little ice-cold water.

Remove from the heat immediately and stir in the orange rind and walnuts. Wait about 5 minutes, or until the mixture cools and thickens slightly.

Pour onto the board or platter, which has been wet with cold water. Spread the mixture with a wet spatula to even it out. It should harden to a stiff, taffylike consistency within 2 to 3 hours. Cut into 1-inch squares to serve.

Yield: About 4 dozen pieces

Vareniki

[Prune, Cherry, or Blueberry Dumplings]

My grandmother made these more often than my mother did. They were usually served with coffee, rarely as dessert after a meal. Any cooked fruit can be used to make them, but stewed prunes or, in season, fresh cherries or blueberries were most often used.

Stewed prunes, cherries, or
blueberries (see below)
1 recipe basic noodle dough
(page 82)

2 to 3 quarts water, lightly salted
Melted butter
Cinnamon sugar

The fruit should be prepared in advance and be at room temperature.

Prepare the noodle dough as described in the recipe. When you have gathered it in a ball, wrap it in a plastic bag and set it aside for at least 30 minutes.

Roll the dough out on a floured board with a floured rolling pin. It should be paper thin but not quite as transparently sheer as for noodles. If you do not have a surface large enough to roll all the dough out in one sheet, divide in half and roll two sheets. Once rolled out, do not let the dough dry. Using a 3-inch round cookie cutter with a plain or scalloped edge, cut circles out of the dough. There should be about 24.

Place 3 cherries, a tablespoon of blueberries, or 2 to 3 prunes on one side of each circle, then fold over to form a half moon. Wet your fingers with cold water and pinch the edges closed very tightly. This pinching should not only seal the seam but should press it so it is not much thicker than the rest of the dough.

Bring 2 to 3 quarts of water to a boil and salt lightly.

Drop about 12 dumplings in at a time and boil rapidly for 10 to 12 minutes, or until the dough is thoroughly cooked but not too soft. Remove with a slotted spoon and place on paper towels to drain. Cook the remaining dumplings.

To serve, place 3 or 4 dumplings each on 6 to 8 individual dessert plates. Pour a little melted butter over each serving. Top with cinnamon sugar and drizzle on a little of the prune, blueberry, or cherry syrup. Serve at once.

Yield: About 24 vareniki

Variation: Vareniki can be baked on a buttered jelly-roll pan (350 degrees for 20 minutes) or deep fried in corn oil (360 degrees for 5 to 7 minutes).

Stewed Cherries

1 pound dark, ripe cherries	2-inch stick cinnamon
½ cup sugar	1 slice lemon
1 cup water, or as needed	

Wash the cherries, then remove stems and pits. Mix with the sugar and let stand in a warm place, preferably in sunshine, for 30 minutes. Place in a heavy saucepan with 1 cup water and the remaining ingredients. Simmer gently for 10 to 15 minutes, or until the cherries are soft but not mushy. Remove the cherries with a slotted spoon, and if the cooking liquid has not yet formed a medium-thick syrup, boil it for a minute or two until it does. Strain and reserve.

Cherries stewed this way can be served with their syrup as a dessert, plain or garnished with sour cream or whipped or unwhipped heavy sweet cream, or over vanilla ice cream.

Cherries and syrup for vareniki (see above) may be used immediately after they are cooked and have cooled.

Yield: 6 to 8 servings as a stewed fruit dessert, or enough filling and syrup for 24 varenikis

Variation: The syrup can also be flavored with a few drops of brandy after it finishes cooking. Pour this syrup over the cherries and let stand in the refrigerator for at least 24 hours before serving.

Stewed Blueberries

Follow the recipe for cherries, using 1 pint of blueberries; blueberries do not have to be pitted. Cook for about 8 minutes.

Stewed Prunes

The best result will be obtained with old-fashioned sour prunes that have not been treated to stay soft. Sweet, softened prunes have so little flavor or body they are hardly worth bothering with.

1 pound dried sour prunes	6 to 8 cloves
Warm water to cover	1 slice lemon
2-inch stick cinnamon	½ to ¾ cup sugar, to taste

Place the prunes in a 2-quart bowl or enameled pot and cover with warm water. Let soak overnight. Cook in the soaking water with the cinnamon stick, cloves, lemon slice, and ½ cup sugar. Bring to a boil, reduce the heat, and simmer for about 20 minutes. Add more water if necessary. Taste and add more sugar if necessary; continue cooking until the prunes are soft, about 10 minutes more. Remove the prunes with a slotted spoon, and if necessary continue to boil the syrup for a few minutes until it is of medium thickness. To prepare prunes for vareniki (see above), remove the pits.

Yield: 6 to 8 servings as a stewed fruit dessert, or enough filling and syrup for 24 varenikis

Variation: The prune syrup may also be flavored with rum or brandy as described for cherries, above.

Candied Grapefruit or Orange Peel

My mother always made this when friends visiting Florida would send us gift crates of citrus fruits. She considered it a very elegant dessert candy and liked to serve it in a cut-glass boat-shaped dish, along with other desserts. It is especially good when nibbled accompanied by freshly brewed tea.

6 large grapefruit or 8 navel	1½ cups boiling water
oranges	2½ teaspoons powdered ginger
4 cups sugar, approximately	(optional)

Select ripe fruit with skins as near perfect as possible. Cut the grapefruit or oranges in half and scrape out the fruit pulp and membranes. (Or use reserved shells from grapefruit or oranges that have been eaten.) Be sure that all membranes are removed but leave the white underskin on the peel. Cut the peel into long strips ¼ to ½ inch wide. Blanch in boiling water for 5 minutes. Drain and repeat the blanching three times, using fresh boiling water each time.

Cook 3 cups sugar in 1½ cups boiling water until a light syrup forms. Add the ginger and peels and stir through the syrup. Simmer gently, partially covered, for about 40 minutes, or until the peels have absorbed the liquid and are tender. Place the peels in a single layer on a sheet of waxed paper. Cool slightly and dredge with 1 cup sugar, or as needed. Let dry in a warm room overnight. Store in airtight containers. Serve as candy or use in recipes.

Yield: About 2 pounds

Note: If you cook both orange and grapefruit peels, cook them separately to retain the flavor of each.

22

A House in the Mountains

Although most of my summers were spent at the Brooklyn beaches, for a few years we rented a big house in the Catskill Mountains, in a tiny hamlet called Shandaken. It was about twelve miles from Fleischmanns, the "big" town where we went to shop, see an occasional movie, bowl, or just walk the streets for the sheer pleasure of seeing other people after so many weeks of seeing only ourselves.

We all loved the house we rented and in later years, my parents often regretted not having bought it. It was huge and sprawling, spread out wide with all of its many rooms on one level. It was built of big gray fieldstones and was furnished with dark wood mission country furniture, many mounted animal heads complete with antlers, and a player piano that was my special delight. In the kitchen was a huge black iron coal stove that had to be kept going with stoking, feeding, and rekindling with wood. This, and the removal of its ashes and the so many other small attentions it required in general, made it the constant subject of conversation and arguments between my city-bred parents, especially if the fire died out in the night. But in

241

the cold country mornings, that stove sent forth a blessed and welcome warmth, and it was on that stove that I was taught to do my first cooking— fried eggs for breakfast when I was about six.

There were mice and chipmunks that worked their way into that house too, much to my mother's horror, and we often found traces of them inside the animal heads, where they made nests, or around the cage of our canary, for mice apparently love bird seeds as much as birds do. Each night my father set traps and each morning cleared them out before my mother would set foot out of the bedroom. I thought chipmunks were adorable, but my mother said they were practically rats, and she had little more affection for woodchucks, who would gnaw at the cushions on the porch furniture.

That porch ran across the whole front of the house, and with its squeaky glider and numerous caned rocking chairs was the place we spent most of our evenings. The house was built high on a hill, and a big stone stairway led down from it to a clear, icy brook that ran and burbled over gold-gray stones, tumbling into a waterfall under which we all sat to let the water pound over us. Sitting behind the falling water was my favorite pastime, for there one did not get wet (as though getting to that point was not enough to leave one soaked) and could not be found, but also because I loved to look through the falling, sun-splashed water and see the trees and sky through that crystal curtain.

I remember the first time my mother found watercress in that brook and gave me some to nibble, I was stunned by the icy pepperiness of it, and to this day never bite into a leaf of it without experiencing an instant flashback to that brook. Speckled rainbow trout ran in it, and since my father loved to fish, we often had the almost live, fresh fish, broiled or tossed with a little salt, pepper and flour or cornmeal and quickly fried in butter.

Trout and watercress were not the only foods free for the gathering, for the area was rich in wild berries—strawberries in late June when we arrived, raspberries and blackberries through most of the summer. We carried aluminum pails and reached through scratchy brambles, trying to avoid poison ivy (and luckily always succeeding) and brought home mounds of berries that were served with sweet cream, over ice cream, or with sour cream and brown sugar. Some went into open tarts, and the surplus was simmered down to thick glistening jams, to be taken home for winter.

Beside food, one of the joys of that house was a big but gently sloped grassy hill alongside it, and when my cousins were there, several of us would join hands and feet to form a long line and roll down the hill. I often did that alone, of course, but it was not quite the same without the tangles and giggles produced by a group of rolling children.

It was customary then (and perhaps now) for anyone who had a house in the mountains to invite other members of the family to it. This my parents did, allowing two weeks each for an assortment of aunts and uncles, cousins and grandparents. Whoever came up from the city brought food, as though my mother hadn't stocked up for the new arrivals. The customary gift from the city was delicatessen—long, heavy salamis, cooked pickled tongues, wide bologna, frankfurter "specials," and towering boxes of cake.

Eating was done on an almost continuous basis—breakfast around eight, coffee and maybe a piece of cake or toasted bagel around ten-thirty, lunch at twelve-thirty, fruit, coffee, and cake in midafternoon, dinner around six-thirty. Then, after card playing and other evening activities, some herring, more cake, a little of this and that around eleven, just before bed.

We went to a local farm for butter, cream, milk, and cheese and during the summers drank the thick, rich raw milk. The most extraordinary product of that dairy was the buttermilk, and I have never tasted any as thick, creamy, and pungent since. I liked it ice cold, with a tiny pinch of salt, and one of the hot, freshly baked corn muffins that my mother often made. The sour cream to be poured over herring or raw vegetables was as rich as whipped cream, and the dry, uncreamed nuggets of pot cheese I remember as being better even than ice cream.

Usually we went to that house for about eight weeks, leaving the day after school closed in late June and returning on Labor Day weekend. Trips to and from "the country" always began before sunrise, when the dew was still on the ground and the sky was a dark, leaden gray. My mother would pack fried egg and bacon sandwiches that we ate along the way, along with thermos bottles full of coffee with sugar and hot milk.

My father generally worked in the city and came up on weekends and for a two- or three-week vacation, but one summer, when he was recuperating from an illness, he spent the whole summer with us and we stayed through the middle of November. For about two and a half months that fall, I attended a local one-room schoolhouse that remains the most memorable and richest of my school experiences. Mrs. Stark, the teacher, taught eight grades in one room, and I was fascinated by the system of giving out assignments to each grade, then hearing the lessons of each in the front of the room while the rest of the group studied assignments and waited for a turn to perform. I was in the third grade, and the history taught to that level in that school was mythology. I was stunned to know that none of my friends in Brooklyn had learned anything about Zeus and Jupiter, Juno and Aphrodite, and my favorite, Loki, whose special province was mischief; my continuing fascination with mythology is something I owe to Mrs. Stark, who made it all come alive.

Most of all I remember the one-mile walk to that schoolhouse, in the early, dew-frosted fall mornings, as colors changed and the mist rose like a gossamer stage curtain. Carrying a lunch box that included raisins and prunes for recess and a sandwich for lunch, I often stopped to pick up and munch on a few ripe, fallen apples. I wished then that I never had to go back to the mundane and stuffy six-story brick Brooklyn school, for I knew I would miss the intimacy and individual instruction I'd found in that simple country schoolhouse.

23

Baking

This is one area where my grandmother's abilities far exceeded those of my mother. My grandmother was, in fact, the best home baker I have ever known, and the variety and intricacies of the cookies, coffee cakes, pies, tarts, and pound and spice cakes she made were seemingly endless. Unfortunately, these have been the most difficult recipes to recreate, since very few of her baked specialties were made by her daughters.

Reproduced here are mostly the recipes my mother used, plus those few of my grandmother's specialties which I was able to approximate from memory and by consulting various Polish, Hungarian, and Jewish cookbooks. I also received help and advice from John Clancy, a professional chef and baker who teaches and writes about baking better than anyone I know. He was especially helpful with the recipe for challah. "Sure," he said when he prepared it for me, "just tell them the Irish John Clancy knows how to make your Jewish grandmother's challah!"

Bagels

More and more, mass-produced bagels are becoming soft, white, fluffy imitations of American rolls. My grandmother baked her own bagels, then stopped when very good bakery varieties became available. Now the wheel has come full circle, and it seems the only way to get really good bagels is to make them. You can, of course, use active dry yeast, but, again, cake yeast will produce far better results, and since you are going to so much trouble, why not go all the way?

1 package active dry yeast, plus ¼ cup warm water and a pinch of sugar, or, preferably, ½ ounce cake yeast, plus 1 tablespoon warm water and a pinch each of sugar and salt
⅔ to ¾ cup warm water
¼ cup peanut oil
Salt
3 cups flour, or as needed
2 quarts water
1 egg, beaten with 1 tablespoon cold water
Coarse salt and/or caraway seeds, for sprinkling (optional)

If using active dry yeast, sprinkle it on top of the ¼ cup warm water and add a pinch of sugar. Set aside in a warm, draft-free corner for 5 to 10 minutes, until the mixture becomes foamy. If using cake yeast, cream it with the 1 tablespoon warm water, a pinch of sugar and salt until you have a syrup. Set aside for 5 to 10 minutes until foamy. Place the yeast mixture in a warm bowl, and stir in ⅔ cup warm water, the oil, and 2 teaspoons salt. Gradually stir in enough flour to make a dough that is stiff but not crumbly and dry and one that is workable; use more water if needed. Knead for 10 to 15 minutes on a floured board, until the dough is satiny and elastic.

Brush the inside of a bowl with peanut oil or melted butter and add the dough to it. Cover loosely with a towel, place in a warm, draft-free corner and let rise for about 1 hour, or until doubled in bulk. The dough has risen enough when an indentation made with your finger remains and does not spring back. The dough should be puffy and spongy.

Cut the dough into 16 to 18 pieces. Roll each to a thin rope about ½ inch in diameter and about 8 inches long. Form each rope into a circle, fastening well at the joining point.

Bring 2 quarts of water to a boil with a handful of salt. Preheat the oven to 450 degrees. Lightly oil a large cookie sheet.

Drop the bagels, two or three at a time, into the gently boiling water. Cook for 2 or 3 minutes on one side, then turn to cook the second side. Remove with a slotted spoon, drain thoroughly and arrange on a greased cookie sheet. Continue boiling the remaining bagels in the same way. When all are on the cookie sheet, brush the tops only with the egg and water combination, sprinkle with salt and/or caraway seeds, and bake for 15 to 20 minutes, or until golden brown. You can break one bagel open as a test to see if it is thoroughly done inside.

Yield: 16 to 18 bagels

Note: Anyone who likes to eat hot bagels is entitled to his choice, but true aficionados prefer them at room temperature, between 5 and 7 hours after they have been baked. They can be frozen and reheated in the oven, and can be made in any size you wish.

Challah

[Braided Sabbath Bread]

My single most unforgettable memory of my grandmother is that of her making this snowy, yeasty, poppy-seed-encrusted braided loaf every Friday morning. I can remember stepping into her small three-room apartment early in the morning when the scents of the coming Friday night meal were already filling the air, and the scene in the kitchen seemed to me overlaid with a gossamer white veil of flour. A small round woman with white hair and very fair skin, my grandmother herself looked as if she were floured right along with her wooden boards and bowls. The dough she made was creamy white in color, gentle, pliable, never sticky but unmistakably alive. I used to help with a brief kneading, and then shape a single small loaf of my own, and the velvety puffiness of the dough is something I can still almost feel.

Her recipe is lost to the family because neither my aunts nor my mother made it (they bought their Sabbath loaves), so I have had to work back toward an approximation. Most challah recipes call for more eggs and sugar, and often for saffron. She used none of those, and one of the outstanding characteristics was the chewy pulliness of the final result.

You can make challah with active dry yeast as indicated below, but the flavor and texture will be far better if you use cake yeast, purchased from a baker or a health food store if you cannot find it anywhere else. This bread is not only delicious plain or buttered, but it makes the world's best French toast (page 106).

2 packages active dry yeast, plus
⅓ cup water and 1 teaspoon sugar,
     or, preferably, 1 ounce cake
     yeast, plus 1 tablespoon warm
     water and a pinch each of
     sugar and salt
½ cup peanut oil
5 teaspoons salt

1 cup boiling water
½ cup cold water
2 eggs, lightly beaten
5 to 7 cups unbleached flour
1 egg yolk, lightly beaten with 1
     tablespoon cold water
Poppy seeds, for sprinkling

Sprinkle the active dry yeast, if using, on the ⅓ cup warm water, then sprinkle on the sugar. Set aside in a warm, draft-free place for 5 to 10 minutes, or until the yeast becomes foamy.

If you are using cake yeast, cream it with the 1 tablespoon warm water, sugar, and salt until syrupy; let stand in a draft-free corner for 5 to 10 minutes, until it becomes slightly frothy.

Combine the oil and salt and stir in the boiling water. Stir, and add the cold water. Beat the eggs into the water and oil mixture and stir in the dissolved yeast. Stir in 5 cups of flour gradually until you have a smooth, very pliable dough that is only slightly sticky. Add more flour as needed.

Turn out on a floured board and knead for about 15 minutes, or until the dough blisters and is elastic and completely nonsticky. Work in more flour; it should take close to 7 cups. Place the dough back in the cleaned bowl, cover with a towel, and set in a warm, draft-free corner for 1 to 1½ hours, or until doubled in bulk. The dough has risen sufficiently when a hole poked into it with your finger remains indented without springing back. (If you have patience, it is better to let the dough rise in a cool room, which can take about 2 hours.) Punch down, knead briefly and let rise again for 1½ to 2 hours.

Turn the dough onto a floured board and knead for a minute or two. Divide into 4 equal pieces. If sticky, knead a little flour into each piece so it will be smooth. Set the dough aside for 5 to 10 minutes while you brush a cookie sheet lightly with peanut oil.

Roll each piece of dough into a strand about 16 inches long. Following the diagram, braid the strands, using four for each loaf, by starting at one end without pinching the ends of the strands and then braiding as shown. Braiding should be firm and compact—not too loose and open, nor tight and pinched. Turn both ends under slightly, also as shown.

Arrange the loaf on the baking sheet and place in a warm, draftfree corner, covered with a towel. Let rise for 1 hour.

Preheat the oven to 375 degrees.

Brush the top of the loaf well with the beaten egg yolk and water combination, and sprinkle liberally with poppy seeds. Bake for 40 to 50 minutes, or until the bread is golden brown on top and sounds hollow when tapped with your knuckles on the bottom. Cool on a rack.

This bread keeps well in the refrigerator and even better in the freezer. After thawing, place in a 375-degree oven for 10 minutes to freshen the flavor.

Yield: 1 loaf

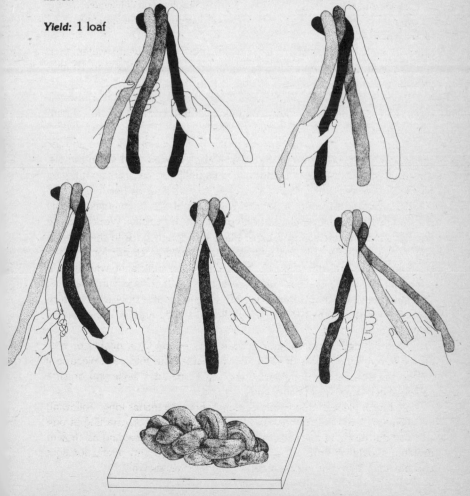

Matzohs

Homemade matzohs have very little to do with the packaged variety but are much closer to the handmade matzohs prepared by Hasidic communities each year before Passover. These matzohs are made very quickly, to avoid the danger of fermentation from the time the flour is wet until the dough goes into the oven. They are circular, not square, and very hard, stiff and crusty. My grandmother used to make a few of her own, but never for Passover, because she could not get the special flour required at that time of year. The recipe below is one I devised after watching the Hasidic bakers in the Williamsburg section of Brooklyn. The version with whole-wheat flour is closer to the authentic schmura matzoh, which is based on milled whole-wheat berries. The final result is a matzoh that is wheat colored and richly flavored. No salt is added to matzohs, nor is the dough allowed to rest before it is rolled. These matzohs look like ancient parchments and have a wonderful toasty flavor. They are good spread with butter, or simply sprinkled with salt or flavored with onion or garlic and reheated, as described on page 251.

The ovens in which the Hasidic bakers make these matzohs are huge, wood-fired, and have stone floors. While it is probably not possible for you to bake them in a wood-fired oven, you can approximate the stone floor by lining a shelf rack in your oven with large, flat, unglazed terra-cotta tiles purchased at a flooring or tile shop. Soak the tiles for 24 hours in water before the first use. I have also gotten very good results baking the matzohs on a heavy cookie sheet. But it is essential that you have a good oven that reaches at least 500 degrees and retains this temperature.

2 cups unbleached flour, more   **½ to ¾ cup cold water, as needed**
   if needed

Preheat the oven to 500 degrees.

Place the flour on a board or in a wide mixing bowl and make a mound with a well in the center. Pour in ½ cup water and begin to stir in the flour gradually, using your fingertips or a fork. Add more water as needed until all the flour is mixed in and you have a soft pliable dough that is just barely sticky. Divide the dough in quarters. On a floured board, knead each portion of dough 8 or 10 times, working in a little flour if it is too sticky to be rolled. Clean the board of all dough scraps, reflour, and with a floured rolling pin roll the dough into a circle about 7 inches in diameter and a little less than ⅛ inch thick. Pierce the surface all over with the tines of a fork, being sure you pierce through the bottom of the dough. This will keep the matzoh from buckling while it bakes.

If you have enough room in your oven or on your baking sheets, you can bake all the matzohs at once. In that case, roll out all the dough and do so. Otherwise bake them one or two at a time, but do not roll out the remaining dough until you are ready to bake it. Lift the pierced dough over a rolling pin and turn onto ungreased baking sheet or tiles. Bake for about 10 minutes. When the matzoh curls, looks very dry, and shows some golden-brown patches and edges, turn and bake the second side for 5 to 8 minutes, or until it too is golden brown. Some very dark edges are desirable, for they add a special flavor. Remove from the oven and cool on a rack.

Yield: 4 seven-inch matzohs

Variations: 1. To make these with whole-wheat flour, follow the above recipe but use more water—probably an extra ¼ cup will do. These matzohs will be a little thicker, but will have a better color and flavor.

2. I have given directions for the 7-inch round matzohs because this size seems more convenient for home baking. However, the matzohs made by the Hasidic bakers are closer to 12 or 14 inches in diameter and are more impressive looking. If your oven or baking sheets can accommodate such sizes, simply divide the dough in half and roll into two big rounds. The larger size is a bit more difficult to handle; be sure the dough does not crease or fold back on itself during rolling or when you place it on the baking sheet or tiles. The folds or creases will form soggy patches.

Baked and Seasoned Matzohs

To freshen the flavor of packaged or homemade matzohs, dampen them lightly on both sides by rubbing wet hands over them. Place on a rack in a 375-degree oven for a few minutes, until dry and crisp and faintly brown around the edges. Coarse salt can be sprinkled on the top side of each after wetting and before baking.

Baked matzohs can also be seasoned with garlic or onion, in which case they are delicious with soup, or cheese and various canape spreads. Rub one side of each matzoh with a cut clove of garlic or onion. Dampen the matzoh slightly, sprinkle with salt, and bake for 6 or 7 minutes at 375 degrees.

Mohn or Zwiebel Kichel

[Poppy Seed and Onion Biscuits]

Whenever my grandmother made these great family favorites, she baked them in huge quantities so they could not only be divided among her sons and daughters in New York, but could be shipped to children and grandchildren all over the country.

Containing both poppy seeds (mohn) and flecks of onion (zwiebel), these crisp, hard, peppery biscuits were referred to in my family by either name, somewhat indiscriminately and almost alternately. There seems to be no reason to make a choice now.

They are especially good with drinks such as beer, whiskey, or young red wine, and go well with cheeses such as Swiss, Cheddar or Muenster. Usually cut into rounds or diamond shapes in the size indicated below, they can also be cut smaller with cookie cutters, if you prefer a fancier, more fashionable version for cocktail parties.

2 envelopes active dry yeast, plus ½ cup lukewarm water and a pinch of sugar, or, preferably, 1 ounce cake yeast, plus 1 tablespoon warm water and a pinch each of sugar and salt
3½ pounds flour, or as needed
3 extra-large eggs, lightly beaten

½ pound very fresh poppy seeds (about 1½ cups)
2½ tablespoons salt
1½ teaspoons black pepper
5 very large or 6 to 7 medium onions, coarsely grated
¾ cup peanut oil

If you are using active dry yeast, sprinkle it into the water with a pinch of sugar. If using cake yeast, mash to a syrup with 1 tablespoon warm water and a little sugar and salt. Let the yeast stand for 5 to 10 minutes, until the mixture begins to foam.

Place the flour in a large, wide mixing bowl or in a mound on a pastry board or wood counter top. Make a well in the center and add the yeast mixture, eggs, poppy seeds, salt, pepper, grated onion, and peanut oil. Beat these ingredients together lightly with a fork, then gradually stir the flour into the liquid mixture until all has been worked in and absorbed. If the dough is too stiff and crumbly, add a little more water. If it is too soft and sticky to knead, which is more likely to be the case, work in more flour until it is light, smooth, very elastic, but not at all sticky.

Working on the lightly floured wood surface, knead the dough very well until it is shiny and blisters form on the surface. This will take anywhere from 15 to 20 minutes, depending upon the temperature in the room and the vigor with which you knead. The process can also be accomplished using the dough hook of a mixing machine, but it will be better if it is finished with hand kneading for at least 5 minutes.

Clean out and grease the mixing bowl. Place the dough in it, cover with a towel, and place in a warm, draft-free corner to rise until it has doubled in bulk. This can take from 1½ to 2 hours. My grandmother preferred even slower rising, and in winter would put the well-covered bowl out on the back porch to rise very slowly overnight. She felt this permitted some of the onion fumes to evaporate, resulting in a more delicately flavored finished product.

Preheat the oven to 350 degrees and brush two or three large cookie sheets with peanut oil.

Punch the dough down, divide it into convenient batches, and using a lightly floured rolling pin on a lightly floured surface, roll out ¼ inch thick. Cut in squares or diamonds with a sharp knife, or, using a glass, cut circles. My mother and grandmother cut diamonds that were about 3 inches in length and circles 2 inches in diameter, but these may seem large by today's standards, so adjust accordingly, to a reasonable portion size.

Arrange the cut kichel on the oiled cookie sheets, leaving a 1-inch space between each on all sides. Prick the entire surface of each kichel with a fork and brush the tops lightly with peanut oil. Bake in a preheated 350-degree oven for about 45 minutes, or until golden brown.

Remove the kichel from the pan as soon as they come out of the oven. Cool thoroughly on a rack, then pack in an airtight container such as a jar or tin box, where they will keep for weeks.

Their flavor strengthens and mellows after 24 hours.

Yield: 50 three-inch kichel

YEAST CAKES

These delicious coffee cakes were really my grandmother's baking triumphs. Always flavored with cinnamon, sugar, and vanilla, her yeast cakes took various forms—sometimes topped with buttery streusel crumbs, other times with nuts and cinnamon or fruit. Our favorite was the one we called "gewickelte" ("entwined") in which the nuts, cinnamon, and raisin filling were rolled into the dough jelly-roll style. She tended to use the richer dough for the plainer cakes and the basic dough for the rolled and filled versions, but that was pure whim. Again, cake yeast is preferable.

Basic Yeast Coffee-Cake Dough

2 packages active dry yeast, plus ½
    cup warm water and a pinch of
    sugar, or, preferably, 1 ounce
    cake yeast, plus 1 tablespoon warm
    water and a pinch each of sugar
    and salt
1 cup (½ pound) sweet butter,
    softened
⅔ cup sugar

1 teaspoon salt
Grated rind of 2 lemons
1½ cups scalded milk, cooled to
    lukewarm
1 jumbo egg plus 5 egg yolks
1 tablespoon vanilla extract
    (optional)
5 to 6 cups flour, as needed

If using active yeast dry, sprinkle it into the ½ cup warm water along with a pinch of sugar. Set aside in a warm, draft-free corner for 5 to 10 minutes, until foamy.

If you use cake yeast, cream it with the 1 tablespoon warm water and a pinch each of sugar and salt until a syrup forms. Set aside for 5 to 10 minutes, until foamy.

Cream the butter with the sugar and salt until light and fluffy. Blend in the lemon rind. Stir in the whole egg, the egg yolks, and vanilla; stir in the cooled, scalded milk. Add the yeast. Beat until thoroughly mixed. Add 3 cups of flour and stir in until smooth. Gradually beat in the remaining flour until you have a dough that is light, pliable, moist, and workable.

Turn onto a floured board and knead for at least 15 minutes, or until the dough is very satiny and elastic. Place in a lightly greased bowl and cover with a towel. Set in a warm, draft-free corner to rise until doubled in bulk, about 1 to 1½ hours. Punch down and let rise again until doubled in bulk. The dough has risen sufficiently if an indentation remains when you press your finger into it. After the second rising, knead lightly, then shape and finish as directed in the following recipes.

Rich Yeast Coffee-Cake Dough

Follow the above instructions, using 12 egg yolks instead of 5, and only ¾ cup milk.

Cinnamon Coffee Cake

Preheat the oven to 350 degrees.

Prepare a rich yeast coffee-cake dough (see above), and after the second rising, knead it lightly and roll or pat it out to fit a buttered 9 x 13-inch pan or a 10-inch round springform. Brush the dough with melted sweet butter and sprinkle liberally with cinnamon sugar. Cover and let rise for 1 hour. Bake in the preheated oven for about 45 minutes, or until the cake is done and the top is golden brown. If you like, slivered almonds or chopped walnuts can be sprinkled over the top with the cinnamon sugar.

Yield: 1 coffee cake

Streuselkuchen

[Crumb Coffee Cake]

Preheat the oven to 350 degrees.

Prepare a rich yeast coffee-cake dough (see above) and arrange in the pan as described for cinnamon coffee cake, just above. Prepare streusel crumbs as described on page 273, doubling the recipe. Brush the dough with melted sweet butter, top with the crumbs, and let rise for 1 hour. Bake about 45 minutes, or until the cake is done and the crumbs are golden brown.

Yield: 1 coffee cake

Gewickelte Cake

[Rolled Coffee Cake]

1 recipe basic yeast coffee-cake dough (page 254)	1 cup sugar
	2 tablespoons powdered cinnamon
Melted sweet butter	2 cups chopped walnuts or pecans
1½ cups currants or raisins	Milk, for brushing

Prepare the coffee-cake dough, and after the second rising, divide the dough in half and knead each portion lightly. Roll each out to a rectangle on a floured board with a floured rolling pin; the dough should be about ⅛ inch thick. Brush with melted sweet butter and sprinkle with a mixture of the currants or raisins, sugar, cinnamon, and nuts. Drizzle a little more butter over the top and roll lengthwise, jelly-roll style.

When the two rolls are ready, place them, seam sides down, on a lightly buttered and floured shallow baking pan, such as a jelly-roll pan. Cover and let rise until doubled in bulk.

Meanwhile, preheat the oven to 350 degrees.

Brush the rolls with milk and bake in the preheated oven for 1 hour, or until golden brown and puffed up. Cool and cut in very thin slices to serve.

Yield: 2 coffee cakes

Poppy-Seed Coffee Cake

Prepare a filling of ¾ pound poppy seeds, washed and ground, mixed with 1½ cups half-and-half milk and cream, 3 tablespoons sweet butter, ¾ cup honey, and the grated rinds of 1 lemon and 1 orange. Simmer in a heavy sauce pan for a few minutes until thick. Cool.

Prepare the basic yeast coffee-cake dough (page 254) and roll exactly as described for gewickelte cake (see above). Brush with melted sweet butter, spread with the poppy-seed filling, roll, and place on a buttered and floured shallow baking pan. Let rise until doubled in bulk. Bake in a preheated 350-degree oven for 1 hour. Cool and serve thinly sliced.

Cheese-Filled Coffee Cake

½ recipe basic yeast coffee-cake
    dough (page 254)
1 pound dry (uncreamed) pot cheese
    or farmer cheese (not cottage
    cheese)
3 tablespoons sweet butter
½ cup sugar

2 jumbo eggs, separated
¼ cup flour, or as needed
⅔ cup sour cream
1 teaspoon vanilla extract
    Grated rind of 1 lemon
1 egg yolk, beaten with a few drops
    of water

Prepare the coffee-cake dough. While it is rising, make the filling.

Rub the cheese through a sieve. Cream the butter with the sugar until light and fluffy, then beat in egg yolks. Combine with the sieved cheese, flour, sour cream, vanilla, and lemon rind, stirring in enough flour to make a puffy but cohesive mass. Beat the egg whites to stiff and shiny peaks and fold into the cheese mixture, gently but thoroughly, using a rubber spatula.

Roll out the dough as described for gewickelte cake (page 255). Brush with melted sweet butter and place the cheese filling in a line, lengthwise along the center of the dough, leaving about 1½ inches empty at each end. Fold the ends in over the cheese, then fold in the long sides until they overlap. Flip the cake over, seam side down, onto a buttered and floured shallow pan. Let rise until doubled in bulk.

Meanwhile, preheat the oven to 350 degrees.

Glaze the dough with the egg yolk beaten with a few drops of cold water. Bake in a preheated 350-degree oven for 1 hour.

Yield: 1 coffee cake

Small Coffee Cakes

Using the basic yeast coffee-cake dough, you can roll it out after the second rising and cut squares anywhere from 4 to 8 inches. Fill them with lekvar (prune filling, page 262), poppy-seed filling (page 256), or cheese filling (page 256). Place the filling in the center, fold the corners in toward the center, and pinch together. Place on buttered and floured shallow baking pans and let rise until doubled in bulk. For a shiny finish, brush with egg yolk beaten with cold water. For a dull patina, brush with plain milk. Bake for about 35 minutes. Four-inch squares will make miniatures. Eight-inch squares will make fairly large pieces.

Knish, Pirogen, or Pierogi

For reasons that have to remain a mystery, the preparation my grandmother called a "knish" is really the big, yeasty, baked roll known as a "pirogen" or "pierogi" (and occasionally as a "piroshki"). I suppose that same dough baked in small squares would look like the conventional knish, which no one in my family ever made. My grandmother always made a huge roll that she turned into a horseshoe shape so that it would fit on the pan. You can cut the basic yeast dough recipe in half to make half the amount, or cut the roll in half if you use the whole recipe and prefer two straight rolls to the horseshoe. It was always an event when my grandmother made this, and she often baked enough to send one over to each of her children who lived in Brooklyn—which meant about five in all. For that amount she used three times the basic recipe. Her filling of chicken livers, kasha, sautéed onions, and the chicken-fat cracklings, griebenes, was savory and delicious. This was always served hot, and is a wonderful cocktail hors d'oeuvre.

1 recipe basic yeast coffee-cake dough (page 254), amended as described below	2 cups finely minced onion
	2 cups cooked fine-grain kasha (see page 219)
2½ pounds chicken livers, trimmed	1½ cups griebenes (cracklings, page 7), crushed or chopped
1½ cups schmaltz (rendered chicken fat, page 7), or as needed	Salt and black pepper to taste

Follow the coffee-cake dough recipe, but omit all sugar except the pinch used to start the yeast. Also omit the lemon rind and vanilla, and add an extra teaspoon salt.

While the dough is rising for the second time, prepare the filling.

Sauté the onion in ½ cup schmaltz until soft and very faintly golden brown around the edges. Remove and reserve. Add the chicken livers to the pan, with more fat if needed, and fry slowly until thoroughly cooked inside and light golden brown outside. Remove from the pan and chop fine, then combine with the sautéed onion, cooked kasha, griebenes, and all the pan drippings and coagulated bits you can scrape up. Add fat if the mixture seems dry. Mix and season with salt and black pepper. Let cool thoroughly.

After the dough has risen for the second time, knead it lightly, then roll out to a rectangle, as thin as possible. Brush with melted schmaltz and spread with the cooled filling. Roll lengthwise, jelly-roll style, and flip over, seam side down, onto a greased and floured shallow pan—a jelly-roll pan is perfect. Fold the ends under. Cover with a towel and let rise for about 30 minutes or until not quite doubled in bulk.

Meanwhile, preheat the oven to 375 degrees.

Bake the knish for 1 to 1½ hours, or until crisp and golden brown. This can be served when it has cooled down slightly, or it can be reheated after it has cooled completey.

Yield: 2 ten-inch rolls or 1 twenty-inch horseshoe

Schnecken

[Cinnamon-Nut Snails]

2 envelopes active dry yeast, plus ¼ cup lukewarm water and a pinch of sugar, or, preferably, 1 ounce cake yeast, plus 1 tablespoon warm water and a pinch each of sugar and salt
½ scant cup sugar
1 cup (½ pound) sweet butter, melted and cooled, plus extra for brushing the dough

½ cup scalded milk, cooled to lukewarm
½ cup sour cream
1 whole egg plus 2 egg yolks
4 to 5 cups flour, as needed
¾ cup brown sugar
2 tablespoons powdered cinnamon
½ cup dried currants
2 cups chopped walnuts

If using active dry yeast, sprinkle it into the ¼ cup lukewarm water, then add a little sugar. Set in a warm, draft-free corner for 5 to 10 minutes, until foamy. If using cake yeast, cream it with the 1 tablespoon warm water and a pinch each of sugar and salt until a syrup forms, then set in a warm, draft-free corner for 5 to 10 minutes, until foamy.

Combine the scant ½ cup sugar with the foamy yeast, melted butter, and lukewarm milk. Stir until dissolved. Add the sour cream, whole egg, and egg yolks. Mix well. Stir the flour in gradually until the dough is pliable but not sticky. Turn onto a floured board and knead for about 10 minutes, or until the dough is satiny and elastic but not blistery. Place in a greased bowl, cover with a towel, and place in a warm, draft-free corner for 1 to 1½ hours, or until doubled in bulk.

Grease two jelly-roll pans. Punch the dough down and divide into pieces that are convenient to roll out. Roll each in a rectangular shape about ⅛ inch thick. Brush the top of the rolled-out dough with butter, then sprinkle generously with brown sugar and cinnamon, mixed, the currants, and walnuts. Roll firmly, lengthwise, jelly-roll style. Using a sharp, thin-bladed knife, cut the roll into ⅓-inch-thick slices and place 1½ inches apart on the baking pans. Sprinkle with cinnamon and sugar. Cover with a towel and let rise until doubled, about 1 hour.

Meanwhile, preheat the oven to 350 degrees.

Bake the schnecken for about 20 minutes, or until a rich golden brown.

Yield: About 3 dozen medium-sized schnecken

Variations: The rolls can be made very small and cut in thinner slices for miniatures.

Rugelach

[Cinnamon Nut Horns]

These are most authentically made with the same yeast dough as used for schnecken (see above). Prepare as above and roll out after the dough has risen. Roll very thin, less than ⅛ inch, brush with a little melted sweet butter, sprinkle generously with brown sugar, cinnamon, currants, and nuts, and cut into triangles that are about 3 inches at the base and 3½ to 4 inches long, tapering of course to a point. Roll the triangles, from base to point, and turn the ends in slightly to form crescents or horns. Place on a greased cookie sheet, cover with a towel, and let rise for 1 hour. Brush the tops of the rugelach with egg yolk beaten with a little milk and bake in a 375-degree oven for 20 to 25 minutes.

Yield: About 3 dozen crescents

Variation: Rugelach are often made with a cream-cheese dough, rather than yeast dough, as follows:

Cream together ½ cup (¼ pound) butter and ¼ pound cream cheese, both at room temperature. Beat in ½ cup sour cream. Stir in a pinch of salt, 2 teaspoons sugar, 1 egg and about 2¾ cups flour, or just enough to make a dough that will stick together. Form a ball, cover with plastic wrap, and chill overnight. Cut the dough in portions that are convenient to handle and roll each out between sheets of waxed paper. Brush with melted sweet butter, sprinkle generously with cinnamon, sugar, currants, and nuts as described above. Cut in triangles. Roll into crescents as above, place on a greased baking sheet, chill for 1 hour, then bake in a 350-degree oven for about 25 minutes.

Yield: About 30 crescents

Hamantaschen

[Three-Cornered Hats for Purim]

I have always wondered why although in German *taschen* means "pockets," these crisp, prune-filled cakes are translated as "hats," symbolizing the tricornered hat worn by Haman, whose well-earned demise is celebrated during Purim, or the feast of Esther. My grandmother always made these the most traditional way with yeast dough; my mother preferred the simpler baking-powder version. Yeast adds more flavor, but choose whichever method suits you.

Hamantaschen may be made with several fillings, most usually with the prune puree known as "lekvar," or with apricot jam or poppy seeds. Only the first was ever used in our family, and it is the only one that tastes authentic to me. Thick prune puree or butter (lekvar) may be purchased ready made in jars in supermarkets, or better yet from barrels in shops found in Jewish and Eastern European neighborhoods. It can also be made at home (see page 262).

Hamantaschen with Yeast Dough

Follow the recipe given for schnecken dough (page 259). After it has risen, roll it out paper thin and cut into circles about 4 inches in diameter. Into the center of each circle place about 1½ teaspoons lekvar. Fold the circles to form three-cornered "hats," as shown in the diagram, pinching the seams tightly closed. Be sure to leave an opening on top so the dark prune filling will show. Arrange on a buttered cookie sheet or shallow baking pan, cover with a towel, and let rise for about 40 minutes, meanwhile preheating the oven to 350 degrees. Bake for about 20 minutes, or until the dough is light golden brown and crisp.

Yield: About 30 Hamantaschen

Note: You will need 1 generous cup of lekvar for this dough.

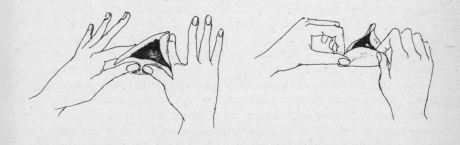

Hamantaschen with Pie-Crust Dough

Double the recipe for rich tart pastry I (page 277). After it is mixed, divide the dough in half, forming a ball with each. Wrap each part in waxed paper and chill for at least 1 hour. Then, keeping one ball of dough in the refrigerator while rolling out the first, roll out to a little less than ¼ inch thick on a lightly floured board; the shape of the rolled-out dough is not important. Using a 3½- to 4-inch round cookie cutter, cut circles from the dough. Scraps may be gathered together and rerolled without chilling if you have worked quickly.

When all the circles have been cut, arrange them on an ungreased cookie sheet. Place 1 well-rounded teaspoonful of filling in the center of each. Moisten the edges of the circles with cold water and shape triangles as shown on the previous page, being sure to pinch the corner seams tightly shut. Bake in a preheated 400-degree oven for about 15 minutes, or until the bottoms are golden brown and crisp and the top crusts are pale golden brown. Remove from the cookie sheet while still warm and cool on a rack.

Yield: 15 to 16 Hamantaschen

Note: For a flaky, softer crust, use the cream-cheese pastry described for rugelach (page 260.) The dough for Grandma Breit's cookies (page 285) was also used for Hamantaschen.

Lekvar

[Prune Filling]

If you buy this ready made, taste it and see if you want to add other flavorings. For 1 pound (2 cups) lekvar, add 2 teaspoons lemon juice, 1 teaspoon lemon rind, ¼ teaspoon cinnamon, and ⅔ cup finely chopped walnuts. It is then ready for use. If you want to (or have to) make your own lekvar, remove the pits from 3 cups of cooked prunes and rub the prunes through a sieve or puree in a food processor. Be very careful if you do the latter, because you do not want to liquefy the prunes; you want a thick, velvety mass. Sweeten with sugar (how much you need will depend on whether the prunes have been cooked with sugar, whether they were sweet prunes or [preferably] sour prunes to begin with, and your personal taste). Cooked, unsweetened sour prunes will require about ½ cup sugar. Stir in a little lemon juice, grated lemon rind, ½ to 1 teaspoon powdered cinnamon, and, if you like, about ½ cup finely chopped nuts.

This is also good as a jam to be spread on hot toast, waffles or French toast, or as a crêpe filling.

Leckach

[Honey Cake]

We loved this cake all year round but of course it has special significance during the Jewish New Year holiday, Rosh Hashanah, when eating honey was considered a promise of a sweet year ahead.

2 cups dark honey
¾ cup black coffee, brewed double strength
3 tablespoons mild vegetable oil, preferably peanut
4 eggs
¾ cup sugar
3½ cups sifted flour
Pinch of salt

1 teaspoon baking soda
1½ teaspoons baking powder
1 teaspoon powdered cinnamon
1 teaspoon powdered ginger
Grated rind of 1 orange
Grated rind of 1 lemon
10 or 12 whole blanched almonds (optional)

Preheat the oven to 325 degrees. Butter a 9½ x 5½ x 3-inch loaf pan. Cut clean brown paper, waxed paper, or baker's parchment to fit the bottom and sides of the pan and butter one side. Place the unbuttered side of the paper against the pan.

Put the honey in a heavy saucepan and bring to a boil. Set aside, let cool, then stir in the coffee and oil. Beat the eggs with the sugar until light and thick so the mixture forms a ribbon when dropped onto itself. Stir in the coffee, honey, and oil mixture. Resift the flour and other dry ingredients into the batter; fold in gently with the fruit rind.

Pour the batter into the lined pan. If you like, make a pattern on top with almonds.

Bake for about 1¼ to 1½ hours, or until the top is golden brown and a tester inserted in the center comes out clean. Let the cake cool in the pan.

Do not peel off all the paper; just peel off what is necessary each time you slice the cake. This cake will develop more flavor if it is kept uncut for 24 hours. It keeps well in an airtight container.

Teiglach

[Honey Nuts]

Again, because of the honey, this symbolized a sweet year ahead. This chewy confection was standard on Rosh Hashanah (New Year's) tables and was a favorite dessert when the Yom Kippur fast was broken. My grandmother made it at other times of the year simply as a confection. It is very much like the Italian Christmas confection, *strufeli*.

3 eggs, lightly beaten	3 pounds dark honey
3 tablespoons vegetable oil, preferably peanut	1½ cups sugar
2 to 2½ cups flour, as needed	2 teaspoons powdered ginger
¼ teaspoon salt	2 teaspoon lemon juice
1 scant teaspoon baking powder	Grated rind of 1 orange
	2 cups coarsely chopped walnuts or hazelnuts

Preheat the oven to 375 degrees. Grease a shallow jelly-roll pan with vegetable oil.

Combine the eggs and oil. Sift together 2 cups flour with the salt and baking powder. Mix the eggs and oil and dry ingredients together, adding enough flour to give you a dough that is soft and workable but one that will not stick to your hands. Knead the dough several times on a lightly floured board until it is smooth and supple. Let rest, lightly covered, for 10 minutes.

Working with convenient amounts of dough, form long, thin rolls about ⅓ inch in diameter. Twist the rolls to form a rope effect. Cut into pieces between ⅓ and ½ inch in length. Arrange in a single layer on the oiled pan and bake for about 20 to 25 minutes, or until the teiglach turn a rich golden brown. When the teiglach are brown, boil the honey with the sugar and ginger for 10 minutes, using a heavy saucepan so it does not burn. Add the baked teiglach and the lemon juice, orange rind, and nuts; mix well.

In most families, the mixture would at this point be poured onto a board that was wet with cold water, or onto a marble slab, and shaped into a single cake or balls about 2½ inches in diameter. My grandmother, however, preferred to pour the mass into wide jars, so that the honey always remained syrupy, and we spooned the teiglach and nuts out and ate them on plates as a small dessert, especially good with tea or black coffee. I am still partial to that softer, more luxuriously gooey version.

Yield: About 5 dozen teiglach

Aunt Estelle's Date and Nut Bread

The real specialist with this recipe was my Aunt Estelle, who at the slightest provocation would send a loaf or two of this moist and delicious bread. She always baked hers in 20-ounce soup, tomato, or juice cans.

¾ cup sugar
1 teaspoon baking soda
½ teaspoon baking powder
1¾ cups sifted flour
1 cup chopped walnuts

1 package (8 ounces) pitted dates,
    cut in pieces
2 eggs
1 teaspoon vanilla extract
¾ cup boiling water

Preheat the oven to 325 degrees. Butter two 20-ounce cans.

Sift the dry ingredients. Combine with the nuts, dates, eggs, and flavoring. Add the boiling water. Stir briefly and allow the mixture to stand for 15 minutes. Stir several times to blend. Half fill the buttered cans and bake for about 1½ hours, or until a toothpick or skewer inserted in the center of the cakes comes out clean. Loosen the sides of the cakes with a spatula. Let cool in the cans for several hours before unmolding. This is delicious spread with cream cheese.

Yield: 2 loaves

Chocolate Almond Torte

1½ cups warm riced or pureed boiled
    potatoes (baking or old
    potatoes are best for this, as
    they are the starchiest)
2 ounces (squares) unsweetened
    chocolate
2 ounces (squares) semisweet
    chocolate
¼ cup very strongly brewed black
    coffee, at room temperature

1¼ teaspoons baking powder
1¾ cups sifted flour
1 cup ground, unblanched almonds
¾ cup (6 ounces sweet) butter
1¾ cups sugar
4 extra-large eggs, separated

Optional garnishes: Whipped cream
    and grated bittersweet chocolate

Preheat the oven to 350 degrees.

Melt the chocolate over hot water. Stir in the coffee. Combine the baking powder and flour and resift together. Add the nuts to the flour and toss together lightly with a fork until thoroughly blended; set aside. Cream the butter with all but 1 tablespoon of sugar. Beat until the mixture is very white and fluffy. Beat in the egg yolks until thoroughly blended and all lumps have disappeared. Stir in the potatoes. Beat in the melted chocolate and coffee.

Whip the egg whites until they begin to thicken, then add the reserved 1 tablespoon of sugar and beat until the whites stand in stiff and glossy peaks. Stir 2 or 3 tablespoons of the whites into the chocolate batter to lighten it. Add the flour mixture and the egg whites. Fold in, gently but thoroughly, using a large rubber spatula. There should be no egg white or flour showing. Turn into a buttered 8- or 9-inch tube pan or kugelhopf mold and bake for about 55 minutes, or until the cake springs back when you press it lightly. Cool in the pan. If possible, invert the pan, standing it on the protruding tube, so the cake "hangs" and remains light. Remove from the pan when the cake is completely cold.

This may be served as is, or topped with freshly whipped cream and grated bittersweet chocolate.

Yield: 10 to 12 servings

Variation: You may also bake it in two 9-inch layer cake pans and spread whipped cream between the layers and over the top. I prefer the higher cake with the side dab of whipped cream.

Passover Sponge Cake

12 **extra large eggs, separated**	**Pinch of salt**
1½ **cups sugar**	1 **cup cake meal (see note below)**
Grated rind of 1 large lemon	¼ **cup potato starch**
Grated rind of 1 medium orange	½ **cup finely ground walnuts**
¼ **cup orange juice**	

Preheat the oven to 325 degrees.

Using a large, clean piece of brown wrapping paper, or baker's parchment, cut a circle to fit the bottom of an 11- or 12-inch springform pan. Then cut a band to fit around the sides. This can be about ½ inch deeper than the pan. Run both pieces of cut paper under the cold water very quickly, slightly dampening both sides of each. Place the circle on the bottom, then fit the band around the inner sides. Set aside.

Beat the egg yolks with 1 cup sugar until they are thick, almost white, and form a ribbon when a little of the batter is allowed to drip back from a spoon. Stir in the grated rinds and fruit juice.

Beat the egg whites with a pinch of salt, and as they begin to thicken, gradually beat in the remaining ½ cup sugar. The whites should stand in stiff and glossy peaks.

Sprinkle the cake meal, potato starch, and ground nuts over the whites. Add the yolk mixture and fold all together gently but thoroughly with a rubber spatula. No egg whites should be showing. Turn the mixture into the prepared pan.

Bake for about 1 to 1¼ hours, or until a tester inserted in the center of the cake comes out clean, and the top of the cake, when pressed with your fingertip, springs back to shape.

Let cool in the pan. After about 2 hours, or just before serving, remove the sides of the springform and peel off the paper. If you are using only part of the cake, remove the paper only from the section to be cut, as the rest of the cake will keep better with the paper on. Stored in the refrigerator, leftover sponge cake can be kept in good condition for a week to 10 days, and can even be frozen with excellent results.

Yield: 8 to 10 servings

Note: Cake meal should not be confused with matzoh meal. Both are made of crushed matzohs, but they differ in texture. Cake meal is fine and floury; matzoh meal is coarser and more like fine cracker crumbs. They are not interchangeable.

Marble Cake

½ cup (¼ pound) sweet butter
2¼ cups sugar
3 extra-large eggs
½ teaspoon vanilla extract
2½ cups sifted flour

1½ teaspoons baking powder
Pinch of salt
¾ cup milk
4 ounces (squares) semisweet
  chocolate, melted and cooled

Preheat the oven to 375 degrees. Butter and lightly flour a 9½ x 5½ x 3-inch loaf pan.

Cream the butter with the sugar until light and fluffy. Beat in the eggs, one at a time, until well blended. Stir in the vanilla. Resift the flour with the baking powder and salt. Add the dry ingredients and milk alternately to the batter, mixing in each addition before the next is added. Begin and end with dry ingredients.

(continued)

Remove one-third of the batter from the bowl and into it stir the cooled, melted chocolate.

Pour half of the plain batter into the prepared loaf pan, top with all of the chocolate and then, finally, with the remaining plain batter. Using a spatula or any knife blade, turn it through the batter gently to create marblelike streaks.

Bake for 1 hour or until a tester inserted in the center of the cake comes out clean and the cake has shrunk a little from the sides of the pan. Cool in the pàn. As with all pound cakes, this will taste better if it is not cut for 24 hours. Wrap in plastic and store in the refrigerator. Let warm to room temperature before slicing and serving.

Yield: 8 to 10 servings

Chocolate Chip Cake

3 ounces (squares) semisweet
    chocolate
½ cup (¼ pound) sweet butter, at
    room temperature
1 cup sugar
2 eggs

1½ teaspoons vanilla extract
2 cups sifted flour
2½ teaspoons baking powder
    Pinch of salt
⅔ cup milk

Preheat the oven to 350 degrees. Butter an 8-inch square baking pan.

Grate the chocolate using a grater, a blender, or a food processor. It should be fine but not powdery, and a few unevenly large pieces will add a pleasant texture.

Cream the butter with the sugar until very light and fluffy. Add the eggs, one at a time, beating in the first before the second is added. Stir in the vanilla. Resift the flour with baking powder and salt. Gradually beat in the dry ingredients and milk alternately—the dry ingredients in three additions and the milk in two—beginning and ending with the dry ingredients and beating each addition in well before the next is added. Finally, stir in the grated chocolate.

Turn into the buttered pan and bake for about 45 minutes or until the top is golden brown, a tester inserted in the center of the cake comes out clean, and the cake has shrunken slightly from the sides of the pan. I prefer this cake as is, but when cold it can also be covered with chocolate icing (pages 291–92).

Variation: The same mixture can be made to make 18 medium-sized cup-cakes. Those should be baked at 375 degrees for about 20 minutes.

Yield: 8 to 10 servings

Whipped Cream Cake

This was one of the simplest and most useful basic cakes my mother made, to be served as pound cake or to be split and served as shortcake with whipped cream and sliced bananas, peaches, or strawberries between the layers and on top.

1 cup very cold heavy sweet cream	1½ cups sifted cake flour (see note below)
2 eggs	
1¼ cups sugar	2 teaspoons baking powder
2 teaspoons vanilla extract	¼ teaspoon salt
Grated rind of 1 lemon	Whipped cream and fruit of your choice (optional)

Preheat the oven to 450 degrees. Generously butter an 8-inch springform pan.

Chill a mixing bowl and beaters for 10 to 15 minutes. Whip the very cold cream until stiff. Add the eggs and beat until the mixture is light and foamy. Beat in the sugar, vanilla, and grated rind. Combine the sifted flour with the baking powder and salt and resift together into the batter. Beat in thoroughly. Pour into the buttered springform pan and bake for 25 to 35 minutes, or until the top is golden brown and a tester stuck into the center of the cake comes out clean. The cake should be slightly shrunken from the sides of the pan. Cool in the springform, then remove the sides. Serve the cake as is, or split into two layers for a shortcake and fill and top with whipped cream and any fruit you choose.

Yield: 1 eight-inch cake

Note: If you cannot find cake flour, substitute ½ cup cornstarch for ½ cup of all-purpose flour.

Helen's Cheesecake

Because this recipe came from my mother's friend Helen, whose last name was also Solomon, it was always called by this name.

1 box of zweiback
⅓ cup melted sweet butter
1 cup plus 3 tablespoons sugar
2 pounds dry (uncreamed) pot
     cheese or farmer cheese
     (preferably the first, and *not*
     cottage cheese)
½ cup heavy sweet cream
½ cup sour cream

2 teaspoons vanilla extract
2 teaspoons grated lemon rind
½ teaspoon salt
7 eggs, separated
2 tablespoons flour
     Confectioners' or vanilla sugar, for
     dusting the cake

Preheat the oven to 325 degrees. Butter the bottom and sides of a 10-inch springform pan.

Pulverize the zweiback to fine crumbs. This can be done in a blender, a food processor, or by putting the zweiback in a paper bag and rolling over it with a rolling pin; the crumbs should be fine and even. Stir well with the melted butter and stir in 3 tablespoons sugar. Mix until well blended. Spread the mixture evenly over the bottom of the springform, pressing it down firmly with your fingertips. Keep in the refrigerator for at least 1 hour, or until ready to fill.

Rub the pot cheese or farmer cheese through a sieve. (Do not use cottage cheese, as it will be too wet.) Mix in the sweet and sour cream, vanilla, lemon rind, salt, and finally the egg yolks. Beat the egg whites until stiff, gradually beating in 1 cup sugar as the whites begin to hold soft peaks. When they are stiff and shiny, turn them on top of the cheese mixture and sift the flour over the top. Fold all together gently but thoroughly, using a rubber spatula. No lumps of egg white should be visible.

Turn into the chilled pan. Bake for 1 hour without opening the oven door. The cake should be a pale golden brown on top, which may require another 15 minutes. Turn off the oven and let the cake remain in the closed oven for 2 hours. Open the door and let the cake stand in the oven 1 hour longer. Serve the cake chilled and dusted with confectioner's or vanilla sugar.

Yield: 8 to 10 servings

May's Sour Cream Coffee Cake

As with "Helen's cheesecake," this is a souvenir of a much-beloved friend, May Horowitz, whom my mother considered to be an extraordinary cook—no small compliment coming from that quarter.

1 cup chopped walnuts	3 eggs, separated
1 teaspoon powdered cinnamon	1 cup sour cream
1¾ cups sugar	3 cups sifted flour
¾ cup (6 ounces) sweet butter, at room temperature	1½ teaspoons baking powder
	½ teaspoon baking soda

Preheat the oven to 350 degrees. Butter a 9- or 10-inch springform pan on the bottom and sides.

Blend the nuts, cinnamon and ½ cup sugar and set aside. Cream the butter with 1 cup sugar until light and fluffy. Beat in the egg yolks and sour cream. Resift the flour with the baking powder and soda. Beat the egg whites, and as they begin to form soft peaks, beat in the remaining ¼ cup sugar. When the whites are stiff and shiny, turn them onto the butter and egg-yolk mixture. Top with the sifted dry ingredients. Fold all in together gently but thoroughly, using a rubber spatula.

Turn half the batter into the pan and top with a sprinkling of half the nut-cinnamon-sugar mixture. Pour in the remaining batter and top with the remaining nut mix. Bake for about 1 hour, or until a tester inserted in the center of the cake comes out clean. The cake should shrink from the sides of the pan and be golden brown on top. Let cool in the pan.

Yield: 6 to 8 servings

Variations: 1. Vanilla or almond extract, with or without the grated rind of 1 lemon, can be added to this batter along with the egg yolks. You can also layer the batter and nuts in thirds instead of in halves.

2. This cake can also be baked in two loaf pans, which will require 5 or 10 minutes less baking time.

Quick Coffee Cake

Although not as fragrantly pungent as a yeast coffee cake, this is a good, quick substitute when you want a cake on short notice. My mother also used it as a base for a fruit coffee cake.

2½ cups sifted flour
⅔ cup sugar
2 teaspoons baking powder
  Pinch of salt
½ cup (¼ pound) cold sweet butter
  cut in small pieces

2 jumbo eggs
⅔ cup milk
1 teaspoon vanilla extract
  Cinnamon sugar and almonds or
    walnuts, or streusel crumbs (see
    below)

Preheat the oven to 375 degrees. Butter a 9-inch square baking pan and sprinkle it lightly with flour, tapping out all excess.

Resift the flour with the sugar, baking powder, and salt. Cut or rub the cold butter into the dry ingredients, using a pastry blender or your fingertips, until you have a mixture that is the texture of coarse meal. Combine the eggs, milk, and vanilla and beat well. Gradually add the dry ingredients, stirring as you do so, until you have a thick, moist mass that can drop from a tablespoon but that is not runny or liquid. Spread the batter evenly in the prepared pan. Sprinkle on the streusel, if using, and bake for 30 minutes, or until the top is golden brown and a tester inserted in the center of the cake comes out clean. Cool in the pan. If you don't use the streusel, bake for 20 minutes, then sprinkle with cinnamon sugar and nuts, and continue baking for 10 minutes more.

Quick Fruit Coffee Cake

Made with peaches, this was a summer dessert favorite. Blue plums were our second choice.

Prepare the batter as above and spread into the pan. Brush the dough with melted butter. Have prepared 6 medium peaches, washed, pitted but not peeled, and cut into quarters; or, about 1 pound small blue plums, washed, cut in half and stoned but not peeled; or 4 large apples, peeled, cored, and cut in eighths. Spread the fruit over dough and brush the top with a little heavy sweet cream. Top with a layer of streusel crumbs (see below) Bake in a 350-degree oven for 30 minutes.

If you prefer, the fruit can be sprinkled with cinnamon sugar and no crumbs.

Serve warm or cold, plain or with whipped cream, or in a deep dish with unwhipped heavy sweet cream poured over each individual serving.

Streusel Crumb Topping

To make crumbs, combine ⅓ cup sugar, ½ cup flour, 2 teaspoons powdered cinnamon and 2 tablespoons melted sweet butter. Mix the butter into the dry ingredients with your fingertips until you have clumps of medium-sized crumbs. More butter will make larger clumps; more flour will make finer crumbs. Sprinkle on the cake just before putting it into the oven.

Strudel

Although I ate my grandmother's strudel often, I only watched her make it twice. But the impact of those performances and the advance preparations for them stand out in memory as great occasions, with as much to-do and flourish as might be expected before some major surgical feat such as a heart transplant.

For one thing, she would work in the dining room, pulling the table away from the wall so she could walk around all four sides to stretch the dough evenly. The table was covered with a long bedsheet that hung to the floor, as the dough almost would later on. She also said the cloth would prevent the table edges from cutting the dough. She removed all jewelry except her wedding ring, which was smooth, and she clipped any hangnails and filed down her fingernails, all in an effort to keep from tearing the dough.

She closed all windows to prevent drafts and never answered the phone once the dough was rolled out. Both measures were intended to keep the dough from drying out.

My mother made strudel many times but always with the ready-made leaves she bought from bakeries or, later on, from the supermarket. You may do that if you wish, but the results will be somewhat less delectable.

Although my grandmother always worked with Hecker's unbleached flour, John Clancy has proven to me that bread flour makes the task easier because its higher gluten content gives the dough more strength and stretch-ability. Other than that, I have not changed her recipe.

2 cups sifted bread flour	1¼ cups melted sweet butter
½ teaspoon salt	2¼ cups bread crumbs, browned
2½ tablespoons peanut oil	in butter
1 jumbo egg, beaten	Filling of your choice (see
½ to ⅔ cup lukewarm water, as	below)
needed	

Resift the flour with the salt onto a pastry board. Make a well in the center and into it pour the oil and beaten egg. Slowly and carefully turn the flour into liquids, mixing as you do so, using either your fingertips or a fork. Trickle water in as needed to make a sticky, very soft dough.

The most critical step is the kneading of the dough, for it is through kneading that you will develop its elasticity. Knead on a lightly floured board, using a pastry scraper to clean up dough that sticks and which should be worked into the overall mass. After kneading for about 10 minutes, lift the ball of dough high and slam it down on the counter top; repeat 110 times, at which point the dough should be satin smooth, supple, and not at all sticky. Place the dough on the counter top or a plate, cover with an inverted clean bowl, and let rest for 40 minutes.

At the end of the resting time, preheat the oven to 350 degrees.

Following my grandmother's method, try to work at a freestanding table (ideally a 48-inch round one) or at the least, one that is free on three sides. You cannot stretch this dough on a counter top. Cover the table with a long pastry cloth, tablecloth, or bedsheet. Sprinkle flour over the cloth, covering it especially well in the center.

Using a floured rolling pin, begin rolling the dough in the center of the table, shaping it into a square as much as possible. Roll evenly from the center out to the edges, lifting the rolling pin a bit at the edge so that that part does not become too thin and tear. Do not roll toward yourself. Up to this point you can keep turning the dough. When it has been rolled as thin as possible, begin to stretch it. Place your hands under the dough, palms down and fingers curved under, almost as though you were about to play the piano. Or, if it is easier, make a rounded fist.

Working out from the center, hand over hand, stretch the dough toward the edges, walking around the table to stretch it evenly. It is important that all this rolling and stretching be done quickly so the dough does not dry. If holes appear, do not try to patch them. They will be covered when the strudel leaves are folded and rolled. The sides of the dough should stretch down like a cloth and the dough should become so thin that you can read the fine print of a newspaper through it. If dry spots appear on the dough, brush with oil or melted butter.

Trim off the thick edges of the dough with scissors and brush the surface with melted butter. Sprinkle with bread crumbs. Place the filling in a row at one end of the dough sheet. Roll once, then fold in the sides and brush them with melted butter. Roll the strudel from the filling end. The cloth beneath it will help you turn and flip the roll. With the last roll, flip the strudel onto a buttered jelly-roll pan. If the roll is too long for your pan, cut in halves or thirds. My grandmother preferred to turn her single roll into a horseshoe shape and bake it that way. Bake in the preheated 350-degree oven for about 1 hour. Brush several times with melted butter. The strudel, when done, should be fragilely crisp and parchment brown.

Yield: 3 ten- to twelve-inch strudels

Strudel Fillings

Because you do not want the strudel dough to dry, have your filling at hand and ready to use as soon as the dough has been stretched. Prepare the filling in advance or while the dough is resting. Any of the fillings below can, of course, be used with strudel leaves purchased ready made. Just spread them with melted butter and proceed as above. If they are frozen, they will have to thaw first, but, if possible, buy fresh leaves, as they are less inclined to be crumbly.

Apple Filling

2 pounds apples, such as Northern Spy, Cortland, Granny Smith, or Greening (in that order of preference)	1 tablespoon lemon juice
	1 teaspoon powdered cinnamon
	Pinch of nutmeg
	½ to ¾ cup sugar, as needed
½ cup melted sweet butter	1 cup bread crumbs
⅔ cup dried currants	1 cup finely chopped walnuts
Grated rind of 1 lemon	

Peel, core, and slice the apples. Combine the sliced apples with all remaining ingredients except the nuts, adding only as much sugar as the apples require. Sprinkle the nuts over the buttered bread crumbs on the prepared strudel dough. Place the filling at one end of the strudel dough and roll as described.

Yield: Enough to fill 3 ten- to twelve-inch strudels

Cheese Filling

¾ cup (6 ounces) sweet butter
¾ cup sugar
3 extra-large eggs, separated
1 pound dry (uncreamed) pot cheese
   or farmer cheese (not cottage
   cheese)

Grated rind of 1 lemon
Grated rind of ½ orange
½ cup dried currants, soaked in a
   little warm water for 10 minutes
1 teaspoon vanilla extract
½ cup sour cream, or as needed

Cream the butter with sugar until light and fluffy, then beat the egg yolks in until the mixture is almost white and thick enough to ribbon. Rub the cheese through a sieve and stir into the egg-yolk mixture along with the grated fruit rinds, well-drained currants, vanilla, and just enough sour cream to make the mixture hold together in a mass. Beat the egg whites until stiff and shiny, then fold gently into the cheese mixture, using a rubber spatula. Fill the strudel dough as described above.

Yield: Enough to fill 3 ten- to twelve-inch strudels

PIE CRUSTS

Rich Tart Pastry

The pastry my grandmother and mother used most often for pies was the German *mürbeteig* ("mellow dough") or what we know as rich tart pastry. It is a wonderfully crisp crust, rich enough to make cookies as well. The type made with whole eggs is a bit harder and sturdier and easier to handle. The variation made only with yolks is more delicate, crumblier because it is shorter (has a higher percentage of fat), but it is even more delicious.

Rich Tart Pastry I

2½ to 3 cups flour	2 large eggs
¼ teaspoon salt	2 tablespoons ice water, or as needed
½ cup sugar	1 tablespoon grated lemon rind
¾ cup (6 ounces) very cold sweet butter, cut into tiny pieces	

Rich Tart Pastry II

2½ to 2¾ cups flour	3 egg yolks
¼ teaspoon salt	2 tablespoons ice water, or as needed
½ cup sugar	
1 cup (½ pound) very cold sweet butter	1 tablespoon grated lemon rind

The method is the same for both mixtures.

Sift the dry ingredients onto a board or into a bowl, using 2½ cups flour. The butter should be very cold. Add to the dry mixture, and working with your fingertips or a pastry blender, or by placing all of these ingredients in a food processor, cut or rub the butter into the dry ingredients until you have attained the texture of a fine meal. Stir in the remaining ingredients, using only enough water to enable you to form a ball that just barely holds together and is not sticky. If too sticky, add a little more flour. If you are using a processor, use it only for cutting in the butter. Once the wet ingredients are added the processor tends to make the dough heavy unless you work with lightning speed.

Turn the ball out onto a floured board and, working quickly, knead it once or twice, until it holds together. Be careful not to overhandle the dough. Once it looks greasy or dark, that means it has been overhandled and will be tough and leaden, rather than light and crisp. It should retain its solid yellow color and look fresh.

Wrap in plastic wrap and place in the refrigerator for at least 1 hour.

You can roll this dough on a lightly floured board using a floured rolling pin. However, it will be easier to roll between two sheets of waxed paper.

Cut the dough in half and roll each section separately, to fit a 9-inch pan. It should be about ¼ inch thick. When rolling between waxed paper sheets, be sure to turn the dough and roll both sides, and to lift the sheets of waxed paper every few rolls so the dough does not stick to them and can expand. If the paper becomes wrinkled, replace it.

Fit the dough into a ungreased 9-inch pie plate or, better yet, a flan pan with a removable bottom. Be sure the dough fits all the way down into the inner rim of the pan. Leave a high edge for crimping or for sealing with a top crust. Roll out the top crust to fit the pie plate and place between sheets of plastic wrap. Cover the filled pie plate with plastic wrap and let both crusts chill for 30 minutes before baking. You can prepare this a day ahead and keep it in the refrigerator.

To bake a pie crust blind, or empty, when this is called for in recipes such as lemon meringue pie (page 280), fit it into the pie plate or flan ring as described above and chill. After 30 minutes prick the bottom of the crust in several places with the tines of a fork. Line the inside of the crust with aluminum foil. Fill lined pie crust with dry beans, rice or the small lead weights sold for that purpose in many cookware shops. Bake for 20 to 25 minutes, or until the crust is pale golden brown.

Recipes calling for prebaked pie crusts will not require a top crust, so make only half the recipe.

Yield: Top and bottom crusts for a 9-inch pie

Variations: 1. When preparing crust for a meat or chicken pie, use only a tiny pinch of sugar for color. To make this crust a bit flakier, as you might want it to be for cookies or a meat pie, sift 1 teaspoonful baking powder in with the dry ingredients.

2. If you are really skillful at rolling and handling dough and want to make the richest possible variation, use 2 raw egg yolks and 2 sieved hard-cooked egg yolks instead of the eggs or egg yolks with the above ingredients.

"American" Pie Crust

Usually, my mother prepared one of the preceding pie crusts, which she called, rightly, European or German or *mürbeteig* crusts. But when she made lemon meringue pie, she used the eggless crust below. Most often she made it with a half-and-half combination of butter and solid vegetable shortening, but I much prefer it made only with butter. The amount below is for a single crust only. If you want to use this for a covered pie, double the recipe.

1 cup unbleached flour
½ teaspoon salt
   Pinch of sugar
6 tablespoons cold sweet butter, cut
      in small pieces, or 3 tablespoons
      cold sweet butter, cut in small
      pieces, plus 3 tablespoons solid

   vegetable shortening, cut in
      small pieces
1 tablespoon distilled white
      vinegar
2 to 3 tablespoons ice water, as
      needed

Sift together the flour, salt, and a tiny pinch of sugar in a bowl, or into the bowl of a food processor. Add the shortening and cut in with a pastry blender, your fingertips, or by turning on the processor using the winged metal blade. When the mixture resembles a fine meal, remove from the processor to a bowl and sprinkle the vinegar and 2 tablespoons water over it. With a fork, blend together, adding a little more water if needed to make the mixture form a ball. The less water you need, the crisper and better the crust will be, so add it carefully. Place the dough on a lightly floured surface and, with the heel of your hand, knead it quickly two or three times. Pat into a round, cover with plastic wrap, and chill in the refrigerator for 30 minutes.

Roll the chilled dough ⅛ inch thick on a lightly floured board, using a lightly floured rolling pin. The circle should be large enough to fit into an 8- or 9-inch pie pan.

Place the dough in an ungreased pan, fitting it down into the corners, then pressing the dough firmly against bottom and sides of the pan. With scissors, trim off overhanging dough, leaving about a ½-inch overhang. Pinch this up onto the rim of the pie pan and flute or press with fork tines. Chill for 30 minutes.

For lemon meringue pie (page 280), this crust should be prebaked empty. To do that, preheat the oven to 450 degrees, prick the bottom of the crust well with a fork, and bake for about 25 minutes, or until golden brown. Cool thoroughly before filling and rebaking as described in the recipe for lemon meringue pie.

If using this dough for a covered, filled pie, double the recipe and roll out two disks, fitting one into the pan as described above and laying the round cover on a sheet of waxed paper. Chill both for 30 minutes, then fill the pie, add the top crust, seal seams closed, and bake as described for apple pie (page 280).

Yield 1 eight- or nine-inch bottom pie crust

Lemon Meringue Pie

No holiday or celebration dinner was considered complete without the appearance of my mother's lemon meringue pie. When asked to dinner at other people's homes, especially members of the family, she always brought one of these pies along. It seems hard to believe that the recipe came from the label on a can of sweetened condensed milk—Borden's Eagle brand, the only one she would use and the only recipe she would follow. If you buy another brand, be sure it is not "filled" condensed milk, which has a brownish color.

1 can (14 ounces) Borden's Eagle brand sweetened condensed milk
½ cup fresh lemon juice
1 generous teaspoonful grated lemon rind
2 eggs, at room temperature, separated

1 half-baked 8-inch "American" pie shell, in the pan (page 278)
⅛ teaspoon salt
¼ teaspoon cream of tartar
¼ cup sugar

Preheat the oven to 325 degrees.

Combine the condensed milk, lemon juice and rind, and egg yolks and stir until smooth and thick. Let stand in the refrigerator for 30 minutes. Pour into the baked pie shell.

Place the egg whites in a mixing bowl with the salt and beat until the whites become frothy. Beat in the cream of tartar. When the whites stand in soft peaks, beat in the sugar, 2 teaspoons at a time, until the whites are stiff and shiny. Do not overbeat, for if the whites lose their gloss and break down, they will deflate and become watery when baked. Heap the whites onto the lemon filling, and using the back of a spoon, spread and peak them until the filling is covered. Spread the whites onto the edges of the pie crust. Bake for about 15 minutes, or until golden brown. Cool at room temperature.

Yield: 6 servings

Apple Pie

1 recipe rich tart pastry I or II (page 277)
8 large green, tart apples
½ teaspoon nutmeg
1 teaspoon powdered cinnamon

¼ teaspoon salt
1 cup brown sugar
1 to 2 tablespoons lemon juice
Grated rind of 1 lemon
2 tablespoons sweet butter

Preheat the oven to 350 degrees.

The unbaked pie crust should be fitted into a 9-inch pan and chilled, along with top crust, which has been laid out on waxed paper. Peel and core the apples, then cut into eighths. Sprinkle with the lemon juice to prevent discoloration. Combine the spices, the salt, and sugar with the lemon juice and rind. Gently turn through the apples. Arrange the apples in layers in the crust, filling it equally all around. Dot the top layer with butter.

Place the top crust over the apples. Seal the edges with the bottom crust and crimp. Cut three or four small gashes in the top crust. Bake about 30 minutes, or until the top crust is golden brown and the apples are tender when pierced with a skewer.

Yield: 8 servings

Variation: Three-quarters cup white sugar can be used instead of the brown sugar if you prefer the milder sweetening.

Deep-Dish Peach Pie

1 recipe rich tart pastry I (page 277), made with 1 teaspoon baking powder

Melted sweet butter, for brushing the crust

2 pounds ripe peaches (6 large peaches)

⅔ cup sugar

1 teaspoon powdered cinnamon

Grated rind of 1 lemon

2 tablespoons flour

2 extra-large egg yolks

¼ cup heavy sweet cream

1 egg yolk, beaten with 1 tablespoon milk

Heavy sweet cream, whipped or unwhipped, for garnish

Preheat the oven to 400 degrees.

Roll out two-thirds of the dough and fit into an ungreased 8-inch square baking pan. The remainder of the rolled-out crust can be used for lattice strips. Brush the crust with melted butter and chill for 30 minutes.

Wash the peaches well, rubbing off the fuzz; they will not be peeled. Dry thoroughly and cut in quarters, discarding the pits. Arrange the peach quarters, cut side up, in the pie crust. Sprinkle with the sugar, cinnamon, lemon rind, and flour. Beat the egg yolks with ¼ cup cream and drizzle over the peaches.

(continued)

Arrange the lattice strips over the pan, sealing the edges to the crust. Brush with the egg yolk beaten with milk.

Bake for 25 to 30 minutes. Serve warm or chilled, with whipped cream or plain cream, if desired, poured over individual servings in deep dishes.

Yield: 8 servings

Cream Puffs

We much preferred these crisp, cream- or custard-filled puffs to birthday cakes, and my mother often made them, not only for us but for her company luncheons as well. Cream puffs filled with whipped cream were the most popular, but she also occasionally used a custard filling. Although she used spoons for the shaping, a pastry tube does a neater, more professional job. I have always disliked the puffs with icing, preferring vanilla-flavored confectioners' sugar.

½ cup (¼ pound) sweet butter
1 cup water
¼ teaspoon salt
1 cup sifted flour
4 large eggs

Whipped cream or custard filling
    (see below)
Vanilla confectioners' sugar, for
    dusting the puffs

Preheat the oven to 400 degrees. Butter a cookie sheet.

Combine the butter, water, and salt in a heavy saucepan. Bring to a boil and cook until the butter melts. Lower the heat and add all of the flour at once, stirring vigorously over low heat until the mixture forms a ball that leaves the sides of the pan.

Remove from the heat. Beat in one egg at a time, being sure one is completely absorbed before adding the next. If using an electric mixer, operate it at low speed. The mixture should stand in a peak when the beater is lifted from it, and be satiny. The puffs may be as large or as small as you like. If shaping with spoons, use two tablespoons and scoop the dough onto the cookie sheet in the desired size and shape—the standard large puff should be a mound about 1½ inches in diameter. This will take a generously rounded tablespoon of dough. For smaller puffs use a rounded teaspoonful. If using a pastry bag, for large puffs use a wide, round no. 9 tube. A no. 7 will do for smaller ones.

Bake in the 400-degree oven for 10 minutes. Reduce the heat to 350 and bake for 25 minutes more, or until the puffs are doubled in size and golden brown. Slide the oven rack out, and with a sharp-pointed knife pierce a hole in one or two places in the side of each puff. Return the puffs to the oven with the heat off and close door. Let them dry out for 15 minutes before removing. If you do not do this, the moisture caught within the puffs will cause them to collapse.

To fill the puffs, you can either split them open and fill with a spoon, or use a pastry tube and fill through a hole in the bottom or side.

Dust with confectioners' sugar when filled.

Yield: 16 medium-sized puffs, 45 small ones

Cream Puff Fillings

Whipped Cream Filling

Simply whip heavy sweet cream flavored with a little vanilla and sugar. Two cups of cream whipped with 2 teaspoons vanilla and 2 tablespoons quick-dissolving granulated sugar will be right for 16 puffs. Chill until just before serving time, then fill the puffs.

Custard Cream Filling

1½ cups half-and-half milk and	4 extra-large egg yolks
cream	1½ teaspoons vanilla extract
3½ tablespoons flour	Grated rind of ½ lemon
Pinch of salt	Melted sweet butter, for brushing
⅔ cup sugar	the top of the custard

Scald the half-and-half in the top of a double boiler set over boiling water. Beat in the flour, salt, and sugar. Continue cooking over boiling water until the mixture is as thick as a medium cream sauce.

Beat the egg yolks with a fork until thin. Gradually trickle 2 or 3 tablespoons of the hot half-and-half mixture into the eggs, beating constantly. Slowly pour the egg mixture into remaining hot half-and-half set over hot (not boiling) water, beating constantly as you pour. Continue cooking and stirring for about 5 minutes, or until the sauce is thick. Do not let it boil. Remove from the heat and stir in the vanilla and lemon rind.

(continued)

Set the pot over ice or cold water so the custard will cool rapidly. Brush a little melted butter over the top of the custard to keep a film from forming until you are ready to use it. Before using to fill cream puffs, beat this butter topping into the custard. Fill cooled, baked puffs when the custard is cool.

Yield: Enough to fill 16 medium sized puffs or 45 small ones.

Orange Walnut Oatmeal Cookies

This is another of my mother's favorite recipes that began with a basic recipe on the side of the Quaker oatmeal cereal box. The oranges, rind, spices, and nuts were her own additions and made all the difference. Do not use anything but old-fashioned oats. The quick cooking types will not give you a crunchy cookie.

¾ cup (6 ounces) sweet butter, at
    room temperature
1 cup firmly packed brown sugar
½ cup granulated sugar
1 egg
¼ cup orange juice
    Grated rind of ½ orange
    Grated rind of 1 lemon

1 cup sifted flour
¼ teaspoon powdered ginger
½ teaspoon powdered cinnamon
1 teaspoon salt
¼ teaspoon baking soda
3 cups uncooked, old-fashioned
    Quaker oats
½ cup chopped walnuts

Preheat the oven to 350 degrees. Lightly butter two large cookie sheets.

Cream the butter with both sugars until light and fluffy. Beat in the egg, then add the orange juice and grated rinds. Resift the flour with the spices, salt, and baking soda and mix thoroughly into the creamed mixture. Stir in the oatmeal and nuts. Drop by teaspoonfuls onto the buttered cookie sheets, leaving about a 1-inch space between cookies. Bake 12 to 15 minutes.

Let cool slightly on the pan, then cool completely on a rack before packing in an airtight container. These will keep for weeks.

Yield: About 5 dozen

Grandma Breit's Cookies

These simple cookies with their crusty toppings of nuts and cinnamon-sugar probably have an official name, but we knew them only by the above. They were always on hand at my grandmother's and were the only cookies I ever knew her to make. They can be cut in any shapes, of course, but hers were always round and were cut with the rim of a water glass. The idea of buying a cookie cutter would never have occurred to her.

3 cups sifted flour	1 tablespoon lemon juice
1 tablespoon baking powder	1 teaspoon grated lemon rind
½ teaspoon salt	½ cup chopped walnuts
½ cup (¼ pound) butter	1 tablespoon powdered cinnamon
1½ cups sugar	1 egg yolk, beaten with 1
3 extra-large eggs	tablespoon cold water

Preheat the oven to 350 degrees.

Resift the flour along with the baking powder and salt. Set aside. Cream the butter with 1 cup of the sugar until light and fluffy. Add the eggs, one at a time, beating until each egg is absorbed before the next is added. Beat in the lemon juice and rind, then stir in the dry ingredients; the mixture should be soft and pliable but not sticky. Gather in a ball, divide in half, and roll out each half on a lightly floured surface, to a thickness of a little less than ¼ inch. Cut into circles with a cutter about 2½ to 3 inches in diameter. (The cookies can be smaller or larger or in other shapes, if you prefer.) Gather scraps, form into a ball, and reroll (see note below).

Mix the nuts, cinnamon, and remaining ½ cup sugar together. Brush each cookie with the egg yolk mixture and sprinkle with the nut-sugar mixture. Lay on an ungreased cookie sheet, allowing about ¼ inch between cookies.

Bake in the preheated oven for 10 to 15 minutes, or until the bottoms are pale golden brown and the tops are just beginning to change color around the edges. Remove from the pan while still hot and cool on a rack. These will keep for weeks in an airtight container.

Yield: About 20 cookies

Note: My grandmother did not reroll the dough. She brushed the uncut sheet of rolled-out dough with the egg wash and then sprinkled on the nuts and cinnamon sugar. When the cookies were cut out and placed on the baking sheet, she then cut the scraps into free-form cookies and baked them. Part of the fun was imagining which animals and flowers the free-form cookies resembled.

Spritz Cookies

One of the great culinary events at our house was the arrival of a cookie press, or "gun," as we called it, that enabled my mother to make saw-toothed "ribbon" cookies, long coiled "snakes," or ridged strips made with the star disc. She made the dough but it was my job and my delight to turn the handle that pressed the dough forms out on the cookie sheets. Directions for all shapes are included in the cookie press package.

1 cup (½ pound) sweet butter, softened to room temperature	2 teaspoons vanilla or almond extract
1 cup sugar	1 extra-large egg plus 1 egg yolk
Pinch of salt	2 cups sifted flour, or as needed

Preheat the oven to 375 degrees. Lightly butter two large cookie sheets.

Cream the butter with the sugar and salt until light and fluffy. Beat in the flavoring, whole egg, and yolk. If the mixture separates, sprinkle in a little flour and mix. Gradually stir in enough flour to make a soft, pliable dough that is not sticky. Pack the dough into a cookie press, and using the disc with the pattern you prefer, press out ribbons, circles, "S" forms, squares, or whatever. If using the plain hole that makes a snake-like rope, try spiraling the dough into pinwheels. Press the dough out directly onto the baking sheets or, if you prefer, onto a board, then lift carefully with a spatula and place on the baking sheets. Bake for about 10 minutes, or until the cookie edges are light golden brown.

Yield: About 5 dozen cookies, depending on size

Soft Passover Almond Macaroons

Most recipes for these gentle, sweet macaroons call for matzoh meal. My grandmother's did not include this starchy ingredient. Instead she used un-blanched almonds, the skins of which took the place of the flour.

2 cups ground, unblanched almonds	Pinch of salt
½ cup sugar	Grated rind of ½ lemon
1 teaspoon almond extract	3 egg whites

Preheat the oven to 350 degrees. Butter or lightly oil a cookie sheet well.

Combine all the ingredients except the egg whites and mix well. Stir in the egg whites gradually to make a dough much like thick, wet sand—medium firm so it can be molded but not dry or shiny with liquid. Take off the dough by teaspoonfuls and roll each spoonful into a ball about 1 inch in diameter. Arrange on the baking sheet, flattening the balls a little. Bake for 15 to 20 minutes, or until the tops of the cookies seem dry and faintly golden brown

Yield: About 2 dozen cookies

Variation: If you like, a whole or split blanched almond can be set in the center of each macaroon as you flatten it before baking.

Pinwheel Cookies

1½ ounces (squares) semisweet chocolate	½ cup (¼ pound) sweet butter, at room temperature
1⅔ cups sifted flour	1 cup sugar
½ teaspoon baking powder	1 extra-large egg
Pinch of salt	1½ teaspoons vanilla extract

Melt the chocolate over hot water; set aside to cool. Resift the flour with the baking powder and salt and set aside. Cream the butter with the sugar, and when light and fluffy, beat in the egg and vanilla. Stir in the sifted dry ingredients and blend thoroughly.

Divide the dough in half and add the cooled melted chocolate to one half. Wrap both doughs separately in waxed paper or plastic wrap and chill for several hours, or until firm and no longer sticky, so they can be rolled.

(continued)

Roll each section of dough out between large sheets of waxed paper or plastic wrap, turning the dough over and rolling both sides; lift and replace the top and bottom sheets of waxed paper between rolls so the dough can move. Each sheet of dough should be rolled to a rectangle approximately 17 × 6 inches. The dough should be rolled evenly to the edges; trim off the thinnest edges.

Peel the waxed paper from one side of each sheet of dough. Invert one sheet of dough over the other, so that waxed paper is on the bottom of the bottom sheet and on top of the top sheet. Be very careful when placing your dough, as it will be too sticky to lift and replace. Match the edges as closely as possible. With the waxed paper still in place, lightly roll over the dough with the rolling pin to press the dough gently together. Remove the top piece of waxed paper. Using the bottom sheet of waxed paper to lift and turn, roll the dough tightly lengthwise and securely as for a jelly roll, being sure you do not roll the waxed paper into it. Wrap in waxed paper or plastic wrap and chill overnight. (This can even be frozen, because it can be sliced without thawing and then baked; so it is a good cookie preparation to have on hand in the freezer.)

Preheat the oven to 350 degrees.

Unwrap the chilled or frozen cookie roll, and with a sharp, thin-bladed knife cut into cookies just a little less than ¼ inch thick. Lay the cookies or an ungreased cookie sheet, allowing about 1 inch between cookies. Bake for 10 to 12 minutes, or until faintly golden brown around the edges.

Cool on a rack before storing in an airtight container.

Yield: About 3 dozen cookies

Pogacsa

[Hungarian Butter Cookies]

I have also seen these written as "pugalchle," "pugachel," and "pogachel." Our pronunciation was the last of the three. In Hungarian, *pogasca* is used for many round, dry, sconelike biscuits, some made with lard and bacon, others buttery, such as the rich version below. They are also made with yeast.

2¾ cups flour

1 scant teaspoon baking powder

¼ teaspoon salt

⅔ cup sugar

1 cup (½ pound) sweet butter, at room temperature

1 egg plus 1 egg yolk

⅓ cup sour cream

Sift together the flour, baking powder, salt, and sugar. Cut in the butter, rubbing with fingertips or using a pastry blender until you have a mixture that resembles a coarse meal. Mix in the egg, yolk, and sour cream until well blended. Wrap in plastic wrap or waxed paper and chill from 1 to 3 hours.

Preheat the oven to 350 degrees. Butter a large cookie sheet.

Roll the dough out on a lightly floured board with a lightly floured rolling pin; the dough should be ½ inch thick. Cut in 2-inch rounds. Place these on the baking sheet 1 inch apart and either prick the surface in three or four places with the tines of a fork or make a crisscross line pattern with a thin sharp knife blade, being careful not to cut through the cookies. Bake about 20 minutes or until pale golden brown.

Yield: 1 dozen cookies

Beatrice's Brown Sugar Cookies

The dry, brown-edged slip of paper that bears this recipe gives no indication why the cookies were named for my mother. When I asked her why, she said just because she made them better than anyone else. They are somewhat like shortbread.

1½ cups (¾ pound) salt butter, at room temperature

½ pound dark brown sugar

2 tablespoons granulated sugar

1½ teaspoons vanilla extract

1 egg, separated

3½ to 4 cups flour

1 cup slivered blanched almonds

Cream the butter with the sugar until well blended, light, and fluffy. Beat in the vanilla and egg yolk. Gradually stir, then work in the flour until the dough is stiff and almost crumbly. Knead the dough until it is pliable and not sticky. Divide in half and roll each half out between sheets of waxed paper to a thickness of ¼ inch. Then, using a pastry wheel, cut into strips about 2 x 3 inches and place on two large buttered baking sheets. Chill for 30 minutes.

(continued)

Meanwhile, preheat the oven to 400 degrees.

Brush the dough with lightly beaten egg white and top each cookie with a few almond slices. Bake for 8 to 10 minutes.

Yield: About 50 cookies

Mandelbrot

[Almond Bread Slices]

4 eggs	3½ cups flour, or as needed
1¼ cups sugar	1 tablespoon baking powder
Pinch of salt	1 teaspoon almond extract
½ cup (¼ pound) sweet butter,	½ teaspoon vanilla extract
softened to room temperature	2 teaspoons dark rum or brandy
Strained juice of 1 small orange	2 cups coarsely chopped,
Grated rind of 1 orange	unblanched almonds
Grated rind of 1 lemon	

Beat the eggs with the sugar and salt until very white and the mixture ribbons when a little of the batter is allowed to drip back into the bowl. With a whisk or beater, blend in the butter until the mixture is free of lumps. Add the orange juice and orange and lemon rinds. Sift 3 cups of flour with the baking powder and add to the mixture. The dough should be soft and workable but not sticky. Add the remaining flour if needed. Fold in the seasonings and nuts and mix well. Let the dough chill in the mixing bowl for 2 hours.

Preheat the oven to 350 degrees. Butter a jelly-roll pan.

Divide the dough in half and shape each batch into a roll about 2 inches in diameter. Place on the jelly-roll pan, which should hold both rolls. Bake in the preheated oven for 20 to 30 minutes, or until golden brown on top. The rolls will be flat on the bottom and curved on top. As soon as the mandelbrot is baked, carefully remove it from the pan and cut into ½-inch zweiback-like slices. Put the slices, cut side down, on the same baking sheet without regreasing it. Put back into the oven for 5 minutes. Turn and bake to toast the second side for 5 minutes longer.

Cool on a rack. When thoroughly cool, store in an airtight container. These can be retoasted to restore crispness.

Yield: About 36 half-inch slices

Chocolate Icing

As a rule we all preferred plain uniced cakes, and I still do. But occasionally on birthdays, or for a special company or Sunday dinner, my mother would use a chocolate icing on the chocolate chip cake (page 268.)

There were two types of chocolate icing my mother made. One we called smooth, the other creamy.

Smooth Chocolate Icing

¾ cup sugar
6 tablespoons water
3½ ounces (squares) semisweet
    chocolate, broken into small
    pieces

1 teaspoon vanilla extract or 1
    teaspoon cold black coffee,
    brewed double strength

Combine the sugar and water in a small, heavy-bottomed saucepan and cook over very low heat until the sugar dissolves. Boil rapidly until the syrup spins a thread when a spoon is drawn out of it, or until it reaches 234 degrees on a candy thermometer. Remove from the heat and stir in the chocolate, beating until it has all melted and is smoothly blended. Stir in the flavorings and pour or spread over the cake while the icing is still warm.

Yield: Enough for the top and sides of a 9- to 10-inch layer cake

Creamy Chocolate Icing

3 ounces (squares) unsweetened
    chocolate
3 tablespoons sweet butter
¼ cup hot, scalded milk
2½ cups sifted confectioners' sugar

Pinch of salt
1 tablespoon vanilla extract or cold
    black coffee, brewed double
    strength

Melt the chocolate and butter in the top of a double boiler over hot, not boiling water. Beat until melted and smoothly combined. Remove from the heat. Combine the hot, scalded milk, sugar, and salt and stir until the sugar dissolves. Beat into the chocolate mixture. Add the flavoring and continue beating until just thin enough for pouring. Pour over the cake while the icing is hot.

Yield: Enough for the top and sides of a 9- to 10-inch layer cake

Table of Metric Equivalents

(Volume and Weight)

Volume (in Common Units)			Weight (in Common Units)		
1 tablespoon	=	3 teaspoons	1 ounce	=	28.35 grams
	=	0.5 fluid ounce	1 pound	=	16 ounces
	=	14.8 milliliters		=	453.59 grams
1 cup	=	16 tablespoons		=	0.45 kilograms
	=	0.5 pint	1 gram	=	0.035 ounce
	=	8 fluid ounces	1 kilogram	=	2.2 pounds
2 cups	=	1 pint			
	=	16 fluid ounces			
	=	236.6 milliliters			
4 cups	=	1 quart			
	=	32 fluid ounces			
	=	0.9463 liter			
1 pint	=	2 cups			
	=	0.5 quart			
	=	4.73 deciliters			
	=	0.4732 liter			
1 quart	=	4 cups			
	=	2 pints			
	=	1.06 liters			
1 gallon	=	4 quarts			
	=	3.79 liters			

Index

PLUME Books You'll Enjoy

(0452)

☐ **CALORIES AND CARBOHYDRATES by Barbara Kraus.** Fifth revised edition. This most accurate and dependable caloric and carbohydrate guide gives counts of many brand-name and fast-food products as well as of basic foods. Recommended by doctors for weight control. (253985—$6.95)

☐ **MEGA-NUTRITION: The New Prescription for Maximum Health, Energy, and Longevity by Richard A. Kunin, M.D.** Foreword by Nobel Prize-winning scientist Linus Pauling. The diet-plus-vitamins program to prevent disease, treat illness, and promote good health.
(254817—$6.95)

☐ **MEGA-NUTRITION FOR WOMEN by Richard A. Kunin, M.D.,** The complete diet-plus-vitamins program that "promotes quick, safe weight loss. Answers beauty problems. Prevents and treats wide range of female health disorders. Try It. You'll feel the results."
—*Ms. Magazine* (255228—$6.95)

☐ **THE SUPERMARKET HANDBOOK: Access to Whole Foods by Nikki and David Goldbeck.** This book will prove invaluable to any shopper concerned with the quality and nutritive value of foods available in today's supermarkets. It will help you to understand labels and select foods with a discerning eye, and provides easy, low-cost ways of preparing and using whole foods in place of processed foods . . . "An enormously useful and heartening work!"—*The New York Times*
(253233—$5.95)

☐ **SHOPPING FOR HEALTH CARE: The Essential Guide to Products and Services by Harold J. Cornacchia, Ed.D. and Stephen Barrett, M.D.** Foreword by William T. Jarvis, Ph.D. This comprehensive, easy-to-use sourcebook gives you the vital information you need to beat the sky-rocketing costs of health care and will help you distinguish reliable, effective health services and products from those that are worthless, dangerous, or harmful—and overpriced. (253667—$8.95)

*Prices higher in Canada.

Buy them at your local bookstore or use this convenient coupon for ordering.

PLUME Quality Paperbacks for Your Bookshelf